Vlasov

Translated from the German by Abe Farbstein

Sven Steenberg

VLASOV

Alfred · A · Knopf

New York

1970

Preface

During the Second World War the Russian General Andrey Andreyevich Vlasov came into prominence as the enemy of Stalin. Vlasov's name is associated with the one attempt to overthrow the Soviet regime that had any chance of success; yet few people know the actual circumstances of the drama in which he played a central role. After the war, propaganda and legend blurred the outlines of his story, so that the significance of this man and the hopes his emergence stirred were shrouded in an obscurity that persists to this day.

The Vlasov case is fascinating for the light it sheds on the psychological and moral reactions of the individual Russian in the face of total dictatorship. Through Vlasov and the liberation movement he represented the true spirit of the Russian people, with all its possibilities and problems, found expression for the first time since the emergence of the Soviet state—at a time when sixty to seventy million inhabitants of the Soviet Union were living beyond the reach of Stalin's power.

The purpose of this work is to rescue Vlasov from obscurity and distortion and to describe his struggle. This book will have fulfilled its aim if it also elucidates the motives that caused hundreds of thousands of Russians to form an alliance with the aggressor against their own government.

The author owes special thanks to those who made available to him their personal accounts and documents. Given the general sparseness of documentary material on the Russian liberation movement, an accurate reconstruction of events would have been impossible without their cooperation.

The author has based his account on information supplied by the following persons: Gunter d'Alquen, Rostislav Antonov, Vyacheslav Artyemyev, Gottlob Berger, Max Bernsdorff, Adeleide

Bielenberg, Werner Bormann, Friedrich Buchardt, Gert Buschmann, Baron Eduard von Dellingshausen, Fritz Delonge, Konstantin Dulschers, Hans Ehlich, Sergei Fröhlich, Werner Götting-Seeburg, Ivan Gordyenko, Nikolaus von Grote, Adam Grünbaum, Walther Hansen, Gotthard Heinrici, Werner Henning, Heinz D. Herre, Ralf von Heygendorff, Heinrich-Detloff von Kalben, Nikolai Kandin, Farid Kapkayev, Alexander Kazantsev, Hans Kehrl, Gert Klein, Baron Helmut von Kleist, Dmitri Kozmovich, Otto Kraus, Theodor Krause, Erhard Kroeger, Robert Krötz, Konstantin Kromiadi, Anatoly Kruzhin, Count Grigory Lamsdorff, Anatol Mikhailovsky, Oldwig von Natzmer, Theodor Oberländer, Manfred von Pannwitz, Herbert von Pastor, Egon Peterson, Gerhard Petri, Klaus Poelchau, Vladimir Poremsky, Vladimir Pozdnyakov, Fritz Prelle, Nikolai Rebikov, Roman Redlich, Viktor Ressler, Baron Georg von der Ropp, Alexander Zaitsev, Mikhail Shatov, Baldur von Schirach, Ferdinand Schörner, Wladimir Schubuth, Helmut Schwenninger, Margot von Schwerdtner, Yurii Zherebkov, Erich von Sivers, Ernst Steen, Wilfried Strik-Strikfeldt, Sun Kuei-chi, Nikolai Tenzorov, and Melitta Wiedemann.

Russian proper names and quotations have been rendered phonetically.

Sven Steenberg

Contents

List of Illustrations

Vlasov

I

THE GENERAL

September 1941. For forty-eight hours, Major General Andrey Andreyevich Vlasov had been trying to contact Moscow by radio. The Kremlin, however, did not respond until the evening of September 18, and then its message consisted of just two words: *Otstupatye—Stalin* ("Withdraw—Stalin"). That very same hour, Vlasov ordered a retreat to the east and the evacuation of Kiev, which he had thus far held against all onslaughts of the Wehrmacht.

Vlasov—a giant of a man with coarse features, a wide, thick-lipped mouth, and a high forehead over intelligent eyes behind thick lenses—had been commander of the Fourth Armored Corps in Lvov at the beginning of the German drive. His unit had been forced to fall back to Berdichev after heavy defensive fighting. At the end of July, Vlasov, then only forty years old, was named commander of the Thirty-seventh Army and of the strategically important Kiev Military Region—a demonstration of the confidence of the top leaders of the Soviet Union in the capacities of this young field commander.

His army was the last to leave its positions on the Dnieper after the Germans, more than a hundred miles to the east, had already completed the biggest pincer movement in the history of warfare. The Germans could thank Stalin for the success of this battle of annihilation in which the entire Russian Army Group Southwest was trapped in an area of 45,000 square miles and in large part destroyed. Stalin had wanted to hold the Dnieper line at any price, even though signs of impending catastrophe were already clearly visible. Turning a deaf ear to Marshal Semyon Budyenny's desperate pleas for a retreat, he threw additional units into the battle. Not until three days after the Germans had closed the ring did he give his approval for a breakthrough to the east.

It was too late. The command structure was collapsing, the armies were already disintegrating, the number of deserters was mounting. Stalin was now paying dearly for his reign of terror. The purges, the slave labor camps, the forced collectivization—all of which had devoured millions of victims—had not been forgotten. A large part of the population greeted the Germans as liberators. Six hundred thousand soldiers surrendered.

Vlasov, however, refused to consider surrender. Equally noteworthy, the core of his army followed him—something not to be taken for granted in those days. He moved eastward in forced marches past dispersed, leaderless, floundering units of other armies, and made a successful escape with a few thousand men.[1] Shortly afterwards, however, he was taken to the base hospital in Voronezh with a serious case of grippe.

At first, none of the local authorities concerned themselves about him. Vlasov was a defeated general and quite possibly in disfavor at the highest level. But in mid-October, Marshal Sem-

---

[1] A thorough and accurate description of the battle for Kiev is contained in W. Haupt: *Kiev*, Podzun-Verlag, Bad Nauheim, 1965.

yon Timoshenko, Budyenny's successor, told him of his appointment as commandant of the Army Rear Area. And when, immediately thereafter, a phone call from Stalin ordered him to
Moscow, the ailing general was remembered; the head of the
NKVD, the commandant of the city, high-ranking military men,
and sundry administrative officials all put in appearances. Vlasov
had not yet been written off, his career might resume its advance
—a career which was exceptional even under Soviet conditions.[2]

Vlasov was born on September 1, 1900, in the small village of
Lomakino in the province of Nizhni Novgorod, the eighth child
of a peasant who also worked as a tailor in order to give his children a better education. In Tsarist Russia, however, the opportunities open to the offspring of a humble man were very
limited. Only the eldest son, Ivan, managed to graduate from
the teachers institute in the city of Nizhni Novgorod. For Andrey, the youngest son, whose intelligence and gift of quick
comprehension had greatly impressed the village teacher, there
was only one alternative: the theological seminary. For the
Orthodox Church took a relatively liberal view and made room
for the gifted without inquiring about their origins. Thus it was
that young Andrey came to attend religious schools, including
the seminary in Nizhni Novgorod. And even this was possible
only through great sacrifices and the assistance of his older
brother.

It was from the seminary that Vlasov witnessed the Revolution. It promised peace, land, freedom, and the elimination of
classes—goals which he could all fully endorse. After graduating
from the seminary, he abandoned his priestly calling, much

---

[2] Vlasov described his career repeatedly after his capture. In 1944 there
appeared a short biography written by V. Arsenyev under the pseudonym of Osokin, based on facts provided by Vlasov (text in *Borba*,
Nos. 11 and 12, 1948 [Russian]). Details on his life for the present
work were also supplied by Baron Eduard von Dellingshausen in an
unpublished manuscript and by Konstantin Kromiadi, Sergei Fröhlich,
Baron Helmut von Kleist, Wilfried Strik-Strikfeldt, and Werner Bormann in interviews conducted by the author.

against his father's wishes, and began in 1918 to study agriculture. In the spring of 1919, however, he was called up for service with the Twenty-seventh Rifle Regiment of the Red Army.

After completing an officer-training course, Vlasov was appointed, in the autumn of 1919, a platoon leader in the Second Don Division, then battling Denikin's White Army. Here he gained the combat experience that brought his military skills to full maturity, and first showed the traits of character which contributed decisively to his rapid rise: He understood how "to win respect, lead men, bind them to himself, and at the same time increase their self-confidence." [3]

By the early days of 1920 the Ukraine and the northern Caucasus had been cleared of White troops. The Second Don Division, in which Vlasov had meanwhile become a company commander, was shifted from the Caucasus to the Crimean front, where the White commander General Wrangel had assembled fresh troops. Vlasov was appointed aide to the division chief of staff and subsequently, at his own request—since he disliked staff work—commander of the reconnaissance detachment. With Wrangel's defeat in November 1920, Vlasov's first active experience of war ended.

He had liked soldiering, however, and decided to remain an officer. Although the Red Army shrank from 6,000,000 to 600,-000 men within two years, he was transferred to active duty as a company commander. On the fifth anniversary of the Red Army, Soviet Chief of Staff Lebedev presented him with an inscribed silver watch in recognition of his company's high level of training. In 1924 he was named commanding officer of the regimental school of the Twenty-sixth Rifle Regiment; he graduated from another officer-training course in 1928 and returned to his old regiment in 1929 as a battalion commander. In 1930 he was appointed instructor in tactics at the Leningrad Officers School, and shortly thereafter was ordered to Moscow to take a course for such instructors. He returned to Leningrad with a glowing

[3] *Red Star*, November 21, 1940.

testimonial and was named deputy to the chief of the instructors staff. It was at this time that, at the urging of his superiors, he joined the Communist Party.

For the next few years, Vlasov served on the staff of the Leningrad Military Region, becoming assistant to the head of its section for military training in 1935. During an inspection tour with the region's deputy commander, General Primakov, the Second Rifle Regiment of the Fourth Turkestan Division was found to be in conspicuously poor condition. Primakov thereupon appointed Vlasov commander of the regiment, and the latter brought the unit up to par in short order. He then assumed command of the 137th Rifle Regiment, which soon won a reputation as the best regiment in the Leningrad Region. His next assignment was as chief of staff of the Seventy-second Division. It was while serving in this post that he lived through, and survived, the purges connected with the Tukhachevsky Affair. This experience, and that of being posted to China in 1938, were of crucial significance for his later development.

The details of the Affair—named for its central figure, the reorganizer and highest-ranking officer of the Red Army, Marshal M. N. Tukhachevsky—remain a mystery to this day. It is not even certain whether there actually was a plot, "whose devastating execution Stalin forestalled only at the eleventh hour," [4] or whether Stalin, taking precautions, simply wanted to eliminate the strongest power center remaining after the purges of the party and secret police—the privileged and critically placed officer clique. Some of Stalin's closest and most influential collaborators, in the face of the steadily accelerating tempo of the terror apparatus's operations, had already tried to bring it to a halt. But they had acted as isolated individuals without adequate power and had paid for their opposition with their lives. The army, however, still represented a source of potential danger to Stalin.

Whether Stalin, as the official version asserts, was warned by

---

[4] Isaac Deutscher: *Stalin*, Verlag Kohlhammer, Stuttgart, 1962, pp. 404 ff. (also, Oxford University Press, London and New York, 1949).

his secret police; or whether he gave credence to a warning of an imminent revolt transmitted by Hitler through Czech President Eduard Beneš, as Nikita Khrushchev has hinted; or whether he himself had provoked Hitler into instigating such a plot, is still unknown.[5] It seems certain, at any rate, that the official indictment—"espionage for a foreign power and preparations for a defeat of the Red Army in a war planned against the Soviet Union"—does not correspond to the facts. It is far more likely that Tukhachevsky—who had repeatedly and urgently stressed the danger that a National Socialist Germany represented for Russia,[6] and shortly before his arrest had visited England and France—had discussed measures to overthrow Hitler with official circles in those countries. The opposition inside the German armed forces may possibly have played a role in these conversations.[7]

Whatever the underlying circumstances, Stalin's reaction was terrifying. According to conservative estimates, about thirty thousand officers were arrested. Three of the Red Army's 5 mar-

---

[5] Walter Schellenberg reports credibly in his *Memoiren* ("Memoirs," Verlag für Politik und Wirtschaft, Cologne, 1956, pp. 48 ff.) that Gestapo leader Reinhard Heydrich received information through a White Russian living in Paris, General Skoblin, that Tukhachevsky was planning to overthrow Stalin, with the knowledge of the German General Staff. However, Heydrich also considered it possible that Stalin had launched such a rumor himself in order to remove the threat to his power posed by the generals. For domestic political reasons it must have seemed preferable to have the pretext for action come from abroad. Moreover, Heydrich offered Stalin forged material through Eduard Beneš. Stalin promptly swallowed the bait and, to Heydrich's surprise, offered money. In mid-May 1937, Stalin paid three million gold rubles for the documents. Tukhachevsky was arrested on June 4.

[6] Report of January 15, 1936, to the Central Executive Committee of the USSR. English translation in: *Soviet Union 1936, Collection of Statements by Stalin, Tukhachevsky, Molotov, and Others,* London, n.d.

[7] Major General Dr. K. Spalke argues in his essay "Der Fall Tuchatschewski" ("The Tukhachevsky Affair") in *Die Gegenwart,* January 25, 1958, that Tukhachevsky was planning a war together with England against Germany, while Stalin wished to stay out of such a conflict. The basic reason for the Red Army purge lay in this disagreement over policy—an interpretation confirmed for Spalke by a Soviet intelligence officer.

shals were liquidated, 13 out of 19 army commanders, more than half of the 186 division commanders. Even their families were not spared. Tukhachevsky's mother, his sister Sophia, and his brothers, Alexander and Nikolai, were killed; four other sisters were sent to a concentration camp.[8]

These events unquestionably influenced Vlasov's attitude toward the Stalin regime—although he was not personally affected, not even arrested. But he learned at firsthand how shaky was the ground on which every high officer of the Red Army stood at the time. One day his divisional commissar pointed to a photo of Marshal Blücher hanging in his office and remarked: "I would remove that picture if I were you." "Already?" Vlasov asked. "Already!" the commissar replied. The photo bore a personal inscription by the marshal, whom Vlasov had met at the military academy.[9]

Vlasov was lucky. He not only escaped arrest, but in the spring of 1938 was promoted to colonel, and appointed head of the military training section of the Kiev staff, by the commander of the Kiev Military Region. However, he did not move out of the danger zone until November of that year, when he received orders to join a group of Soviet advisers going to China.

This new assignment afforded Vlasov his first acquaintance with a non-Communist country. He went first to Chungking, then the seat of the Chinese government. The Russian advisers at the front wore Chinese uniforms without insignia of rank, the others civilian clothes. Most of them used pseudonyms— Vlasov himself took the name of Volkov. He immediately established rapport with the Chinese and quickly won their respect

---

[8] Cf. Boris Levytsky: *Vom roten Terror zur sozialistischen Gesetzlichkeit* ("From the Red Terror to Socialist Legality"), Munich, 1961; Yepishev in *Voyenno-istoricheskyi Zhurnal* ("Journal of Military History"), 1963, pp. 4–5; Malinovsky in *Red Star*, February 23, 1963; O. Reile: *Geheime Ostfront* ("Secret Eastern Front"), Verlag Welsermühl, Wels, 1963, pp. 249 ff.; *Die Moskauer Schauprozesse 1936–1938* ("The Moscow Show Trials, 1936–8"), dtv-Dokumente, Stuttgart, 1963.

[9] Vlasov described this incident in a conversation on April 19, 1943, with Sonderführer Klein (interview with author).

and liking, distinguishing himself by his brilliant lectures at the Chinese military academy in Chungking.

The Kremlin was pursuing a twofold policy in China. On the one hand, it supported Chiang Kai-shek against the Japanese; on the other, it sought to strengthen the Chinese Communists. Vlasov received a corresponding hint from the Soviet Secret Service, but ignored it, since nothing of the kind had been mentioned in his official instructions. He was repelled by the idea of abusing the hospitality and trust of the Chinese.

From February to May 1939 he served as adviser to Marshal Jen Tsi-shan, commander of the Second Military Region of the northwest front in Shansi province. The task was a delicate one. The marshal had used different pretexts to sabotage many directives from the General Staff. He was considered clever, scheming, and headstrong, and was a master at politely distorting the facts. His army was supposed to participate in a large-scale operation, and it was Vlasov's job to convince him of the necessity of the operation. Through skillful diplomacy he succeeded in winning the marshal's confidence and was given permission to inspect his troops.

The advice and support of his personal interpreter, Sun Kuei-chi, were of great value to Vlasov in this enterprise. Sun, then twenty-nine, had originally been a lawyer and had been assigned to the Russian mission by the Press Bureau of the Foreign Ministry. He was an intelligent and cultivated man, with whom Vlasov soon struck up a genuine friendship. Sun was impressed by Vlasov's extraordinary ability to concentrate on the task at hand. The Russian let nothing distract him and never drank when on duty. He repeatedly displayed great personal courage. On reconnaissance operations there was danger of capture by the Japanese, and he instructed Sun, who was always right behind, to shoot him if they were caught in an ambush.

Off duty, Vlasov was cheerful and relaxed. He refrained from engaging in political discussions and never propagandized for Communism. He would evade direct questions with a joke: He was a simple soldier; let the politicians who knew more about it talk about politics. He avoided criticism of conditions in the Soviet Union—although it could be deduced from many of his remarks that he was not an enthusiastic supporter of Stalin's methods.

The Chinese ponies were too small for a man of Vlasov's stature, so that he presented a somewhat comic figure. "Fate is everything," he once said enigmatically to Sun. "I am Don Quixote and you are Sancho Panza." After completing his mission with Jen Tsi-shan, he was named chief of staff of the advisory group. He was finally recalled in November 1939, after just under a year's stay in China. At a farewell party in his honor, Marshal Chiang Kai-shek awarded him the Yun Hui ("Propitious Cloud") decoration, and Madam Chiang presented him with a gold watch. However, at the stopover in Alma-Ata, on the way home, all gifts were taken from him and his companions, supposedly to be "registered"; they were never seen again.[1]

Vlasov found a changed situation at home: The nonaggression pact had been signed with Germany; Poland had been partitioned; Latvia, Estonia, and Lithuania had been incorporated into the USSR; the Finnish War was going badly for the Red Army. And over everything, like a shadow, lay Stalin's terror. The disparity between what the Revolution had been supposed to bring, and what it actually had brought, oppressed Vlasov. But he refused to tackle political problems which he could neither influence nor solve; he buried himself in his work. There was more than enough to do when, shortly after his return, he was named commander of the Ninety-ninth Rifle Division. In this division, considered the worst in the army, served soldiers of five different nationalities, some of whom could barely speak Russian.

It was not easy at that time to be a Red Army commander. In addition to normal duties, valuable time had to be spent at meetings of "party activists," at which attendance was obligatory

---

[1] Sun Kuei-chi has reported on Vlasov's stay in China in an interview with, and letters to, the author. Sun is now a member of the Yuan (legislature) of the Republic of China. He confirms Vlasov's account, which is repeated by Bormann, Strik-Strikfeldt, von Dellingshausen, and Kromiadi. Cf. footnote 2, page 5.

for all party members. Every member, whether cleaning woman or groom, could offer criticism on matters of which he or she had not the slightest understanding. One day, for example, the man who fired the furnaces criticized Vlasov's conduct as divisional commander. When Vlasov objected that the comrade was in no position to judge, he was told that all party activists were equal and that he had better fulfill his duties.

If this incident was not to make him a laughingstock, Vlasov decided, he would have to take countermeasures. The next morning he entered the staff offices an hour before the day's duties began and found the fireman asleep and the offices unheated. He promptly sentenced the man to twenty days in the guardhouse for neglecting his job. This did the trick: Vlasov's prestige was restored. Still, there were intrigues, informers on all sides, and the need to be on good terms with the divisional commissar, who had the right to review all orders and could, if he so desired, countermand them.

The government had established the system of political commissars because of its distrust of the military, its fear that someday the army might turn its weapons against the regime. In 1928, Ivan Unschlicht—a prominent leader of that time—had declared, on the occasion of the tenth anniversary of the Red Army: "Comrades, do not forget that the foundation of our Workers' and Peasants' Army consists of peasant youth who enter its ranks with all the sentiments that prevail in the village . . . and these sentiments are hostile to us!" [2]

Despite all the strains and unpleasantness, Vlasov succeeded in steadily raising the level of discipline and efficiency of his division. On June 4, 1940—a few months before his fortieth birthday—he was promoted to major general. [3]

Shortly afterward he spent his first leave in his native village

---

[2] Quoted in Vitov: "Die Achillesferse der Sowjetarmee" ("The Achilles' Heel of the Soviet Army"), *Schweizer Rundschau*, February/March 1958.

[3] *Pravda*, June 7, 1940. The announcement was published with a photo of Vlasov.

since returning from China. Days at home during leave were always an expensive affair. He was the pride of his many relations and the entire village. His appearance was an event, and gifts and invitations were expected of him. Although it ruined his budget for several months, he did not wish to rob his relatives of their pleasure. Besides, his aged father did not believe that he depended completely on his pay. "In my time," he would say, "you could make enough money just from the oats for a squadron to buy a nice little house." He had served in a Tsarist cavalry guard regiment, had been discharged as a sergeant, and would reminisce enthusiastically about those days. A monarchist, he made no secret of the fact that the new social order didn't please him.

In 1933, Vlasov had married a young doctor from the neighboring village. She had borne him a son while he was in China. His wife's parents' property had been expropriated on the ground that they were "kulaks"—rich peasants—and she had had to repudiate them so as not to endanger her husband's career. Secretly, however, Vlasov supported his destitute parents-in-law. The fate of his oldest brother, Ivan, who had been shot in 1919 for participating in a plot, was another closely guarded secret.

In the summer of 1940 the higher echelons of the Red Army stiffened their resistance to the power of the military commissars, blaming them for the reverses of the Finnish War. Vlasov took part in this struggle, which marked his debut in the political-military arena. At conferences of army political cells in the Kiev Military Region he espoused the view that political propaganda must not be an end in itself but should be subordinated to the main goal, that of increasing combat readiness.[4]

The authority of the commissars was greatly reduced in August 1940. From then on the military commander had exclusive power of decision in military matters. This facilitated Vlasov's work, and he succeeded in whipping his division into such excellent shape that it won honors as the best division

[4] *Red Star*, December 4 and 9, 1940.

in the Red Army. Marshal Timoshenko presented him with an inscribed gold watch, and he was cited in ten issues of the army newspaper, *Red Star*, as well as in *Pravda*. Timoshenko wrote on September 27 that Vlasov and his division had "shown their ability to solve tactical problems under especially difficult conditions."

General Meretskov, the Red Army's chief of staff, also praised the division following a personal inspection. Vlasov was lauded as the "commander of an exemplary division, as a soldier and human being," in one of the publications issued by the political administration of the Kiev Regional Command.[5] Special emphasis was placed on his ability "to achieve coordination in the use of all types of weapons and a high state of troop readiness under simulated emergency conditions." *Red Star*, in its issue of November 21, called on all divisions to take the Ninety-ninth as a model. Vlasov published a long article, "New Methods of Troop Training," which also appeared in pamphlet form.[6] His name became known throughout the army, which was especially unusual since, after the Tukhachevsky Affair, senior officers were seldom singled out in this way. Vlasov received another honor in December 1940: He was assigned as cospeaker with General Meretskov, who was to address the senior officer corps of the Red Army on the tasks of military preparation for the coming year. In January 1941, Vlasov became commander of the Fourth Armored Corps in Lvov, and in February, on the occasion of the twenty-third anniversary of the Red Army, he received the Order of Lenin.

The retreat at the beginning of the war and the defeat in the battle of Kiev disillusioned Vlasov profoundly. He had experienced a failure of leadership and organization that pointed to basic flaws in the Soviet system. Nevertheless, there existed no alternative for him at that time to the struggle against German aggression. Perhaps the inevitable growth of the

[5] *Novoye v Podgotovke Voisk*, Kiev, 1940.
[6] A. A. Vlasov: *Noviye Metody Boevoi Uchoby*, 1940.

army's power during the war would force indispensable changes in the system. But he could not yet imagine any other solution. And so, barely recovered from his illness, he boarded the plane which carried him to his meeting with Stalin.

II

STALIN'S
FAVORITE

By October, Moscow was in a state of panic. Much of the population was wavering between fear of what was to come and hope for Stalin's downfall. Looting began. Government records, administrative agencies, the ministries, and the diplomatic corps were evacuated to Kuybyshev. The privileged of the regime, who had received priority travel orders, jammed the Kazan Railroad Station, the only one from which trains for the east still departed. Trains rolled uninterruptedly toward the east, holding up the arrival of fresh troops from Siberia. Stalin remained in Moscow, as did the members of the Politburo—most of whom owed their positions to the liquidation of their predecessors. Besides Stalin himself, only three of the fourteen members and alternate members of the first Soviet Politburo were still living: Molotov, Voroshilov, and Kalinin.

When Vlasov reached Moscow on November 10, 1941, the vanguard of the Siberian divisions was disembarking. Stalin had restored relative order through Draconian measures. The secret police had been instructed "to shoot on sight provocateurs, spies, and enemy agents who [were] violating law and order." Newly organized worker battalions were being marched off to the front, and women were being dragooned to build fortifications on the city's outskirts.

Vlasov received orders—as was the rule with Stalin—to report at midnight. He drove to the Kremlin with Marshal Voroshilov and General Shaposhnikov, chief of the General Staff. After passing through a number of checkpoints, they entered the office of Pozkrebyshev, that strange and mysterious man who had enjoyed Stalin's absolute trust for many years. Vlasov, who was meeting Stalin for the first time, could not repress a certain nervousness. After a short while he followed Voroshilov and Shaposhnikov into Stalin's command bunker. Stalin's gigantic desk stood in a corner. A long conference table covered by a red cloth ran parallel to the side wall, and seated at it were Beria, Zhukov, Malenkov, and Stalin. Stalin rose and greeted the newcomers with brief handshakes. He moved silently, lithely, and quickly. He was of no more than medium height, and Vlasov, a full head taller, towered over him.

"Comrade Zhukov," began Stalin, speaking in a remarkably soft, though very clear voice. Marshal Zhukov delivered the most unpleasant report imaginable. The Germans in the central sector were twenty-five miles from Moscow. In the south, General Guderian's armored troops had almost reached Tula. With the end of the mud season, which had given the badly mauled Red Army a breathing space, the Germans would resume their attack. It had to be assumed that Colonel General Hoth's Third Armored Group to the north and Guderian to the south would together envelop Moscow. Although Siberian troops were arriving in growing numbers, it seemed doubtful whether there would be enough time to throw them into the fighting.

When Zhukov had finished, Stalin turned to Vlasov: "What do you think of the situation?" Slowly and reflectively, Vlasov pointed out that a mobilization of untrained workers without the aid of regular troops was useless. If the Siberian troops arrived in time, a breakthrough to the west should be attempted —this would be the only way to win time. The Russian winter would take care of the rest. "Anybody can defend Moscow if he has troops," Stalin answered brusquely. The several million inhabitants of the city had to be mobilized to defend it, block by block. In addition, Beria would provide ten thousand criminal prisoners.

"And tanks?" Vlasov interjected. "I have no tanks," Stalin said, and suddenly smiled. "Comrade Malenkov, how many tanks can we give Comrade Vlasov?" "Fifteen," replied Malenkov. "Well, you get fifteen tanks. I don't have more." He then appointed Vlasov commander of the new, yet-to-be-organized Twentieth Army. He got up. The discussion was over. Vlasov had been greatly impressed by Stalin's calm and objectivity, the absence of all poses, of any sign of nervousness, as he gave his orders in this desperate situation; most of all, that Stalin could smile over the fifteen remaining tanks in such an hour! [1]

Vlasov drove with Shaposhnikov to army headquarters to discuss the problems facing him as he assumed his new command. The worst difficulty was the lack of transportation. Vlasov's solution was to hitch long rows of heavy sleds loaded with munitions and weapons to the fifteen tanks—not one more and not one less—he had been given. Many other problems had to be tackled with the most primitive means and methods, though that was nothing new. The German offensive had gained so much ground, however, that the Twentieth Army had to go into action even before it was completely organized. To the north, a German tank group had traversed the Krasnaya Polyana district and reached the outskirts of the city; in the northwest and center sectors, the front had advanced to a point less than twenty miles away; in the south, Guderian's tanks stood arrayed before Kashira. Moscow's fall seemed inevitable.

[1] Vlasov described his meeting with Stalin many times. Informants agree on all essential points.

Defense along a wide front was out of the question. Despite his inferior forces, Vlasov decided to counterattack. It was risky, but an attack appeared to be the only way to disrupt the German advance and slow its tempo. With the few tanks, of which he had taken personal command, and some motorized troops, he succeeded in breaking through the German lines. A few hours later, however, he found himself surrounded, cut off from the rest of his army. By radio he ordered a diversionary attack for the next morning and moved forward to match it with a strike from the west. This maneuver also succeeded, and the two spearheads met near Shimki.

The Germans halted their advance; precious time had been won. But soon afterward they pushed forward again, and it seemed they would still make the breakthrough to Moscow. Vlasov's reserves were gone, and the reports from the northern sector sounded increasingly ominous. At this critical moment a Siberian relief brigade showed up, ready for battle. Its commander had received orders to reinforce the neighboring army to the north, but had lost his way in the snowstorm. Vlasov immediately placed the brigade under his own command. He was well aware that this unauthorized act might cause him future unpleasantness; but time pressed and the needs of his own army seemed more important to him. He allowed the new troops a two-hour rest and then ordered them to start off for the most endangered position on his main firing line.

This move proved to be a turning point: The forward drive of the German armies was blunted. Snowstorms and three-foot-high drifts blocked supply lines; motors failed; clothing was insufficient, and thousands of soldiers suffering from frostbite had to be taken back to base areas. The suicidal advance ordered by Hitler was at last exacting its toll. The German divisions fell back, no longer capable of coping with counterattacks by fresh forces. They did manage to halt the Russian thrust, and for the moment the situation was stabilized.

The next day, December 6, Vlasov made a second decision which determined once and for all the outcome of the battle for Moscow. Despite the risks involved, and without exact knowledge of the enemy's condition, he ordered the counter-attack resumed. The exhausted Germans thereupon retreated. Vlasov's Twentieth Army drove forward some 120 miles through Volokolamsk to Rzhev. The neighboring Russian armies also advanced.[2] For the first time the German *blitzkrieg* divisions had been successfully mauled. Moscow had been saved, and one of its saviors was Vlasov.

Zhukov, to be sure, held over-all command on the central front, and alongside Vlasov's Twentieth Army had been many other units—Lelushenko's Thirtieth Army, Kuznetsov's First Shock Army, Rokossovsky's Sixteenth, Govorov's Fifth, Boldin's Fiftieth, and Golikov's Tenth Army. But it was Vlasov's Twentieth that had stood at the center and initiated the crucial turn in the tide of battle.

His fame now spread abroad, and journalists sought him out for interviews. The American correspondent Eve Curie wrote: "This is a man who knows how to fight not only with reso-lution, not only with courage, but with passion as well." [3] Ilya Ehrenburg visited him and published an article on this meet-ing.[4] Vlasov was awarded the Order of the Red Banner,[5] and was promoted to lieutenant general on January 24, 1942.[6]

[2] *Pravda*, December 13 and 15, 1941.
[3] Eve Curie: *Journey Among Warriors*, Doubleday, Doran, Garden City, 1943.
[4] *Red Star*, March 13, 1942. Ehrenburg describes this meeting once more in the fifth volume of his memoirs *Menschen—Jahre—Leben*, Kindler Verlag, Munich, 1965, pp. 353 ff. (also *People and Life*, Alfred A. Knopf, 1962). He calls Vlasov an "interesting, ambitious but brave person," very popular with his men. When Ehrenburg learned that Vlasov had received command of the shock army, he thought: "It's not a bad choice." Yet, Ehrenburg attributes Vlasov's subsequent op-position to Stalin and his regime to base motives, believing that "He had no convictions, just ambition." Vlasov, in his view, aspired to become "commander in chief or minister of war in a truncated Russia under the aegis of a victorious Hitler." He has long been "forgotten by everyone, even by his hirelings who fled in good time to the American occupation zone."
[5] *Izvestia*, January 3, 1942.
[6] *Izvestia*, January 25, 1942.

★

The unusually cold winter yielded very slowly to spring. The mud was thicker than it had been in years. It made fighting impossible and lengthened the breathing space during which the Red Army was able to replenish its strength. Vlasov received several days' leave at the end of February and saw his wife and child for what was to be the last time. Stalin summoned him again on March 6, and—in the presence of Molotov, Beria, Voroshilov, Malenkov, and the head of the Air Force, General Novikov—appointed him acting commander in chief of the northwest front, so that he could, as Stalin phrased it, "create order" where General Meretskov had failed.

At the end of the discussion, after the military situation had been analyzed, Stalin said that the political unreliability of the population and parts of the army had created a critical situation in the first months. Fortunately, however, "the Fascists themselves had cured these people quickly." Vlasov was startled—never before had the facts been admitted so frankly. This remark of Stalin's indicated his recognition of the dangerous possibility that the Germans might mobilize elements of the population hostile to him. As early as July 16, 1941, he had been forced to reveal, in his Secret Order No. 0019, that: "There are many elements on all fronts who even run to meet the foe and throw away their weapons on their first contact with him . . . while the number of reliable commissars and commanders is not very large." [7]

How pessimistic Stalin really was and how little faith he had in his own troops is shown by his bid to Roosevelt and Churchill to have American and British troops operate on Soviet soil. Harry Hopkins, Roosevelt's special envoy, reported six weeks after the war began that if the United States would enter the war, Stalin would welcome the deployment of American troops

---

[7] Quoted in Alexander Dallin: *Deutsche Herrschaft in Russland 1941–1945*, Droste Verlag, Düsseldorf, 1958, p. 78 fn. (also, *German Rule in Russia*, St. Martin's Press, New York, 1958).

on every sector of the front, even if they remained under exclusive control of the American high command.[8] And in September 1941, Stalin cabled Churchill:

> In my opinion there is only one way out—the establish-
> ment of a second front in the Balkans or France this year,
> which will divert thirty to forty [German] divisions from the
> eastern front. At the same time, thirty thousand tons of
> aluminum must be supplied by October and four hundred
> planes and five hundred tanks must be delivered monthly.
> Without these two kinds of help the Soviet Union will
> either suffer a defeat or be so weakened that it will be de-
> prived for a long time of the capacity to support its allies
> through its own operations at the front in the struggle
> against Hitlerism.

When Churchill indicated that creation of a second front
was, for technical reasons, not feasible at that time, Stalin
cabled back:

> . . . I do not doubt the wish of the British Government
> to see the Soviet Union victorious. . . . If it considers the
> creation of a second front in the west impossible, cannot
> some other way be found to actively support the Soviet
> Union in the field? In my opinion, Great Britain could land
> twenty-five to thirty divisions in Archangel without risk or
> move them across Iran to southern Russia. In this way mili-
> tary cooperation between the armed forces of the Soviets
> and those of Great Britain could be initiated in the territory
> of the USSR. . . .[9]

This appeal was of truly unprecedented political significance.
Troops of capitalist states under their own commands in the

[8] Robert Sherwood: *Roosevelt und Hopkins*, Wolfgang Krüger Verlag,
Hamburg, 1950, pp. 268 ff. (also Harper and Row, New York, 1950).
[9] Winston Churchill: *Memoiren*, Parnass-Verlag, Stuttgart, Scherz und
Goverts, 1951; Sherwood, op. cit., p. 304.

Soviet Union, which until then had been hermetically sealed off from the outside world? It is no wonder that Soviet historians never discuss this confession of Stalin's weakness.

By the end of 1941 the German Wehrmacht occupied territories in which lived nearly one third of Russia's population—about sixty million people. These areas were the source of sixty-five per cent of the country's coal, sixty-eight per cent of its iron ore, fifty-eight per cent of its steel production, and sixty per cent of its aluminum. Moreover, forty-one per cent of the USSR's railroad tracks were located in these sections. In the second half of 1941 total Soviet industrial production declined by more than half, and steel production by two thirds.[1] Under these conditions a political mobilization of anti-Stalinist forces by the Germans would have proven truly decisive.

On March 9, 1942, Vlasov, Voroshilov, Malenkov, and Novikov met with Meretskov at the latter's headquarters. They found him quite downcast: Stalin had openly expressed his dissatisfaction, and the general knew what that could mean. The situation was indeed critical—but it was hardly Meretskov's fault. At the beginning of the year, Stalin had personally ordered an offensive aimed toward Leningrad, and for this purpose the Second Shock Army, reinforced by fresh troops, had been mobilized. This advance was risky because it had to pass through a sparsely settled, swampy area spanned by nothing but a few bad roads, while the Germans had dug into well-fortified positions all around it. Such an attack had a chance of succeeding only in winter—with the onset of the thaw the terrain would become trackless and impassable.

At the end of January, after weeks of bloody fighting, the German lines on the banks of the Volkhov were penetrated, and an advance of over fifty miles was achieved. But the drive had exhausted the army. German resistance had hardened, and it proved impossible to widen the narrow breakthrough points

[1] Nikolai Voznesensky: *Voyennaya Ekonomika SSSR* ("War Economy of the USSR"), Moscow, 1948, p. 42.

—there was an imminent danger of the "bottleneck" being plugged. The thaw had begun, and a catastrophe could only be avoided by a withdrawal of the army to the east bank of the Volkhov. Vlasov proposed such a retreat; but Stalin categorically rejected it and instead ordered continued attack. All objections, even a flight to Moscow, were in vain. Finally Vlasov yielded; it would have been suicide to ignore the order.

Shortly afterward, on March 19, what he had feared occurred: The Germans plugged up the breakthrough points, and the army was cut off from the main front. Vlasov personally assumed command of the army and flew into the cauldron on March 21. On March 27 he succeeded in re-establishing a line of communication with the front, even though it consisted only of a narrow funnel no more than a mile and a half in width. Again he urgently requested permission to retreat; again Stalin refused and ordered him to continue the assault. The Red Army soldiers attacked "through swampy, trackless woodland, often up to their waists in snow or up to their knees in water." [2] But the force of their attack was soon decisively broken, and the army had to go on the defensive.

It was at this time that a woman named Maria Voronova suddenly appeared and delivered a letter from his wife to Vlasov. The outline of his son's tiny hand had been traced on the back of the envelope as a greeting and talisman for him. It was the last letter he would receive, and he carried it with him until his death.

The letter contained another piece of news: *Gosti byli*— "Guests were here." The secret police had searched his home —despite his services, despite his decorations from Stalin. It was a bitter realization, one of the experiences that would lead him eventually to a crucial decision.

Maria was a strong-willed woman of thirty whose husband had vanished into Siberia. For several years she had been helping Vlasov's wife with her housework and the care of the child. Now she said she was going to stay at Vlasov's headquarters

[2] *Bitva za Leningrada,* Voyenizdat, Moscow, 1964, p. 146.

and cook for him. He was still weak from his illness, and his wife had enjoined her to take care of him. She remained, despite Vlasov's misgivings about the situation at the front.

Meanwhile, the army's situation was becoming increasingly hopeless. Supplies dwindled, the German attacks increased in fury, casualties mounted. But Stalin did not give the signal to retreat until May 14. With enormous effort, Vlasov succeeded in passing several divisions through enemy lines. On May 20, however, the Germans finally disrupted all communications among Vlasov's forces. Nine divisions and seven brigades went to their destruction. Fourteen thousand men fell in the Botetskaya-Myasnoi-Bor Chudovo area alone. Thousands lay drowned, bleeding to death, or starving in the swamps and woods. Only 32,000 men survived the battle and were taken prisoners. Vlasov's own headquarters was knocked out of operation by a surprise artillery barrage that killed or wounded most of his staff officers. Help failed to materialize, as Stalin had abandoned the army. He did order Vlasov and his staff rescued by paratroops, but these units could not find his headquarters and were themselves wiped out.[3]

Vlasov ordered an attempt at escape in small groups. He himself, however, was unable to make it through the enemy lines. For weeks he wandered with a few faithful aides through swamps and woods. The nights were sultry and damp, the days scorching hot. The stench of decaying corpses often made breathing impossible; hunger became sheer torment. There was an abundance of only one item—time, a great deal of time. And Vlasov used it to attempt to clarify things which he had never before really thought through to a conclusion. Work, profession, career—these had been his life. Now he drew up a balance

---

[3] Kyril Meretskov: *Voyenno-istoricheskyi Zhurnal* ("Journal of Military History"), No. 1, 1965, pp. 54–70. Meretskov describes the course of the battle and asserts that blame for the defeat of the Second Shock Army rested solely with the Soviet High Command—that is, Stalin. Until the death of Stalin all mention of Vlasov's name was forbidden. He has subsequently appeared in Soviet historical writings as an isolated individual who turned traitor.

sheet. A great deal became evident which consciously or un-
consciously he had pushed aside, had repressed: the mistakes
of the government, the terror, the meaningless sacrifice of tens
of thousands, as at Kiev and now at the Volkhov.[4] He saw
no way out for himself. Should he shoot himself? For whom?
For Stalin?

Thus he continued to vegetate, waiting for whatever fate
had in store. Perhaps some chance to cross the front would
present itself. He never even considered the idea of surrendering. In a few weeks his group dwindled down to Maria; his
chief of staff, Vinogradov; and the latter's orderly. When
hunger became unbearable, they begged for bread at some lonely
farmhouse. Their situation finally became altogether hopeless,
and they decided, as a last resort, to throw themselves on the
mercy of some villagers. Perhaps the peasants would hide and
feed them until the German troops moved on, until they found
a chance to cross the front lines.

On July 11, Vlasov and Maria entered the small forest village
of Tukhovetchi while Vinogradov and his orderly tried the
neighboring village of Yam-Tezovo. They had removed all insignia of rank. Vlasov had given his coat to Vinogradov, who,
wounded and sick with malaria, was always cold. The Tukhovetchi village elder agreed to help them and locked them in a
windowless shack of the fire brigade. Then he informed the
Germans. The following is an account by the interpreter of the
German Thirty-eighth Corps, Klaus Poelchau, of the strange
circumstances of Vlasov's capture:

> At dawn on July 12 the corps intelligence officer, Captain
> von Schwerdtner, awoke me with the news that Vlasov had
> been shot the previous evening near Yam-Tezovo by two

---

[4] After his capture, Vlasov described the course of the battle on the
Volkhov many times. The account here is based on information supplied in an unpublished manuscript of von Dellingshausen's and in
interviews with Bormann, Fröhlich, Kromiadi, and Strik-Strikfeldt.

sentries and had to be identified. Though we were skeptical
—the search for Vlasov had been going on for weeks and
we had had many false alarms—we started out immediately.
As we passed the village of Tukhovetchi, the Russian mayor
asked us to take along two partisans who had been imprisoned the previous evening when they asked for food.
Since we first had to complete our mission, we promised
to do so on the way back.

In Yam-Tezovo, to which the corpse had been brought,
the local commander told us that the dead man's orderly,
slightly wounded, had been captured. The first thing we did
was to interrogate this man, who affirmed that he had been
Vlasov's *denshchik*, his orderly. Together with Vlasov's cook,
he said, they had wandered about for weeks in the hope
of being able to reach their own front lines. Hunger had
repeatedly forced them to visit villages in which they con-
jectured there were no Germans. They had done the same
thing this time, too, but they had been shot at and Vlasov
killed. He did not know what had happened to the cook.

The dead man wore the coat of a lieutenant general; all
other marks of identification also jibed, including a gold
tooth mentioned in a "wanted" circular. We had not the
slightest doubt that it was actually Vlasov, and so filled out
an official form and released the corpse for burial. Corps
headquarters was informed by radio.

We had already passed Tukhovetchi on the return trip
when we remembered the partisans. We turned back, and
the mayor led us to a house bolted on the outside but otherwise unguarded. We posted two men with submachine guns
in front of the door and, when the mayor opened it, I
yelled in Russian into the pitch-dark room for the man to
come out. A bass voice immediately responded in broken
German: "Don't shoot, General Vlasov!" And a man
emerged who bore a puzzling resemblance to the one we had
just buried. He wore an officer's uniform without insignia
and handed me identification papers bound in morocco

leather, and personally signed by Stalin, which confirmed that he was the acting commander of the northwest front and commander of the Second Shock Army. He then drew a Belgian pistol from his trouser pocket and handed it to Captain von Schwerdtner. When I asked who the woman was, he replied, his cook. I then told him we had just identified a corpse as that of Vlasov and that one of the identifying marks had been a gold tooth. Vlasov showed us a gold tooth in the same place and said the dead man might be his chief of staff, Colonel Vinogradov, who resembled him. We were still not completely convinced, and on the return trip, Captain von Schwerdtner asked him various trick questions, which he answered in such a manner as to eliminate all our doubts.

It appeared from Vlasov's statements that he had recognized the hopelessness of the situation and preferred capture to suicide. He asked whether in the German view a general in his situation should have shot himself. Schwerdtner replied that capture was no shame for a general who had fought with his unit to the last moment. Corps headquarters was initially reluctant to accept our prisoner as the real Vlasov. But everything was cleared up when the man claiming to be Vlasov's orderly admitted he had wished to protect Vlasov and was actually Vinogradov's orderly. The next day we started out under heavy guard for the headquarters of the Eighteenth Army in Siverskaya. Colonel General Lindemann, the army's commander, and Vlasov's antagonist in the battle of the Volkhov, treated Vlasov correctly and politely. The generals discussed the course of the battle at length.[5]

[5] Letters to the author whose factual details have been confirmed by communications from Frau Margot von Schwerdtner and staff doctor Werner Henning.

III

POLITICAL ABOUT-FACE

On July 15, 1942, at the Siverskaya railroad station, Vlasov said goodbye to Maria, who was being shipped off to labor service. He himself was escorted to the Army High Command (OKH) in Lötzen by MP Lieutenant Ernst Steen and two MP's.

Vlasov was silent during the journey. He seemed depressed and inwardly tense, though he observed everything very carefully. Not until they reached the border station of Eydtkuhnen, where obligatory delousing took place, did he shake off his numbness. The occasion was the appearance of a group of little girls in bright summer clothes who, led by their kindergarten teacher, passed by singing. Moved, Vlasov spontaneously grabbed his escort's arm as he watched the small band. This peaceful scene apparently dissolved the tension which had gripped him for the past few days and weeks; his eyes were moist as they moved on. From then on, he smiled occasionally. As they crossed East Prussia, he observed the villages, fields, and cattle, and suddenly he said approvingly: "Deutschland khorosho!"— "Germany is good!" [1] They arrived in Lötzen on July 17. Some days later, Vlasov was taken to Vinnitsa, where the OKH had been located since the beginning of the summer offensive and where its special interrogation camp had also been transferred. This installation—set up without the knowledge of top-level officials—had been authorized by Count Klaus von Stauffenberg, head of Section II of the Administrative Branch of the General Staff.

The camp commandant was a German Balt, Captain Egon Peterson, who had a knack for quickly establishing rapport with his prisoners. Like all the officers in the Foreign Armies East Department, he was an opponent of the official *Ost* (East) policy. The camp always held from eighty to a hundred select prisoners, who were well treated by the standards of the time: Generals occupied individual rooms, while two or three colonels shared one room. They all received German rations.[2]

Vlasov met other high-ranking Red Army officers in the camp. Understandably, many prisoners at first viewed captivity as a kind of inner liberation despite their anxieties about the future. A close relationship developed from Vlasov's meeting with Colonel Vladimir Boyarsky, who while serving as a General Staff officer and as commander of the Forty-first Guard Division, had been wounded and taken prisoner. Boyarsky, an impulsive, intelligent man, was a fanatical nationalist. He declared that he hated the Soviet regime and that he considered its overthrow possible with German help. He would be ready for honest collaboration, however, only if liberation, not conquest, was the goal.

He and Vlasov clearly grasped the possibilities that existed for overthrowing the regime. They knew the general state of mind prevailing among Red Army officers and understood that

---

[1] Ernst Steen, report to the author.
[2] Egon Peterson, interview, and letter to the author.

the majority—like themselves—would not desert. The situation would be fundamentally different, however, if instead of the Germans, they confronted a Russian national government and a Russian liberation army which could credibly claim to represent Russia's national interests.

After much discussion they drafted a memorandum[3] on August 3, 1942, in which they declared that the majority of both the population and the army would welcome the Stalin regime's downfall—provided the new Russia was accepted as an ally on an equal footing. For this purpose a "Center for the Creation of a Russian Army" should be established. Only such a liberation army, fighting for Russia's interests, could avoid being stigmatized as a band of traitors.

Vlasov and Boyarsky were, in fact, expressing a view that had already been advocated before them. It had become plain during the advance that the majority of the people in the occupied areas were quite ready to cooperate with the Germans, whom they regarded as liberators from Stalin's terror.

This population had been compelled to sacrifice ten million people to the collectivization of agriculture.[4] It had endured the purges of GPU (Secret Police) chief Yezhov—the so-called *Yezhovchina*—from 1936 to 1938. Eight to ten million people had been dragged off each year to the slave labor camps.[5] While these terrible blows had made organized resistance impossible, they had given vast numbers of people—the relatives and friends of those who had fallen victim to the terror—personal reasons for hating Stalin. It would probably be difficult to find another example in history of a regime so hated and feared by so large a part of its subjects. This is the only explanation for the fact that millions of Soviet citizens, who were certainly no less nationalistic in thought and feeling than citizens of other

[3] Dallin, op. cit., p. 569, fn. 1.
[4] Stalin cited this figure in a conversation with Churchill in May 1942. Cf. W. Churchill, op. cit.
[5] American Federation of Labor: *Slave Labor in Russia*, Report to the United Nations, 1949.

states, were prepared to make a compact with the invaders against their own government.

Innumerable examples make clear how far opposition to the regime extended at the beginning of the Germans' eastern campaign. An American, Charles W. Thayer, describes thus the reaction of peasants in a village 130 miles southwest of Moscow when they heard the news of the German attack: "At last!" they said. "Just let the Kremlin give us weapons. We already know which people we'll shoot. When Hitler comes across the bridge to the front of the village, we will all be there and receive him with bread and salt." [6]

In the autumn of 1941, about two thousand men, mostly students from Leningrad, fled to the woods near Gatchina to avoid being drafted into the Red Army. They looked forward to the Germans' arrival in the hope of participating in a struggle against the Stalin regime. They were also hoping for a political program that could replace Bolshevism. The Germans, however, banned all political activity and proposed that they serve in the base zone as drivers and kitchen help. Part of this group went over to the partisans at the end of 1943, when German policy was becoming increasingly disastrous for the Russian nationalists.

In Pogegen, near Tilsit, where one of the first POW camps in Lithuania was located, twelve thousand men—half the camp inmates—signed a memorandum stating that the time had come to turn the war into a civil war against the Stalin regime and that they were ready to take up the struggle. At the end of 1941, when the inmates of an officers' camp in Minsk were about to be transported to Germany, they shouted, "We don't want to go to Germany! Give us weapons! We want to fight Stalin!" [7] Similarly indicative is an entry, dated January 14,

[6] Charles W. Thayer: *Guerrillas und Partisanen*, Verlag Rütten & Loening, Munich, 1965, p. 67 (also, *Guerrilla*, Harper and Row, New York, 1963).
[7] Dmitri Kozmovich, interview.

1942, in the captured diary of a Red Army captain: "Almost half the village has collaborated with the Germans. The partisans were not only not supported, but betrayed and fought." [8]

Millions of Russians faced the dilemma of whether to go along with the Germans because it seemed the only way possible to overthrow Stalin, or whether to defend their country and thus strengthen a hated government. There is very little information about the anguish and mental suffering the situation entailed. In large measure the decision depended on how the Germans treated the Russians or the idea the Russians had of the Germans. If they believed the Germans really intended to liberate them, they became dedicated, self-sacrificing fighters. If the initial encounter was negative in character, they chose the lesser evil and defended their country.

Some elements, however—the best-known example is the forty-thousand-man Ukrainian Insurgent Army, the UPA—after being disillusioned by the Germans, turned on both them and the Soviets and continued an underground struggle against the Stalin regime for years after the war ended.

Unquestionably, Vlasov's own attitude was influenced by the humane and considerate treatment he had received from General Lindemann, his antagonist in the battle of the Volkhov. However, his meeting in Vinnitsa with the representatives of the OKH's Foreign Armies East Department, and above all, with Captain Wilfried Strik-Strikfeldt, played the crucial role in his decision.

By the time Vlasov arrived in Vinnitsa, the Wehrmacht, after having smashed the Red Army's attempts to breach the front the previous winter, had taken Sevastopol. At the beginning of May an attack by Marshal Timoshenko—initiated near Kharkov with forty fresh divisions—had been blunted, and his forces isolated. The Wehrmacht had then launched its new

---

[8] Quoted in Paul Carell: *Unternehmen Barbarossa*, Ullstein Verlag, Frankfurt-Berlin, 1963, p. 340 (also, *Hitler Moves East*, 1941–3, Little, Brown, Boston, 1964).

summer offensive in the Caucasus and on the Volga. Enormous new territories with millions of inhabitants fell under German domination.

Meanwhile, however, the German political leadership was further removed than ever from establishment of a uniform and realistic *Ost* policy. Behind the monolithic facade of the totalitarian state there raged a struggle of power cliques of which the outside world had scarcely an inkling. At the Führer's headquarters one goal prevailed despite the winter's reverses: ruthless subjugation and colonization. In the Reich Ministry for Occupied Eastern Territories, Alfred Rosenberg tried to implement his idea of dividing the Russian domains into autonomous satrapies, including the Ukraine, White Russia, Caucasia, and Turkestan. However, the "Reichskommissare" whom Hitler had appointed—especially Gauleiter Erich Koch in the Ukraine—pursued a policy of brutal exploitation and extermination that destroyed any chance of bringing these plans to fruition. Heinrich Himmler dreamed of a Greater Reich in which the Slavic *Untermensch* (subhuman) would play the role of an illiterate robot. Joseph Goebbels had envisioned various such alternatives but lacked either the power or the will to implement them.

Finally, there was the group that rejected and fought these megalomaniacal and unrealistic ideas not only on military grounds but for reasons of conscience as well. This group had become openly active since the winter and was attempting in various ways to effect a change in *Ost* policy. Count Klaus von Stauffenberg (later one of the conspirators in the plot to assassinate Hitler) called it the "Association for the Struggle Against Mortally Dangerous Idiocy." It included—in addition to a number of army commanders and staff officers campaigning in the east—the majority of the top officers of the OKH, among them General Eduard Wagner, the Quartermaster General; various officers in the Propaganda Department of the OKH; Admiral Wilhelm Canaris, the head of German military counterespionage; and a group of diplomats led by the former ambassador to Moscow, Count Friedrich von der Schulenburg. Even members of the Waffen-SS fighting on the eastern front, and individual members of the SS (Secret Service) offices III (Domestic) and VI (Foreign), began to perceive the irrationality of the *Ost* policy. To be sure, many of them were motivated not by considerations of conscience but by the expediencies of power politics.

In this undertaking, only the Wehrmacht circles had any real prospect of success at this time. Showing great moral courage, they set to work with all the means at their disposal. The Supreme Headquarters of the Armed Forces (OKW), and especially Field Marshal Wilhelm Keitel and Colonel General Alfred Jodl, obeyed Hitler unconditionally and had instructed the army not to meddle in political questions. Thus, there remained but one way to break through what Stauffenberg called a "wall of idiocy and blindness": to collect accurate and convincing intelligence reports that would unequivocally prove the impossibility of executing a policy based on force. Furthermore, *faits accomplis* had to be carried through which could not be undone without shattering the structure of the eastern front. Heretofore, however, the Foreign Armies East Department had not been working energetically enough in the desired direction.

In April 1942, General Franz Halder, army chief of staff, had appointed Lieutenant Colonel Reinhard Gehlen, an officer on the General Staff, as head of Foreign Armies East. Gehlen, long a bitter foe of Hitler's violent methods, believed that the only chance of overthrowing the Soviet regime lay in an honest alliance with the Russian people. He had attracted a number of younger, like-minded General Staff officers, all with experience at the front and a knowledge of Russia. The department soon had a large quantity of authentic intelligence on hand. In addition to interrogation records and military intelligence reports concerning conditions on the Russian side, petitions and memoranda were piling up from different sections of the Wehrmacht and from various autonomous administrative bodies—all urgently demanding a change in *Ost* policy if everything already accomplished was not to be risked, or the cooperative attitude of the population to be turned into hatred and rejection.

It became increasingly apparent that Communism could not be conquered by its own methods, but instead by the attraction of a better social order. The indispensable cooperation of the peoples of Russia could be won, in the long run, only through the formulation of social and political goals they would find worth fighting for. The conditions for such a development had existed now for quite a while. The local military authorities had been forced to make urgent decisions with the silent consent of the OKH but without the knowledge of Hitler's headquarters. In so doing, they had simply started from the fact that a surprisingly large part of the population was ready to collaborate. Colonel General Schmidt, commander of the Second Panzer Army, was the first army leader to comment on this situation, in a memorandum dated September 18, 1941: "On the Possibility of a Blow at Bolshevik Resistance from Within." Armed local militias had sprung up spontaneously after the retreat of the Red Army, to wage their own struggle against groups of functionaries and partisans who had been left behind, and these local units were permitted to operate temporarily as "people's militia" and later as "order police." German divisions at the front were increasingly employing deserters and prisoners as drivers, mechanics, and ammunition carriers and for other auxiliary jobs. These men wore German uniforms without insignia, in most cases bore arms, and fought alongside the Germans when needed. The designation *Hilfswillige* (Hiwi)— "auxiliary volunteers"—was invented for them, and their numbers swelled to several hundred thousand.

Starting in July 1941, the 134th Infantry Division offered all its prisoners full status as soldiers, so that by the end of 1942 almost half the division consisted of former Soviet troops. Though this experiment, with its far-reaching implications, remained an exception, it nonetheless demonstrated the possibilities that existed.[9] Fully equipped volunteer battalions organized under German command were deployed in fighting partisans as well as in guarding communication routes in rear areas. In two instances larger Russian units were organized under exclusive Russian command: the Russian National People's Army (RNNA) in Ossintorf and the Russian People's Liberation Army (RONA) in Lokot.[1]

All in all, in the fall of 1942, about 800,000 to 900,000 members of Russia's various nationalities were bearing arms against their own government, without Hitler's having knowledge of the fact. Since every attempt to effect a direct change in *Ost* policy had failed, the opposition within the Wehrmacht now rested its hopes, first, on the persuasive power of unavoidable reverses and, second, on the opportunity to present to the other side a respected and well-known personality as leader of a Russian liberation movement—a Russian Charles de Gaulle, perhaps.

Into this atmosphere of tension, disillusionment, and impatience came the news of Vlasov's capture. Here was one of the ablest and best-known Russian generals, one of the saviors of Moscow. His emergence as Stalin's enemy would have unpredictable repercussions. What was essential was to discover the extent of his opposition to Stalin and whether he would be ready to face the consequences of turning against him. To determine this, the right man had to be found—one who not only knew the Russian people but who had sufficient tact, sensitivity, and knowledge of human nature to present the situation in such a manner as to win Vlasov's confidence.

For this task, Gehlen chose Captain Wilfried Strik-Strikfeldt. Strikfeldt, a German Balt, had been a Tsarist officer during the First World War. Gehlen had secured him from the staff of Army Group Center for his own headquarters after learning that Strikfeldt had advocated ideas similar to his own since the start of the eastern campaign.

[9] Cf. Dallin, op. cit., p. 551, with sources cited.
[1] Cf. pp. 57 ff. and 78 ff.

In October 1941, Strik-Strikfeldt had been assigned by General Staff officers von Tresckow and von Gersdorff to draw up a plan for the creation of a Russian liberation army of 200,000 volunteers. Through Colonel von Tresckow, then operations officer of Army Group Center, and with the approval of AGC Commandant Fedor von Bock, the plan was passed on to Field Marshal Walther von Brauchitsch, then commander in chief, and through him to the Führer's headquarters. The final impetus for this report had been supplied by a memorandum to Hitler signed by the Russian mayor of Smolensk and ten other notables of the city. This document proposed to ensure the speedy overthrow of the Soviet regime through a guarantee of Russian independence, the establishment of a rival government, and the organization of a liberation army.

In November, however, a laconic reply came down from Keitel: "Political problems are in principle none of the army's business. Such ideas are, in any case, out of the question as far as the Führer is concerned." [2] A few days later the memorandum came back to headquarters with Brauchitsch's marginal note: "I regard this as crucial to the outcome of the war." Shortly afterwards, Hitler dismissed both Brauchitsch and Bock, and Keitel's negative reply stood as final. When General Greiffenberg presented the mayor of Smolensk with two freight cars of medicine in the name of the army group and then began talking about the memorandum, the mayor abruptly interrupted him: "If four weeks can go by when a question so crucial to the outcome of the war is involved, then the answer can be anticipated." [3]

It was about this time that Strik-Strikfeldt wrote another memorandum, together with some officers of Army Group Center who had been impressed by the friendliness of the population toward the Germans and were concerned over the in-

---

[2] Heinz D. Herre, diary; Strik-Strikfeldt, interview.
[3] Strik-Strikfeldt, interview. Strik-Strikfeldt was present on this occasion as an interpreter.

tolerable conditions in the overcrowded POW camps. The memorandum proposed the release of all POW's who were natives of the occupied territories, with the exception of party functionaries, and the creation of armed people's militias. This plan, if it had been carried out, would have refuted Soviet claims of mistreatment and execution of POW's and would have resulted in a sharp rise in the number of deserters, in the destruction of the then still-weak partisan groups, and above all, in the possibility of adequate food and housing for the remaining prisoners. But the Führer's headquarters ignored these arguments and rejected the proposals, even though the Soviet scorched-earth policy was quite clearly making it impossible either to care for the prisoners adequately or to evacuate them elsewhere. On a note from Admiral Canaris about this time, protesting the illegal treatment of POW's, Keitel had written: "The scruples are those of a soldier fighting a chivalrous war. But here it is a question of annihilating an ideology. I approve of and support these measures."

The consequences of this attitude were harsh indeed: During the winter a high percentage of the POW's died of hunger and epidemics, and disappointment and disillusionment spread among them. Many became irreconcilable enemies of the Germans. Oppressed by his awareness of the situation, and recognizing that the turning point had to come soon, Strik-Strikfeldt approached Vlasov.

Vlasov, meanwhile, had been trying to sort out his ideas and feelings. His disparate impressions confused him. He had to balance reports from fellow prisoners on conditions in other POW camps against his almost friendly relationship with Lindemann and the courteous and correct treatment accorded him in Lötzen and Vinnitsa. Which was an inherent part of the system, which was intentional, which was merely abuse of the kind that occurs in every war?

On his first visit to Vlasov, Strik-Strikfeldt learned the external circumstances of the Russian's life. He heard about the poverty of his parents' house, of his enthusiasm for the Revolution which aspired to better everything, and the successful career which the peasant's son had enjoyed as a Red Army officer; the regime had granted him the opportunity to rise and had not injured him personally in any way. Strik-Strikfeldt soon sensed, however, that everything was not so simple, that much of what the man had experienced and learned had been shunted aside, lest his work or career be harmed. But it had not been forgotten—it had surfaced again in the inferno of the Volkhov battle and in the weeks of deep reflection that followed. Probably for the first time he had clearly and soberly thought things through to the end, and then, after talks with captured companions, had made the inner break, the break with Stalin and the system.

It did not seem important to Strik-Strikfeldt that this decision would never have been made without the ordeal of Volkhov or without his capture. What mattered was that it had been made and that he could count on this fact. It was now up to him to show the way, to explain how understanding could be transformed into the liberating act. After days of probing, of growing familiarity and comprehension, he at last decided to speak with a frankness he could display toward few Germans in this period. Only thus, he sensed, could the confidence of this man be won.

Slowly a new and completely strange world opened up for Vlasov. He realized with surprise that, in contrast to the situation in his homeland, not all decisions here depended on a single man's will; that other plans could be pursued more or less openly; that circles existed which wished to prod Hitler into doing what they considered rational and correct. Yet, Hitler too was a dictator. Wasn't this sympathetic captain a candidate for death, a man it would be best to avoid?

The decision to head a liberation movement was not an easy one for Vlasov to make. He knew he was taking a path on which there was no turning back, one he would have to travel to the end, whatever happened. But he also saw the possibilities. What was crucial was whether the Germans would give him the freedom of action that was indispensable for success. In the end, it was his faith in Strikfeldt that settled the issue; for Vlasov was a good enough judge of men to trust implicitly in the other's integrity. And so he concluded a pact with him which both regarded as a personal commitment, and for which they were ready to take the consequences. Vlasov had become an ally—an ally not only against Stalin but Hitler as well.[4]

Soon afterward, when the OKW's Propaganda Department sent Lieutenant Dürksen to Vinnitsa to become acquainted with Vlasov and arrange his journey to Berlin, Vlasov was frank and cooperative. Gehlen decided to have Strik-Strikfeldt remain with Vlasov and, therefore, assigned him also to the Propaganda Department. Gehlen foresaw that Vlasov would be subject to strains he would be unable to withstand without the friendly support of a German he trusted completely. In addition, Strikfeldt was to supplement the somewhat abstruse activity of the Propaganda Department with his practical experience and in this way, also, promote proposals for a basic change in *Ost* policy.

Strikfeldt reached Berlin several days before Vlasov's arrival. There he met with the inmates of a small compound which had been set up in the wing of a house at 10 Viktoriastrasse for specially selected anti-Stalinist prisoners and deserters. He spoke to them frankly—so frankly, in fact, that at first, some of them suspected him of being a provocateur. But finally they recognized that this was a man of great moral courage who was criticizing *Ost* policy on the basis of his knowledge of the situation and for reasons of conscience. Once, when someone voiced the fear that the German leadership might make a pact with the anti-Bolshevik Russians only in order to exploit and then double-cross them, one of those present said, half-aloud, that

---

[4] Strik-Strikfeldt, interview.

then they would flee to the forest and fight as partisans against the Germans. Strikfeldt answered: "In that case we will probably meet in the forest." [5]

To the inmates of the special compound, the importance of propaganda and political struggle in wartime was axiomatic. Therefore, they thought it a bad joke or a camouflaging tactic when they learned that the OKW's active propaganda in the east was actually being prepared by no more than two men: Captain von Grote and Lieutenant Dürksen. Grote was really predestined for this work—an intellectually gifted man with great skill in negotiations. He was a Balt and, like the Russian ethnic German Dürksen, knew the Russians and their problems. Moreover, in Colonel Hans Martin, head of eastern propaganda activity, he had a superior who, though initially he had followed the official line, had quickly recognized what was at stake and was also willing to fight for it. Martin promoted and facilitated the employment of Russians, to whom fell a substantial share of the department's work. In addition to the occupants of the special compound, "old émigrés" of the First World War were also recruited. These were free staff members, not subject to any outside German authority.

This also held true for Alexander Stepanovich Kazantsev, who played a far more important role in the Russian liberation movement than his position might have indicated. He was one of the leaders of the émigré organization NTS, the Russian Solidarists, established by the youth of the old Russian emigration. They had banded together in the recognition that the mass of Russia's population could not be won over by such aims as the restoration of the monarchy and large estates, that new ideas had to be employed in the struggle against Communism. The NTS had a tight organization and started sending its members into the occupied areas right after the Russian campaign began. They were allowed in—without the knowledge of the

[5] Alexander Kazantsev: *Tretya Sila* ("The Third Force"), Frankfurt, 1952, p. 154.

German political leadership—to recruit new members from among the population and war prisoners, to encourage the organization of autonomous local administrations and militias, and to collect intelligence on the possibilities of a popular uprising against Stalin.

The NTS, having learned quite early the real aims of Hitler's *Ost* policy, rejected National Socialism. Nonetheless, it continued to cooperate with the Germans, because an end to the Soviet system seemed inconceivable without their help. On the other hand, the NTS also believed that the Germans would get nowhere without the help of the Russian people and that they could be forced ultimately to renounce their plans of conquest and colonialization. The NTS thus saw itself as representing a "Third Force" whose strengthening was its major task.

The NTS did not officially collaborate with the German authorities, but many of its members worked as individuals for various government and military agencies in order to pursue their goals more effectively; for example, in the Propaganda Ministry, the Economy Ministry, the Propaganda Department of the OKW, and above all, Rosenberg's Eastern Ministry, into which they had been brought by Leibbrandt, director of the Political Division, and Knüpffer, director for Training Camps. Unlike Leibbrandt, who supported Rosenberg's policy, Knüpffer rejected the Hitler-Rosenberg program and deliberately gave the NTS people a free hand.

There were always several thousand deserters and prisoners in the training camps, where they were prepared for employment in the occupied territories, in the fields of administration, propaganda, and security. These camps afforded the NTS a splendid opportunity. Not only could suitable people be selected from the POW camps and trained, but there was also the possibility of getting them into the occupied areas and thus establishing contact with the inhabitants and recruiting them into the organization. The NTS was in great demand because it was the only Russian group that had played an active role in the eastern campaign.[6]

Alexander Kazantsev helped put out leaflets and newspapers in the OKW Propaganda Department and was thus in a position to influence the inmates of the Viktoriastrasse compound in favor of the NTS. This influence turned out to be quite far-reaching in its effects, since many leading figures of the liberation movement first passed through the compound. Because Kazantzev had not yet visited the occupied eastern region, however, he had no idea how deeply elements of the German army deployed there opposed, and indeed obstructed, the official *Ost* policy. He closed his mind to the fact that the "Third Force" could only be strengthened through sincere cooperation with this part of the German people.

Vlasov arrived in Berlin on September 17. Here he met Mileti Alexandrovich Zykov, a distinguished, though enigmatic, figure in the Russian liberation movement. Zykov would ordinarily have been liquidated by the German Security Service after his capture near Bataisk in April 1942, because he was a political commissar and had, moreover, an oriental appearance. Luckily for him, however, the intelligence officer of Army Group South, Lieutenant Colonel Baron von Freytag-Loringhoven, was impressed by his acute mind and assigned him to the OKW Propaganda Department after he had been processed at the Vinnitsa camp. There Zykov had immediately proclaimed himself a passionate enemy of Stalin who had seized the first opportunity to desert in order to submit a sweeping action program for the overthrow of the Soviet regime to the German leadership. He declared further, however, that he was also a Russian and would only cooperate with the Germans if they intended to liberate Russia, not enslave it.

Grote and Dürksen had described the political situation to him in detail and tried to persuade him that he could best serve

---

[6] On the NTS, see Kazantsev, op. cit.; Vladimir Poremsky, Roman Redlich, and Alexander Zaitsev, interviews.

his country by supporting the sensible elements within the German leadership. After requesting time for reflection, Zykov had completed, within thirty-six hours, a report on the structure and organization of the Soviet economy, particularly of the armaments industry, which far surpassed anything German intelligence officers had ever read. It was the report of an expert with an enormous store of facts, combined with an astonishing ability to interpret them. Eight days later he had submitted an "Organizational Plan for the Practical Mobilization of the Russian People Against the Stalinist System." This displayed an accurate knowledge of existing conditions and of the psychological situation in the Soviet Union and confirmed the correctness of the ideas of the circle around Stauffenberg, Gehlen, and Grote. Zykov also considered it important to have a future Russian opposition regime initially headed by a Red Army general whose popularity would rest wholly on his exploits. He was convinced that such a man would be found as soon as Germany was ready to enter an honest alliance. Once this condition had been met, the downfall of the Stalin regime would just be a matter of time.

Zykov—just turned forty, a well-groomed man of average height with a somber face and a soft, always self-controlled voice—quickly became the center of a small circle. People admired his intelligence and respected him; but only a few really liked him. His superiority was too evident, his encyclopedic knowledge too dazzling, his response to irrelevant arguments too curt, his personality too impenetrable. Yet, strangely enough, the icy intellect was combined with a highly romantic sensibility. The cool, always controlled intellectual was also an artistically gifted individual who recited poetry flawlessly. Even if he spoke reluctantly of his past, even if what he was concealing or distorting remained a puzzle, one thing was evident: A man had turned against Stalin who had to be counted as part of revolutionary Russia's intellectual forces.

Born in Odessa, the son of a merchant of modest means,

Zykov had come into contact with the intellectual elite of the Revolution at an early age. He had known Lenin and the other leaders of the Revolution personally, and was one of the first to be decorated with the Order of the Red Banner. He had advanced quickly from the post of chief editor of a provincial newspaper in Uzbekistan to that of assistant to N. Bukharin, editor-in-chief of *Izvestia*. Married to the daughter of A. Bubnov, the minister of education, Zykov moved in the highest party circles. He sometimes delivered lectures on the history of literature. When Bukharin and Bubnov both fell victim to a purge, he himself was sentenced to three years of forced labor in Siberia. In 1940, however, he was readmitted to the party and assigned as a political commissar with the Red Army. Such had been the career of this convinced Socialist, who made no secret of the fact that the future Russia he dreamed of would be Socialist.

This, and his rejection of the old émigrés from the First World War, set him apart from most of Stalin's other foes, especially the NTS. His views occasioned many sharp debates with Kazantsev, who nonetheless recognized Zykov's superior qualities. Grote and Dürksen also appreciated the value of this collaborator. Grote quieted the Security Service's suspicions that Zykov might be a secret agent by pointing out that the Soviets would hardly have employed a Jewish-looking political commissar for such a mission.

Zykov himself had neither acknowledged nor denied being a Jew. Once, during a session of drinking and card-playing, a companion questioned him directly on this point. Zykov reflected and then calmly replied: "You can't talk about such things while playing. When the game is over, we'll discuss it." [7] He did not make clear whether he meant the card game or the game of life and death he played daily.

When Vlasov arrived, Zykov had already been in Berlin for several months. The inmates of the special compound had ex-

[7] Mikhail Kitayev, unpub. ms., p. 5.

46

haustively discussed every possible way to overthrow the Stalinist dictatorship; but hope that attention would be paid to their proposals had steadily declined. With Vlasov, a turning point at last seemed possible. Knowing what decisive consequences his appearance could have, they awaited him with the greatest excitement. And after their first talks with him, no one could doubt that he had all the qualities required in this situation: personal integrity, popularity with the army, persuasiveness, and a proletarian origin. Not even the ordinary Red Army soldier would believe he had become Stalin's enemy out of opportunism. Vlasov became the center of the small circle almost naturally, although at first, characteristically, he merely listened and observed.

At last he began to speak about his life, his talks with Stalin, the battle of the Volkhov—in the process achieving a detachment which now enabled him to analyze his experiences, something he would have been incapable of doing a few weeks earlier. He had no difficulties in agreeing with Zykov on political plans. Collaboration with this man—whose knowledge, capacity for work, and exceptional gifts for propaganda and psychological strategy he quickly recognized—was fruitful for him in many respects without impairing his own talents and independence.

A short time later, Strikfeldt arranged to have sent to Viktoriastrasse another individual destined to play a crucial role in the circle around Vlasov: Major General Vassily Feodorovich Malyshkin. If Zykov embodied the intellectual, Malyshkin represented the ideal staff officer. He was a strong, cheerful fellow with an infectious optimism and great energy. The son of a bookkeeper in Novocherkassk, he had plunged into the Revolution as a young and very idealistic noncommissioned officer, had joined the party, and after graduating from the military academy, had become a professor there. He was chief of staff of the Siberian Military Region when his commander, Velikanov, was arrested and shot in connection with the Tukhachevsky Affair. Shortly afterward he himself was arrested and for months was so intensely "interrogated" that more than once he had to be carried unconscious back to his cell. But he possessed an iron constitution and an iron will, and he survived this period without signing a "confession." Finally, after fourteen months, he was released and sent to a sanatorium to recover his health. Subsequently he was permitted to return and teach at the military academy. When the war started, he was chief of staff of the Nineteenth Army and while serving with it was captured by the Germans near Vyazma.

Malyshkin deeply hated Bolshevism—hated it because it had destroyed all the hopes he had lodged in the Revolution. He could not forget the humiliations of his imprisonment, although he never mentioned the subject. Malyshkin quickly established good relations with the Viktoriastrasse inmates. He loved to recite the poems of Esenin, who had been a personal friend and had said that Malyshkin could recite his poems better than he himself.

While still in Vinnitsa, Vlasov had written, after discussions with Strikfeldt and Colonel Freiherr von Roenne, an initial leaflet in which he made a general appeal for struggle against the Stalin regime. The OKH wanted to use this to "prove" to the Führer's headquarters the kind of impact a man like Vlasov could have on the Red Army. Reports on the leaflet's success reached them shortly after his arrival in Berlin—and it exceeded all expectations. The number of deserters had multiplied; almost all of them had asked for Vlasov and wanted to meet him.[8] On the basis of this favorable outcome, Grote decided, with OKH approval, to go one step further. For this he needed Vlasov's agreement in principle to head a liberation movement and army. After days of discussion with Strikfeldt and Grote, Vlasov consented. However, he laid down the condition that it must be a political, not simply a propaganda, operation.

Since premature disclosure of the plans might endanger the

[8] Dallin, op. cit., p. 570; Herre, interview.

entire project, the first proposals were limited to the formation of a liberation committee and army under Vlasov's leadership. The decisive argument was that only Vlasov, a man known to all Russia, could properly step forward at the head of such a movement. It was hoped that the success of these measures would at last bring in its wake approval for an opposition regime, a guarantee of independence, and the delegation of power to a civilian administration in the occupied territories. In the meantime, Vlasov, Zykov, and Malyshkin drafted the text of a proclamation.

They awaited the reply from the Führer's headquarters in a state of extreme tension. These ideas seemed so logical, irrefutable, and compelling, they promised such complete success, that their advocates—despite previous experience—could not conceive of their being turned down. This showed how little they knew Hitler's frame of mind. For the incomprehensible occurred: The proposals were rejected.

Martin and Grote returned to the attack over and over again without success. Keitel's answers, written with his lilac pencil, all said the same thing: "Politics is not the army's business— as much propaganda as you wish, but no politics—know the Führer's attitude. Out of the question!" And finally, irritated: "More suggestions of this kind forbidden!" That was how October passed.

At the beginning of November, Grote succeeded twice more in channeling memoranda to Keitel through Colonel von Wedel, head of the OKW Propaganda Department. These petitions spoke almost beseechingly of this unique opportunity. But Keitel brusquely turned Wedel down, and forbade "definitively and irrevocably" any further impositions of this kind. At last the propaganda officers had to admit that what seemed to them a providential solution did not appear as such to the Führer's headquarters, that further attempts would be pointless, and that their plan had been shattered by Hitler's pigheadedness. Hitler's attitude was basically consistent: He was not prepared to change his plans of colonialization and subjugation; it was therefore illogical to encourage national aspirations, because any anti-Stalinist national government and army would also turn against Germany the moment they recognized that enslavement, not liberation, lay ahead.

Keitel, the only channel through which members of the Wehrmacht could reach Hitler, was a primitive man without the slightest political instinct, who not only failed to support the Wehrmacht's efforts, but rubbed his own salt in the wounds caused by Hitler's rejections. He lacked, in any case, the backbone to defend his own views against Hitler's. His function was that of a senior military clerk who served Hitler almost like an automaton and no longer possessed any authority of his own. Nor did the OKW exercise any autonomous command functions; it merely served, instead, as Hitler's military staff. Keitel's subjective dependence on Hitler's will was so great that he renounced all criticism and would not even intercede for higher officers. He was well aware of his weakness and once said to General Westphal: "Well, you know, one has become such a scoundrel." [9]

Strik-Strikfeldt suffered most in this situation. What was he to say to Vlasov now, how could he explain matters to him? It is testimony to the personal courage and uncompromising dedication of Martin, Grote, and Strikfeldt that again they sought to find a path, hoping perhaps to reach their goal by detours, that they continued to believe in the correctness of their ideas. But they failed to grasp how very much the *Ost* policy they fought so hard was a consequence and integral part of National Socialist ideology and how hopeless their efforts were.

Lieutenant Colonel Baron von Roenne, Head of Section III of Foreign Armies East, once asked Strikfeldt why he was doing all this, why he was exposing himself to such danger. Strikfeldt

[9] Walter Görlitz: *Generalfeldmarschall Keitel—Verbrecher oder Offizier* ("Field Marshal Keitel—Criminal or Officer"), Musterschmidt Verlag, Göttingen, 1961, p. 407.

replied that he felt duty-bound: (1) before God and his own conscience; (2) because it was politically correct; and (3) because he had a high regard for the Russian people and wanted to help them liberate themselves from Bolshevism. Whereupon Roenne answered in his curt fashion, going—as always—to the heart of the matter: "1 doesn't apply nowadays, 2 is correct, 3 is treason." And then, with a fleeting smile: "But, of course, you are right." [1]

Vlasov had drawn his own conclusions from the news which had finally reached him, although he was in no position to measure the full magnitude of the catastrophe. He was disturbed by the thought that his name might still be misused, that he might be pushed along a path leading him and the entire project to sure destruction. Strikfeldt, sensing his distrust and agitation, made no attempt to gloss over the situation. But at the same time he insisted that they must not give up, that the struggle to change the *Ost* policy must continue.

Strikfeldt outlined a new plan that he, Martin, and Grote had worked out. While as yet it was impossible to organize the committee and liberation army, they at least had to pretend that these were a reality. A liberation movement already did exist in the form of millions who were ready to fight against the Soviet government. A proclamation announcing a liberation committee and army, fictional though they might be, would still spark local reactions that not even Hitler could ignore for long. Up to now they had tried to establish a policy first and then proceed to propaganda. Now they had to try to conduct propaganda in such a way as to suggest that a policy stood behind it.

A long time passed before Vlasov decided to take the risk. There was no guarantee German *Ost* policy would change, and his confidence in Strikfeldt would vanish forever if the program remained a propaganda trick. Zykov argued that only this subterfuge offered an opportunity; only through the power of a

[1] Strik-Strikfeldt, interview.

fait accompli could anything really be accomplished. And Strikfeldt pointed out that despite all prohibitions the proclamation
would become known in the occupied areas.

The final version of the "Proclamation of the Smolensk
Committee" drafted by the occupants of the special compound
was ready by the beginning of December. Zykov had played an
important part in its writing. The name "Smolensk Committee"
had been chosen because the first impulse toward organization
of a liberation movement had originated in that city in the fall
of 1941. Vlasov and Malyshkin signed the proclamation. It
called for the elimination of the Communist system and the
signing of an honorable peace with Germany. Among other
things, it promised freedom of movement for workers, restoration of free enterprise, the return of the collectivized farms to
the peasantry, and an end to forced labor; it also guaranteed
freedom of speech, press, and religion, and security of person
from arbitrary arrest or detention.

Ten days later the OKW approved the manifesto as a piece
of propaganda, on condition that it not be publicized on the
German side of the front; moreover, since it involved a political
program as well, it had to be submitted to the Reich Ministry
for the Occupied Eastern Territories. There followed a week
of haggling with representatives of that ministry, even though
the Stalingrad disaster was now looming ominously on the
horizon. The ministry officials feared that the leaflet, despite
its fictitious nature, would encourage "Great Russian" chauvin-
ism and might offend the representatives of the Russian minori-
ties they were sponsoring.

While they waited from one week to the next for Rosenberg's
decision, Strikfeldt arranged for Vlasov to meet three other captured generals. One of them was the former commander of the
Nineteenth Army, Mikhail Lukin, who at the end of 1941 had
expressed his willingness to fight the Stalin regime. However,
he had insisted on an agreement to establish an opposition government and a Russian liberation army. Lukin told Vlasov he

had lost faith in the sincerity of the Germans and would not cooperate with him without a binding declaration from Hitler.[2] This was also the position of the other two generals.

At this time a report was received from Major Heinz Herre, a staff officer of Foreign Armies East, on the interrogation of Krupennikov, the captured chief of staff of the Third Guard Army. Krupennikov had asked why the Soviet POW's had not been called upon to fight Stalin. To Herre's question as to whether he himself was prepared to do this, he had replied: "Perhaps I would like to return to Russia, not Soviet Russia. Many of us are tired of life under Stalin." At the same time he had stressed the need for a well-formulated program to save the Russians from conflicts of conscience. If such a policy were adopted, he had asserted, perhaps seventy per cent of the captured officers would fight against Stalin. They or their families had suffered personally under that regime. He had also suggested creating a national liberation army, which would certainly make a better showing than Germany's other allies, whose fighting qualities he denigrated contemptuously.[3]

Vlasov refused to talk to Krupennikov, since he too would ask for guarantees. Looking at the shabby, ill-fitting suit Strikfeldt had found for him, he remarked caustically, "You can't even give me the right-size suit, and you want to conquer the world!"[4] Vlasov did not question Strikfeldt's good will; but he was growing increasingly doubtful about what the German officer could actually accomplish. Even so, he did not suspect how impotent his German friends really were.

In those days of waiting a man joined Vlasov who would soon become one of his closest colleagues: Georgi Nikolayevich

[2] After the war, Lukin returned to the Soviet Union, but was not restored to active duty. In 1965 he wrote a biased and distorted description of his experiences in German captivity. Cf. MiD (*Materialy i Dokumenty ODNR v Gody Vtoroi Mirovoi Voiny* ("Materials and Documents of the ODNR in the Second World War"), pp. 97 ff., All-Slavic Publishing House, New York, 1966).

[3] Cf. Herre, diary, and letter to the author; E. Peterson, interview.

[4] Strik-Strikfeldt, interview.

Zhilenkov. The thirty-three-year-old Zhilenkov had been a high Communist Party functionary and, as secretary of a Moscow district, had ruled over 400,000 people with an almost free hand. When the war broke out, he had been posted as a brigade commissar to the Thirty-second Army, which the Germans encircled near Smolensk. Captured with the rest of the shattered army, he had disguised himself as a rank-and-file soldier, been enrolled in a German unit as a *Hilfswilliger*, and employed as a munitions driver. He did not reveal his identity until he was about to be shot with a group of other Hiwis on suspicion of sabotage. By order of Foreign Armies East, he was sent to the Lötzen special camp and then to the house on Viktoriastrasse, where he became friendly with Kazantsev and Zykov.

Zhilenkov was pre-eminently a product of the Soviet system. An orphan, he had been reared and educated at government expense. His superior intelligence and imposing appearance had insured a rapid rise in his career as a party functionary. It was strange, then, that this man, who owed everything to the Soviet state, should remain with the Germans—even though there had been several occasions during the turbulent winter retreat when he could have crossed over the front lines.

His reasons were typical of many Russians. Zhilenkov described them in conversations with Kazantsev: For a man in a prominent party post, what was unbearable was not so much the day-to-day feelings of uncertainty and insecurity as the unremitting obligation to show, by word and deed, enthusiasm and unshakable faith in the leader Stalin and his actions. Mere approval was not enough; one had to be passionate about it. Because of his position, Zhilenkov spoke at meetings three or four times a week—which meant he had to play the role of crusader three or four times a week. This was hard enough even for a true believer; it was unendurable for those outside the faith. The majority did not believe in Stalin's infallibility or his terroristic measures. But they, too, were forced to lie in word, gesture, attitude, and conduct.

A party member could not resign. For those of Zhilenkov's standing, only two paths were open: to continue up the ladder or to descend into the grave. "It sounds paradoxical," Zhilenkov said, "but I felt like a free man for the first time in a foreign, enemy world, in captivity—I, an important party official, who had every prospect of becoming a member of the Central Committee. What then did an ordinary person really feel! I learned that during the days and months I wandered with them through the forests, and later when I worked for the Germans. I had never realized what crimes the regime had committed, never suspected how much the party is hated by the average man, the peasant and worker. I learned it only when for the first time we could talk freely. I have no desire to spend the rest of my life in Siberia. Just a few hours as a prisoner is enough to convince me of that. The regime shows so little faith even in those who have dedicated all their energies to the Revolution." Earlier, in Lötzen, Zhilenkov had declared: "Treat us decently, as equal friends and allies, and we are yours. I am yours; you will have most of the generals and half the party apparatus." [5]

Zhilenkov's stay on Viktoriastrasse was brief. In mid-August—shortly before Vlasov arrived—he and Boyarsky, whom he had met in Lötzen, were assigned to lead the first large-size unit consisting exclusively of war prisoners and deserters and organized under Russian command: the so-called Experimental Formation Center. [6] The formation of this unit was illustrative of the mood

[5] Information on Zhilenkov may be obtained in Kazantsev, op. cit., pp. 140 ff., and Dallin, op. cit., pp. 544 ff. For the present work, details were also supplied in letters to the author from E. Peterson and Georg von der Ropp, and in interviews with Zaitsev and Bormann.

[6] No details have been published as yet on the origin and purpose of the Experimental Formation Center. Dallin makes a brief reference to its existence (op. cit., p. 545). Jürgen Thorwald describes only the last phase before its dissolution and states that Zhilenkov assumed command in mid-October—although he actually did so on August 26, 1942 (J. Thorwald: *Wen sie verderben wollen . . .* ["Whom the Gods Wish to Destroy . . ."], Steingrüben-Verlag, Stuttgart, 1952). Kazantsev also refers briefly to the organization's last phase and says

of a great many Russians during the first phase of the eastern campaign—it required just one encouraging move to bring them to the point of wanting to fight for liberation from the Soviet dictatorship.

The initiative for organizing the Experimental Formation Center had come from an émigré, Sergei Nikitich Ivanov, who had excellent connections in Nazi Party and Wehrmacht circles and had propagandized there for the creation of a Russian liberation army. Only, however, with Wehrmacht intelligence, which had more freedom of movement than other service branches, did he achieve any success. Admiral Canaris saw the potentialities in creating a unit which would be cloaked as a reserve for commando operations on the other side of the front and perhaps later might form the core of a Russian liberation army. He sent Ivanov to Smolensk to see the head of Intelligence Service Command 203, Lieutenant Colonel Dr. Werner Götting-Seeburg, who immediately promised his support.

In Berlin, Ivanov recruited two more émigrés for the enterprise: thirty-year-old Igor Sakharov, son of a Tsarist general, who had been decorated several times for bravery in the Spanish Civil War and been awarded a lieutenant's commission from Franco; and a former regimental commander, Konstantin Grigorievich Kromiadi. Kromiadi, however, made it clear that he would not serve with mercenary troops; that he would collaborate only if a national Russian army were organized, with equal rights, its own uniforms, and the goal of fighting for Russia's liberation.

The unit was established at the beginning of March 1942. Ivanov was appointed its political leader and was also made responsible for liaison with the German authorities. His repre-

---

that the unit was organized in the summer of 1942 by Zhilenkov and deserted en masse to the partisans in the winter of 1942 (Kasantsev, op. cit., p. 143; and 1963). This account, however, does not jibe with the facts as supplied to the author in interviews with Dr. W. Götting-Seeburg, Kromiadi, Lamsdorff, and Mikhail Shatov, and in a letter to the author by Viktor Ressler.

sentative was Sakharov. Kromiadi, adopting the pseudonym of Sanin, assumed military leadership as camp commandant. The unit was listed as "Russian Battalion for Special Duty" under the code name of "Operation Gray Head."[7] It was stationed at Ossintorf—the site of a former peatworks on the Orsha-Smolensk railroad line—which was situated amidst huge swamps and had enough barracks to house ten thousand men. The unit was organized on the Russian model, and its equipment consisted of captured weapons. The men wore Soviet uniforms to which shoulder straps had been added (something that did not then exist in the Red Army) and white-blue-red cockades.

The Russians, convinced that this represented at last the beginnings of a liberation army, called their unit the Russian National People's Army, abbreviated RNNA (*Russkaya Natsionalnaya Narodnaya Armiya*). The RNNA was three thousand strong in July 1942 and had grown to about seven thousand by the end of the year. Its central staff had the same number of ranks as a division staff. It consisted initially of four infantry battalions, an artillery battalion, and an engineer battalion, and there were plans to expand the battalions to regiments. Each battalion had a noncommissioned officers training school, and the central staff had an officers school. A library and an officers club were built. Propaganda was conducted from a nationalistic Russian point of view, and the RNNA even published its own newspaper, *Rodina* ("The Fatherland").

Soldiers and officers were picked from the POW camps. There was no shortage of volunteers. As soon as the RNNA representatives announced their program, more men applied than could be accepted. Even partisans got in touch with Kromiadi: "We would all join you, but we don't trust the Germans. They will shoot you and us."[8]

Besides Kromiadi, Ivanov, and Sakharov, three other émigrés

---

[7] So named for the gray-haired Ivanov—not for Sakharov, as Dallin incorrectly assumes (Dallin, op. cit., p. 551 fn.).
[8] Kromiadi, interview.

joined the unit: Lieutenant Viktor Ressler, Lieutenant Count Grigory Lamsdorff, and Lieutenant Count Sergei von der Pahlen. The rest of the officers and men, however, had all belonged to the Red Army. There were excellent staff officers among them, seven of whom had held the rank of colonel or regimental commander on either divisional or army staffs. A former General Staff officer, Major Ril, became chief of staff; Colonel Gorsky, commander of the artillery battalion; Colonel Kobtsov and Majors Ivanov, Golovinkin, and Nikolayev, battalion commanders; Major Bocharov, chief of intelligence.

Most of the recruits arrived at Ossintorf in a pitiful, semi-starved condition. Many, in fact, had joined principally to escape starvation in the camps; but, as almost everywhere, when the Russians could exchange views freely and believed a real opportunity existed to fight the Stalin regime, they quickly became convinced members of the liberation movement.

Lieutenant Colonel Götting-Seeburg, an opponent of the Ost policy, fully supported the build-up of the unit. He was held in great affection by the Russians, who nicknamed him Dyedushka ("Little Grandfather"). Tresckow, operations officer on the staff of Army Group Center, and Gersdorff, an intelligence officer, strongly backed his efforts. They were in a position to point out to Field Marshal Guenther von Kluge the success of the unit's commando operations and its proven political reliability.

The unit's first big action, carried out by three hundred men under Bocharov's command, took place in May 1942 in the Yelyenya area. Its mission was to probe the strength and morale of the corps commanded by General Belov, which the Germans had encircled, but which, from forest areas, still maintained contact with the Red Army. Despite some critical moments—a clash occurred with units of the corps and Major Bocharov was temporarily captured—the operation was a complete success. Among other things, a reconnaissance detachment commanded by a "Hero of the Soviet Union," First Lieutenant Knyasev, went over in a body to the RNNA. (However, Knyasev and twenty of his men subsequently changed sides again when he concluded that the Germans would not be sincere allies. He discussed the situation frankly with Kromiadi, explaining to him that Stalin was certainly bad but that subjugation by the Germans would be even worse.)

More victories were scored by units led by Lieutenant Count Lamsdorff, Major Ril, and Major Grachov. In addition, one RNNA battalion was transferred to Shklov to protect that district. The German officials shifted administrative power to the Russians in a formal ceremony. This lifted the mood of the population, since it now looked upon the RNNA as its own national army. There was great hope of further progress in terms of Russian national interests. The local militia considered itself part of the RNNA, and a large number of men tried to enlist. The Soviet leaders began to watch this experiment closely. Agents were dispatched to infiltrate the RNNA and demoralize it.

General Wöhler, chief of staff of the Army Group, inspected the unit in June. A clash soon followed between him and Götting-Seeburg. Wöhler, whose irascible temperament and rudeness were common knowledge, accused Götting-Seeburg of lying because the latter had allegedly supplied the RNNA with more weapons than were necessary. Götting-Seeburg requested arbitration of the dispute. Berlin, however, feared the prospect of ensuing tensions and transferred him. His successor, Colonel Hötzel, maintained his distance, and his relations with the Russians were cool. Nor did he champion the cause of the unit to the same degree as his predecessor had. The situation was aggravated by the tactlessness and blunders of the German authorities, so that the Russians' irritation and bitterness deepened. They suffered another shock when the order came down that all old émigrés had to leave the occupied territory—an order that took in, among others, the very popular Colonel Kromiadi. His final order of the day, issued on August 26, 1942, was typical of the spirit that prevailed in the unit. Containing not a single reference to the Germans, it was devoted to the theme of liberating the homeland. It ended with the declaration: "Never forget that you are Russians, that your tormented Russia cries out for succor." [9]

How strongly the Russians distrusted the Germans, how desperately they were wracking their brains for a way out, is shown by a much-discussed plan of what to do should the unit be disarmed or broken up. In such a contingency they would vanish into the forest and from there deliver an ultimatum to the Germans demanding the right to fight on a separate and equal basis. The Germans would have to reckon with the power of this well-armed unit located just a short distance behind the front. Calmer reflection would have made it obvious that such a move would inevitably result in the destruction of the unit and a weakening in the position of the Russian nationalists. But such was the mood that gripped them.

This was the situation Zhilenkov and Boyarsky found when they arrived. They did not come without their own preconceptions—they feared that the "old" émigrés wanted to promote German interests and create a band of mercenaries. The unit, in turn, received the new commanders with distrust. Zhilenkov had been a party functionary and commissar, and to make matters worse, his first speech to the troops teemed with propaganda phrases and flattered the Germans. The distrust was so great that several officers asked Kromiadi for permission to liquidate Zhilenkov—he was obviously an agent provocateur.

A private conversation between Boyarsky and Kromiadi finally cleared up the situation; their views coincided. Boyarsky assured him that Zhilenkov also shared these views, but that as a former commissar he was endangered by the unpredictability of the Germans and teetered constantly between life and death. For this reason he felt it imperative temporarily to say things he did not believe. With Zhilenkov and Boyarsky in command, the Ossintorf brigade was attached to Army Group Center under the

[9] The author is in possession of the text of this order.

designation of Experimental Formation Center. Both men soon realized that the unit would form a suitable core for a liberation army and had the potential to demonstrate, by action at the front, a significant political impact to the German authorities.

The brigade was combat-ready by the beginning of December. When, on December 16, an urgent need for reinforcements arose, Tresckow suggested to Field Marshal von Kluge that the unit be sent to the front. Kluge immediately visited the encampment, inspected the troops, and was favorably impressed. But then, as if this were a routine matter, he ordered that the Russian troops be apportioned, in battalion strength, among various German units and that they be supplied with German uniforms. All Tresckow's representations, his argument that serious psychological damage would be done, were useless. Kluge knew Hitler's attitude and refused to take risks.

In the end, Gersdorff had to journey to Ossintorf to break the news to Zhilenkov and Boyarsky and try to win their acceptance of the new situation. Boyarsky flew into a rage— better, he felt, to be shot than become a mercenary. The two addressed a statement to Kluge in which they emphasized that the brigade was part of a future Russian army and would fight only in that capacity. It had been organized to liberate Russia from Bolshevism and considered its relation to the German army as that of an ally. To the Germans, however, this was mutiny. That night, rudely bypassing Tresckow and Gersdorff, Kluge sent an ultimatum to Zhilenkov: Either obey the order or face a court martial and disarming of the unit.

At this critical point, Tresckow again intervened. He and Gehlen agreed on Zhilenkov's and Boyarsky's recall to carry on activities in Berlin aimed at creation of a liberation committee. They would be officially designated as "propagandists," which would remove them from prisoner status. Tresckow then sent for the two men, but they refused to come until they had been given safe conduct. He explained to them how much the cause and its goals would suffer if Kluge's orders were flouted, how the enemies of a sane *Ost* policy would exploit the incident, and promised that he would personally continue to look after the unit. They dropped their resistance and left the RNNA the next day. Major Ril, promoted to colonel, became commander, and Major Besrodny chief of staff.

The situation was still extremely tense, and the mood of the troops threatening. Three hundred men fled to the partisans on the night the order was announced for the breakup of the brigade and the wearing of German uniforms. But the rest remained and were shifted to the Bobruisk-Mogilev area to carry out security duties and to fight the partisans.

Thus ended the RNNA. The first attempt to build a national Russian liberation army had failed almost at the outset.

Zhilenkov and Boyarsky were sent into Foreign Armies East to remove them from the line of fire. When it seemed certain that Kluge would not insist on further measures against them, they were dispatched to Berlin. Zhilenkov stayed on in Viktoriastrasse, while Boyarsky was appointed head of a propaganda detachment in the northern section of the front. Zhilenkov's report to Vlasov confirmed the latter's own belief in the possibilities for liberation on the one hand; on the other, it strengthened his fears concerning Hitler's attitude, especially since no decision had been forthcoming yet on the Smolensk Proclamation, and the attitude of the Reich Ministry for the Occupied Eastern Territories remained unreasonable.

While the Eastern Ministry continued to resist the stubborn pressures of the OKW Propaganda Department and other Wehrmacht agencies, memoranda were steadily piling up from eastern army units, urgently demanding, on the basis of their practical experience, an immediate and radical change in *Ost* policy. During the advances to the Volga and in the Caucasus, the population had shown even greater eagerness to collaborate than in the central sector. There were no partisans in these territories. On the initiative of the intelligence officer of Army

Group South, Lieutenant Colonel von Freytag-Loringhoven, Cossack units were immediately organized to strengthen the German front in the enormous expanse between the Don and the Volga. Sixteen Kalmuck squadrons were formed on the Kalmuck Steppe, and individual Turkestani, Azerbaizhani, Georgian, Armenian, and North Caucasian volunteer legions soon appeared.[1]

By March 1942 the Germans were ruling over sixty to seventy million Soviet citizens. The intelligence, tact, and fairness of the German military and civil authorities would determine whether collaboration would grow or would turn into hostility and hatred. Awareness of these alternatives gradually crystallized army opinion against current administration methods and the colonialization plans. Reports were written by General von Rocques,[2] Colonel Gehlen,[3] and Colonel von Tresckow,[4] on the basis of hundreds of memoranda submitted by the staffs of smaller army units.

The commanders of the army rear areas, knowing that Keitel's negative attitude blocked access to Hitler, requested a conference with Alfred Rosenberg, Reich Minister for the Occupied Eastern Territories. This was held in Berlin on December 18, 1942. The commander of Army Group Center's rear area, Gen-

[1] After the Germans retreated, these peoples had to pay dearly for their collaboration. The Kalmuck Soviet Republic was dissolved on December 27, 1943. The "liquidation" of the Moslem peoples of the Northern Caucasus was ordered on February 11, 1944, and carried out to the letter. The Crimean Tartars, Kalmucks, Chechen-Ingush, Karachays, and Balkars were exiled en masse to Siberia, as were the 1,500,000 inhabitants of the German Volga Republic. Cf. Dallin, op. cit., pp. 263 f.

[2] Commander of Army Area (Rocques) to OKH/Quart.-Gen., September 14, 1942, cited in Dallin, op. cit., p. 558 f.

[3] Foreign Armies East (Gehlen): "Dringende Fragen des Bandenkrieges und der 'Hilfswilligen-Erfassung'" ("Urgent Questions of Guerrilla Warfare and Mobilization of 'Hiwis'"), November 25, 1942; Dallin, op. cit., pp. 559 f.

[4] Army Area Center: "Erfahrungen in der Verwaltung des Landes und politische Zielsetzung" ("Experiences in Regional Administration and Political Goals"), December 25, 1942, cited in Dallin, op. cit., pp. 562 f.

eral Count Schenckendorff, painted a brutal picture of the conditions which had arisen as a result of the policies of Rosenberg's own colonial governors (Reichskommissare) and the measures of the Economic Ministry and SS Security Service staffs. The generals pointed to the growing danger of partisan activity as the consequence of these official actions, and to the conflicts that would surely develop within the native volunteer units.

The finer distinctions between Hitler's and Rosenberg's views on *Ost* policy were a closed book to the generals. They emphasized Germany's need to live on friendly terms with the Russian people in the future as well, and the fact that Germany was then doing its damnedest to completely foreclose this prospect. They presented an unsparingly candid outline of the military situation and stressed the increasing weakness of the German position, which could be rectified only by cooperation with the population. Schenckendorff asked Rosenberg to tell the Führer the plain truth. He could not believe, he declared, that Hitler had an accurate notion of actual conditions in the Soviet territories occupied by the Wehrmacht and administered by the Eastern Ministry.

Rosenberg was visibly impressed. Besides the commanders of the army rear areas, every department of the General Staff was represented, and all these officers were obviously of one mind. A view long held by the circle around Vlasov had been elevated to the level of a German military judgment: "Russia can only be conquered by Russians." Lieutenant Colonel Schmidt von Altenstadt argued that without a basic change in the German attitude the half million Russians attached to the Wehrmacht constituted an incalculable danger. There was not the slightest doubt, he added, that the people were still willing to fight against Stalin's regime—if they were convinced by concrete evidence that the current policies had been totally scrapped.

It was no accident that all the officers presented military, rather than moral, reasons for altering *Ost* policy. They knew that moral arguments would be meaningless to Hitler. Nor was it an accident that not one of them spoke of breaking up Russia. To them it was axiomatic that Stalin's dictatorship could be overthrown only by the combined strength of all regions and that plans to carve up the country would merely benefit the Soviet regime.

Rosenberg promised to work for a change in *Ost* policy.[5] On December 21 he sent Hitler a memorandum in which he summed up the main points of the conference and requested permission to report personally on the affair. Hitler received him shortly afterwards, but stressed the usual argument that it was the business of generals to wage war, not dabble in politics. Nevertheless, it is probable that the arguments the Wehrmacht had fired at Rosenberg were responsible for Hitler's approval of the Smolensk Proclamation on January 12, 1943. He prohibited, however, any distribution of the proclamation on the German side of the front.

The campaign swung into action the very next day, since the OKW Propaganda Department had made preparations for this down to the last detail. Millions of leaflets were dropped on all fronts, and some of them—as secretly planned—fell "accidentally" as well into occupied territory. The operation's success exceeded even the expectations of the optimists in the Gehlen–Grote circle. The first reports from the several fronts announced a sharp rise in the number of deserters, who almost without exception were asking to be taken to Vlasov and his liberation army. The first dispatches from the occupied eastern regions followed a little later. They reported "deep interest and universal approval"; the population awaited "further steps in this direction"; it was "urgently necessary to give the Liberation Committee real power to act so that our propaganda will not lose its credibility." [6]

---

[5] The conference was held on December 18, 1942. The minutes of the conference are dated January 4, 1943. Dallin, op. cit., pp. 163 and 560.

[6] Quoted in Dallin, op. cit., p. 580.

A wave of expectant excitement had seized large sections of the populace. After all the doubts about the sincerity of the German leadership, indeed the despair caused by its political irrationality, it now seemed that, at last, a change had occurred. Those Germans in the occupied territories who met with Russians, who had established relations with them, kept hearing the same hopeful and impatient questions. The Russian volunteers demanded that they be assigned to the liberation army, the ROA (*Russkaya Osvoboditelnaya Armiya*).[7] None of them knew that the ROA did not yet exist, that the Smolensk Committee was a creature of paper; their reaction, however, had become a political reality with which the opponents of the official policy hoped to strengthen their position. "The genie has popped out of the bottle, now let them try to stuff him back in," Zykov declared,[8] expressing not merely the hopes but the malicious satisfaction of Vlasov's circle.

The day the Smolensk Proclamation was approved can be considered the real birth date of the Russian liberation movement. For the first time its latent energies had been given a program; for the first time the goals of the struggle had been stated, not merely the identity of the enemy. It is interesting to note that this document, despite its Hitlerite sponsorship, expressed democratic ideals.

The Soviet propaganda apparatus continued to maintain its silence. However, the order went out to hand in all such leaflets immediately, and the death penalty faced anyone who circulated them. Stalin understood the danger the liberation movement represented to his government, as was shown by a far-reaching change in the political line. Overnight the Soviet people were summoned to a national struggle for the Fatherland. The churches, bitterly fought till then, were reopened by a government that had murdered thousands of priests. Epaulets, reviled as marks of the bourgeoisie, were restored; decorations bearing

[7] Author's diary.
[8] Kitayev, op. cit., p. 6.

the names of the old national heroes, the Tsarist generals Suvorov and Kutuzov, were introduced; and the Comintern was dissolved.

For almost a quarter of a century the party had sought to fashion a "new Soviet man"; it seemed now that it had failed. Stalin could not appeal for the defense of a Communist social system and a struggle for international Communism, but had to propagandize, instead, for defense of the Fatherland. This propaganda was not without effect, owing to disillusionment with the Germans. Many began to believe that under pressure from a victorious army Communism would change. The partisans spread the rumor in the occupied territories that neither a Liberation Committee, nor an ROA, nor Vlasov were actually to be found on the German side; that it was all a German propaganda trick. And the more time passed without any news of further progress by the movement, the greater was the credence given to such reports.

IV

THE FIGHT FOR FREEDOM OF ACTION

Increasingly worried by this situation, the army groups became more and more convinced that it was imperative to have Vlasov visit the occupied areas. Kluge and Schenckendorff agreed to assume responsibility for the move so that no time would be lost in exchanges with higher echelons. Vlasov's presence had become crucial with respect to the attitude of the population and the volunteer units. Although Kluge and Schenckendorff had given assurances, and Vlasov's tour would be officially masked as "propaganda," Martin and Grote knew perfectly well how risky the venture was for them and their cause. Nevertheless, they got preparations under way for Vlasov's tour.

Vlasov at first declined to make the trip. As long as the committee lacked official approval, as long as the liberation army remained a fiction, he could promise nothing of what was expected from him by the people and volunteer armed units. Long discussions with other Russians, however, persuaded him not to give up. If even the Smolensk Proclamation's success had not swayed the Führer's headquarters, Vlasov's appearance, it was felt, would occasion such a forceful demonstration of the feelings of the people that they would be impossible to ignore.

Considering Vlasov's importance and his public stand against the Soviet regime, there is something almost grotesque about the petty obstacles that consumed the energies and time of his German patrons on the highest staff levels of the Wehrmacht. For example, several Propaganda Department officers had to pay for his uniform out of their own pockets because he could not appear publicly in his shabby suit. Vlasov would not wear a German uniform; a Soviet one was out of the question because of the bad effect it would have on the population; and a Russian liberation army uniform was as nonexistent as the army itself. And so it was that the uniform Vlasov was fated to wear to the end of his days was a figment of the imagination to which chance stood godfather. The material Strikfeldt collected, after days of tireless scavenging, consisted of black pants with a general's red piping, a dark-brown jacket minus tabs and shoulder straps, and a similarly colored coat with red lapels. In Smolensk, Captain Peterson snipped off the silver buttons sewn on originally and replaced them with the gold buttons of a general's uniform.

No longer classified as a war prisoner, Vlasov occupied a small, poorly furnished room in the Russian Court, a second-rate hotel in the center of Berlin. At Strikfeldt's request he started his tour on February 25, 1943, in the company of Schenck-endorff's intelligence officer, Lieutenant Colonel Wladimir Schubuth, and of Captain Peterson, whom he had already met in Lötzen and who was to serve as his interpreter.[1] From Berlin's Silesian Station they traveled in the sleeping car of a courier train to Lötzen, and from there in a furlough train to Smolensk.

[1] Information on Vlasov's trip supplied in interviews with Peterson and W. Schubuth.

General von Schenckendorff received Vlasov in his head-quarters on the city's outskirts. They discussed the possibilities and necessities of the political struggle. Vlasov then visited the cathedral, which, until the Wehrmacht had occupied the city, had been used as a granary. There he held a long conversation with the priest. That evening a festive affair took place at the theater. For the first time since his capture, Vlasov spoke to a large group of Russians.

Vlasov's deep, resonant voice filled every part of the hall. He spoke simply, choosing apt comparisons, and immediately established rapport with his listeners. Himself a man of the people, he knew how to hold this audience. He radiated authority, confidence, and the power of conviction.

He began by briefly describing his career in the Red Army and his reasons for turning against Stalin. He spoke of the aims of the liberation movement and, once they were achieved, of the European commonwealth of nations in which a free Russia would take her place. He emphasized that it was the business of the Russians themselves to overthrow Stalin. Although the Germans would be allies in this struggle, he stated that National Socialism could not be transplanted to Russia. The Russians could not wear a foreign coat. The form of government that would emerge after victory would be one that fitted Russia's conditions and requirements. He concluded by calling on those present to express their views.

The first to rise was the acting district chief of Smolensk. He said that the population in the occupied territories had hoped for much and received little, and he asked questions which countless Russians had posed in vain since the beginning of the war: Was it true the Germans intended to turn Russia into a colony and Russians into slave laborers? Were those people right who said they would rather live in a wretched Bolshevik Russia than under the German knout? They were always being told what they should fight against, but not what they should fight for. Nobody had yet announced what was planned for their country after the war. Why hadn't the Germans consented to

Russian administrations in the occupied areas? Why didn't the volunteers, who were fighting alongside the Germans, have their own headquarters and Russian commanders? They would like to know why none of these things had happened.

Vlasov had feared these very questions. All he could offer in reply was hope. He pointed out that his own public activities demonstrated growing understanding among the Germans. He argued, as he did also in later speeches, that initially the Germans felt the majority of the people were fighting for Communism. This distrust had led them into error, but many Germans had now come to recognize their mistake. He was working with them to clear up misunderstandings and accomplish the things which had to be done. It was nonsense to assume that 190 million people could be enslaved. But German help was needed to eliminate Stalin's Communism, and it was not treason to accept this aid, since a majority of the people desired Stalin's overthrow. The aims had been clearly stated in the Smolensk Proclamation. Vlasov needed the trust and help of the people if he was to fulfill his mission, if he was to succeed in convincing the German leadership of the measures that had to be adopted. The stormy applause that followed his remarks showed how deeply these people had suffered from uncertainty, how much these hopeful words meant to them.[2]

The next day, Vlasov inspected a volunteer unit and visited the editorial offices of the local Russian newspaper. Then he met with a White Russian, Major Dmitri Kozmovich, who had become famous in the administrative region of Army Group Center for sweeping large areas around Bryansk and Smolensk clean of partisans. Kozmovich, one of the small group of intellectuals produced by the White Russian peasantry, had emigrated early and joined a political organization in Belgrade whose aim was to fight for an independent White Russia. He had returned to his homeland at the beginning of the eastern campaign to pursue this goal with German assistance.

This was Vlasov's first meeting with such an advocate of radi-

[2] Details of the meeting supplied by Peterson in interview.

cal separatism. Kozmovich expressed his willingness to cooperate if Vlasov and the Liberation Committee would guarantee White Russia's independence. Vlasov argued in vain that first the common enemy must be beaten, that the people would decide this question later, and that to proclaim Russia's division would be to give Stalin his best trump card in the political struggle. On this discordant note the two men parted.

Nonetheless, the meeting was valuable for Vlasov. Kozmovich had proven how easy it was to mobilize the populace and what could be accomplished if the Russians themselves, not the Germans, assumed administration of the occupied eastern territories. At the time Kozmovich had arrived in Smolensk, the large forests surrounding the city had been occupied by a partisan brigade almost two thousand men strong. It was difficult to fight the brigade because it maintained contact with the Red Army from the forests around Demidov, where there was no fixed front. It requisitioned cattle and food from the villages and harassed the population, which finally turned to Smolensk with a plea for protection.

The German army commander and city commandant, General Pohl, authorized Kozmovich to organize a self-defense network. The first step was to protect the nearby villages. In each village 100–150 men were armed from stores of booty. Bunkers were built, and a signal system to alert neighboring units in case of surprise attacks was devised. Kozmovich's most pressing need was for officers and noncommissioned officers who could train the peasants. Sixty officers, including many regular officers up to the rank of colonel, were picked from a prison camp. These men hated Stalin, but they had become embittered and disillusioned by the Germans as well. The experiment, therefore, was not without risk, since with partisan help they could desert to the Red Army at any time. Yet there was not a single defection.

In an expanding circle with Smolensk at the center, one village after the other was armed and thus withdrawn from the reach of the partisans. Starting in June 1942, the local militias—

officially designated *Ordnungsdienst* (OD), or "Order Police" [3]
—also temporarily took over bunkers in the forests around Demidov, which had in effect become the front lines. In Smolensk
itself, Kozmovich organized a motorized task force which could
be quickly thrown into emergency situations. The total strength
of the local militia in the Smolensk region ultimately amounted
to almost 3,000 men, and in the entire rear area of Army Group
Center, to about 100,000. Kozmovich, appointed inspector of the
Ordnungsdienst, organized them into battalions under command
of a general staff so as to expedite their incorporation into the
projected liberation army. Shortly thereafter, however, the OKW
forbade centralization of any kind. This was not just another
disappointment for the Russians, but also for the German commander of the army rear area, who had greatly exceeded his
authority by supporting Kozmovich's plans.[4] Kozmovich was
operating with a simple approach whose success depended on a
single assumption: the readiness of the population to collaborate.
The extent to which they had done so again confirmed the
validity of the experiment.

Vlasov's tour lasted three weeks. He spoke in villages and
cities and to volunteer formations. Everywhere he was received
with great enthusiasm; his appearance visibly raised flagging
spirits and revived almost-shattered hopes. His visit left an especially strong impression on the Kononov Cossack regiment in
Mogilev. While tens of thousands of men had deserted to the
Germans in the first year of war, they had all come individually
or in small groups. The Soviets' sophisticated network of informers seemed to preclude altogether the defection of whole
units. However, Major I. N. Kononov, commander of the 436th
Infantry Regiment of the 155th Infantry Division, had managed
to bring over his regiment to the Germans in a body—the one
such instance in the entire war.

[3] Text of Administrative Regulation No. 20 of December 1, 1942/
April 30, 1943, on organization of Order Police (indigenous local
police) is in author's archives.
[4] D. Kozmovich and Nikolai Kandin, interviews.

Kononov was a graduate of the Military Academy, a party member since 1927, a veteran of the Finnish War, and a holder of the Order of the Red Banner. Like Vlasov, he had not himself been persecuted by the government but had watched Stalin's terror destroy the best officers of the Red Army. And he knew the mood of his regiment. While his unit was bringing up the rear during a retreat, he sent one of his most trusted men to the enemy with a message offering the cross-over of his regiment—provided the Germans agreed to let him take part in establishing a Russian liberation army to overthrow the Stalin regime. The Germans accepted the offer. He thereupon called in the officers of his regiment and informed them that he was an enemy of Stalin's government and had decided to begin the struggle against it for Russia's liberation. Those who wanted to go with him were welcome to do so, those who didn't could remain and nothing would happen to them. With the exception of a few commissars, everyone was willing to join Kononov. He then addressed the regiment as a whole, informing them of his decision. Each man had the choice of staying with the Red Army or following him. They all followed. On August 22, 1941, he led the regiment without incident through the German lines.

Kononov had the good luck to get General Schenckendorff for his collaborator. Schenckendorff promised to do everything in his power to win the approval of the High Command for the creation of a large Russian liberation army. Meanwhile, on his own authority, he sanctioned the formation of a Cossack regiment. Schenckendorff well knew that at this particular time he would never receive approval for a Russian regiment.

Kononov, himself a Don Cossack, agreed "temporarily" (as he thought) to organize such a unit. He did not doubt that the German leadership would quickly recognize how easily the Stalinist regime could be brought down with the help of the Russians themselves. Schenckendorff gave Kononov authority to act with complete independence and appointed Lieutenant Count Rittberg as liaison officer between them. Rittberg soon won Kononov's confidence and friendship, and remained with the regiment until the end of the war.

Eight days after switching sides, Kononov visited the POW camp in Mogilev, where he asked for volunteers to join the first unit of a Russian liberation army. More than four thousand of the five thousand POW's wanted to sign up, but of these, Kononov picked only five hundred, of whom four hundred were Cossacks. He promised the rest they would have their chance later. The same pattern repeated itself in the camps at Bobruisk, Orsha, Smolensk, Propoisk, and Gomel.

On September 19, 1941, scarcely four weeks after the defection, the new Cossack regiment became a reality, with a complement of 77 officers and 1,799 men. Kononov had to dismiss one group of his former soldiers because they were not Cossacks— although non-Cossacks in fact constituted forty per cent of the regiment's strength. The men dismissed, however, were not sent to POW camps but were assigned, instead, either to the civil administration or to police units.

In the meantime, Schenckendorff had allocated arms and equipment for the regiment and personally read to the assembled unit the OKH's Order of the Day authorizing a Cossack regiment to be designated the 120th Don Cossack Regiment. The regimental standard-bearer was a Don Cossack named Belogradov who had spent twelve years in Stalin's concentration camps and whose two brothers and four sons had been murdered by the secret police.

Kononov's hopes for the speedy organization of larger units, however, did not materialize. In fact, on January 27, 1943, he was informed that Russian units could not be approved above the battalion level and that his regiment therefore had to be renamed the Six-hundredth Don Cossack Battalion—although it then contained about two thousand men and was due to receive another thousand in February. Subsequently a special armored detachment called the Seventeenth Cossack Armored Battalion was formed. It was assigned to the German Third

Army and was repeatedly engaged in front-line combat. One hundred twenty men from Kononov's battalion, dressed in Soviet uniforms, infiltrated the Russian lines near Velikie Luki. They succeeded in capturing a Soviet military tribunal with five military judges and a twenty-one-man guard, liberating in the process forty-one Red Army soldiers already sentenced to death, and carrying off important documents.

Vlasov's visit filled the battalion with new hope. They interpreted German approval of his activities as a sign of growing understanding. Kononov and Vlasov quickly established rapport, agreeing on the creation of a Cossack force within the framework of the projected liberation army. Kononov, who was always hostile to separatist aspirations, advocated this idea to the end.[5]

In Bobruisk, the next stop on the journey, the local propaganda unit had planned to have Vlasov speak over the radio. Higher-ups in the Propaganda Ministry, however, vetoed this idea. To spread word of Vlasov's presence as widely as possible, therefore, the news broadcasts reported that he had arrived to inspect the radio station. Vlasov also received in Bobruisk a detailed description of the only large area within the occupied territories that was under Russian administration. This area, located in the administrative region of the Second Panzer Army, near the front lines, encircled Lokot on the eastern rim of the great forest stretching south from Bryansk. Here, too, the Wehrmacht had demonstrated more understanding of political necessities than the German civil authorities. The experiment in the Lokot area provided one of the most convincing examples of what was possible and could be accomplished if reason and insight into the realities, rather than utopian schemes, were the determining factors.

The situation in this area, in the middle sector of the front, exemplified all the problems that had to be solved in the occupied territories. Primeval forests flourished in the region, and

---

[5] Cf. Chap. V, pp. 182–3. On Kononov, see also Konstantin Cherkassov: *General Kononov* (in Russian) published by the author, Melbourne, 1963, 2 vol.

partisans lurked in their trackless depths. Fertile fields tilled by the peasants lay near the big cities of Orel and Bryansk. Here the first and largest Russian-administered district came into being, and the first Russian volunteer units were organized and activated. The initiative and moral courage shown by the commander of the Second Army, Colonel General Schmidt—who did not shrink from ordering required measures without the knowledge and against the desires of the Führer's headquarters —fostered a relationship of mutual trust between the military administration and the populace.

The mood was unequivocally anti-Soviet. The peasants had divided up the collective farms as soon as the Red Army retreated. They armed themselves with the weapons abandoned by Red Army men in order to defend their villages from reprisals by scattered soldiers and partisans. This attitude had its effect as well on the Red Army men who after the siege of Bryansk wandered by the thousands through the forests. Many disappeared into hiding in the surrounding villages, where labor shortages existed. Others surrendered to German units and were put to work, or joined local militias. In this fashion a kind of popular movement against the Stalin regime evolved in the area even before the Germans took over its administration. The first person to exercise authority in the Lokot district was a tall, handsome engineer named Voskoboinik, a man of remarkable intelligence and a gifted speaker. He managed to set up, in a few weeks, a kind of autonomous administration which was initially protected from the partisans by an armed self-defense unit of five hundred men.

This was the state of affairs the arriving Wehrmacht came upon, and that General Schmidt legitimized, confirming the area's status as an autonomous, Russian-governed region. Full executive authority was bestowed upon the Russians, and all German troops and administrative units were withdrawn from the area, except for a small liaison staff. The Russians assumed the obligations of maintaining order, driving off the partisans, and supplying the Germans with stipulated quantities of food.

With the passage of time the region was expanded until it finally embraced eight districts with more than 1,700,000 inhabitants, and had at its disposal a Russian-led brigade of more than 20,000 men that kept the territory free of partisans until the German retreat. The brigade—whose men wore Soviet uniforms with national insignia and epaulets—comprised five infantry regiments, one armored brigade with twenty-four T-34 tanks, one engineer battalion, one guard battalion, and one anti-aircraft artillery battalion. The Russians, regarding this brigade as part of a future liberation army, formally designated it the Russian National Liberation Army (*Russkaya Osvoboditelnaya Narodnaya Armiya—RONA*). Partisans frequently deserted to RONA, sometimes coming from more than sixty miles away. As late as the spring of 1943 an entire detachment of eighty men, led by their commander, turned up in Lokot.

After Voskoboinik fell fighting the partisans, an engineer named Kaminsky became head of the region and brigade, and General Schmidt appointed him a brigadier general. Under Kaminsky, who handled his relations with the Germans with a sure touch, the region developed into a model of what the Russians could accomplish without German interference. It published its own newspaper, and a theater, a bank, several factories, and two hospitals under Russian medical supervision were set up. The area even had its own tax board. The region's economy revived swiftly as a result of the immediate restoration of private property, and the population had a standard of living higher than that in any other occupied area. Its deliveries of food and raw materials to the German army were exemplary.

A "National Socialist" party was planned, though this never got beyond the initial stages. This prospective party was not, in any case, infected by German National Socialist ideology, of which the Russians had not the slightest conception.

Although Himmler had no authority in army-administered territory, General Schmidt sought added security by use of an SS-Security Service liaison man assigned to the army.

At the end of 1942, Kaminsky submitted a memorandum to

General Schmidt which summarized achievements and proposed future measures. The document did not fail to note that continued refusal to enunciate positive political goals could lead to an unfavorable shift in the popular mood. Its proposals were essentially the same as those already contained in hundreds of German and Russian memoranda: Russian autonomous administration in all occupied territories, a Russian-led liberation army, a Russian opposition regime, and guarantees of Russia's independence within its 1938 borders. General Schmidt personally brought up these proposals with his superiors—and was promptly transferred from the eastern front.

All this was going on barely sixty miles behind the front. Some Germans felt that RONA would someday desert; but evidence to the contrary was repeatedly noted. Thus, the brigade was sent into action when the Red Army broke through the German front lines near Dmitrovsk in the summer of 1943, and it repulsed the Soviet attack in a two-day battle. Not one man deserted. The following autumn the Fourth Regiment of the brigade was assigned to hold the city of Sevsk until the general withdrawal had been completed safely. The Soviets, however, encircled the area after a surprise attack led by tanks, and in two days of bloody fighting slaughtered the RONA troops down to the last man. Not even the wounded were spared; the regiment's injured commander, a young major, was tied to the back of an armored scout car and dragged to his death through the streets of the town.

This occurred in connection with a general pullback by the Germans to the Dnieper at this time. Most of the brigade—more than fifty thousand men in all—joined in this withdrawal and, on its completion, were quartered in the Lepel area. It was at this point, however, that demoralization began to set in as the plans of the German leadership became known.[6]

A visit to Lokot had not been included in Vlasov's itinerary,

---

[6] During the period from January 1942 to the autumn of 1943, the author was assigned to report to the staff of the Second Panzer Army,

since the district was then no longer under Schenckendorff's jurisdiction. Nonetheless, Vlasov's tour strengthened his conviction that unified leadership, consistent guidelines, and—most important—complete freedom of action would transform the potential willingness to collaborate into a powerful liberation movement.

Vlasov completed his tour with visits to four volunteer battalions which had been organized out of RNNA when Kluge ordered it broken up.[7] The men of these units had already been compelled once to bury their hopes for a great Russian libera-

---

and later to that of the Ninth Army, on whatever happened in their respective sectors. At the same time he was responsible for maintaining liaison with the autonomous Russian administrative bodies. His notes were preserved. He was responsible for a message center in Lokot headed by Sonderführer Adam Grünbaum. Very few reports have been published on the Lokot experiment or on Kaminsky, who is viewed, in the main, as a mercenary and Nazi. He was neither. He and his comrades-in-arms turned against the Stalin regime out of conviction, and none of them had any notion of the nature of National Socialism. The Germans regarded his self-confident behavior as a piece of arrogance. The sentence he received was basically prompted by excesses committed by elements of his brigade during the crushing of the Warsaw Uprising. These are most certainly not to be excused, but they may be explained by the demoralization which was already widespread at this time, caused by the desperate situation and German stupidity.

The mood of the population in the Orel-Bryansk area was essentially the same as that in other occupied areas of Russia. This mood has often been inaccurately depicted, either deliberately or out of ignorance. Thus the unusual eagerness with which the population was ready to join the Germans against the Stalin regime is largely ignored in Alexander Werth: *Russland im Krieg 1941–1945*, Droemersche Verlagsanstalt, Munich, 1966 (also, *Russia at War, 1941–1945*, E. P. Dutton, New York, 1964). Werth says: "The general impression was that in the victorious days of 1941/42 a number of Russian adventurers, camp followers of the Germans, toyed with the idea of playing a role in Germanicizing pure Russian territories, as, for example, the area around Orel." The same author writes of the Russian volunteers: "The Germans organized from Russian war prisoners a 'volunteer army' commanded by Vlasov. Unquestionably a large part of the 'volunteers' heeded the call of the Germans because the only alternative seemed to be starvation." This generalization ignores the fact that neither the members of the Kononov Regiment, the Kaminsky Brigade, nor the local militias and Hiwis had ever been in POW camps.

[7] Cf. Chap. III, pp. 61–2.

tion army; but the appearance of Vlasov—in whose existence they had almost ceased to believe—aroused these hopes once more. His visit made a deep impression, and the battalions remained faithful to their ideal to the end.[8]

Field Marshal von Kluge received Vlasov before the latter's return to Berlin. Although far more reserved than Schenckendorff, Kluge discussed Vlasov's aims with candor and promised to support him as much as possible. Vlasov's tour left a strong impression not just on the populace and the volunteer units, but also on the military and civil authorities. It was now widely recognized that Vlasov represented in political terms a powerful trump card—as was shown by Field Marshal Küchler's statement that Vlasov's mission would fail unless clear German directives regarding Russia were issued immediately. Litzmann, Generalkommissar of Estonia, called for the strengthening of collaboration with the anti-Bolshevik elements of the population, who had to be told what the future held for them. Litzmann was one of the idealists who had been profoundly disillusioned by the development of National Socialism under Hitler. "Heaven knows my father and I had other ideals when we joined the party," he told Dr. Kersten, Himmler's physician.[9] And even Goebbels wrote in his diaries: "Vlasov has been pretty much put on ice by the Eastern Ministry. This shows an astonishing lack of [political] instinct on the part of our central Berlin authorities."[1]

Officials of various autonomous Russian administrations also drafted memoranda—among them Axionov, district chief of the Ostrov region; Professor Soshalsky; and Pavlov, head of the Pochep district, who wrote:

It is strange that the German leadership should see a danger in establishing an opposition government. Such a regime

---

[8] The author has obtained an unpublished report on Vlasov's visit to the "Volga" Battalion, written by its commander, Colonel A. Doshkevitz.

[9] Felix Kersten: *Totenkopf und Treue* (Death's Head and Loyalty"), Mölich-Verlag, Hamburg, 1953, pp. 247 ff.

[1] Dallin, op. cit., p. 581 fn.

would be able to assume administration of the occupied territories and create an army to fight shoulder to shoulder with the Germans until the final annihilation of Bolshevism. A Russian government is necessary to convince the Russian people that the German army has not come to conquer the country but to liberate it from Bolshevism. It should be remembered that the majority of the Russian people did not want war with the Germans and at the beginning, entire units laid down their arms. The Germans made the mistake of treating these prisoners in an unfriendly fashion. If Russian soldiers could be shown that they would no longer be received as at the start of the war, and if a Russian regime existed here to protect them, they would surrender as before.[2]

None of these officials realized that enslavement of the Slavic *Untermensch* was an essential part of the National Socialist plan of domination.

On his return to Berlin in mid-March, Vlasov wrote a report in which he almost imploringly emphasized how greatly the popular mood had changed, that this change had resulted from German blunders and mistakes; how fear was spreading that the Germans did not wish liberation but the destruction of the Russian state and enslavement of the Russian people; how Stalin's skillful propaganda was reinforcing this fear; that it was high time, and perhaps the last chance, to change policy. Today it was still possible to win a majority of the population; tomorrow might be too late.

Lieutenant Colonel Schubuth, who had escorted Vlasov on his tour, also wrote a report, which he hoped would reach Hitler. He basically asked for the same measures as Vlasov, and added:

General Vlasov's tour, word of which spread quickly through city and countryside, is widely viewed as the last round of

[2] The author has in his possession the original of this memorandum, dated February 11, 1943.

inspection before the onset of decisive events. Hope for a solution of the question of the future has risen sharply. A mystique about Vlasov has taken hold of the volunteer units; they see in him the man capable of leading them to a new and better life. Now is the time—the crucial moment to act resolutely. The consequences of a new disappointment are incalculable.[3]

Important Wehrmacht circles continued to push for a change in *Ost* policy. Himmler, however, complained in a letter to Martin Bormann, dated March 4, 1943, about the Wehrmacht's actions in establishing a Russian Committee and a liberation movement, and he requested a decision by the Führer.[4] The continuing confidence of the circle of officers working for a realistic *Ost* policy was demonstrated by the creation of a "planning center." Outstanding members of the liberation movement were brought together in this center so as to create a leadership elite and a cadre of reliable officers. The center was also to draft political and economic plans for the struggle against the Stalin regime and for Russia's reconstruction. Here, as elsewhere, the driving force was Strik-Strikfeldt, extremely alarmed to see time slipping away unused. Strikfeldt had consultations with Gehlen, and eventually approval was received from Stauffenberg for the organization of an "East Propaganda Section, F.S.D.,"[5] comprising 1,200 Russians. Suitable people were picked from volunteer units, POW camps, even slave labor camps. The project was camouflaged as a training camp for selected members of the volunteer units and as a propaganda school. Strikfeldt found a livable barracks camp in Dabendorf, less than twenty miles south of Berlin. A flag with the cross of St. Andrew was hoisted as the symbol of the liberation movement.

A small group of Germans managed economic and technical

---

[3] This report, dated March 16, 1943, is quoted by Thorwald, op. cit., p. 209.
[4] Quoted by Dallin, op. cit., p. 586.
[5] F.S.D. = for special duty.

affairs, while the Russians themselves had exclusive charge of camp operations and instruction. Subsequently, the occupants of the special compound on Viktoriastrasse moved to Dabendorf. An additional thirty-five men were transferred from Wuhlheide, where a training camp under the joint jurisdiction of the Propaganda Ministry and the OKW Propaganda Department had existed since October 1941. Its director and organizer, Baron Georg von der Ropp, had been given the title of "instructor." Significantly, Wuhlheide did not provide better food rations than other POW camps, so it could not have been material advantages that attracted the propagandist trainees. Ropp had recruited several captured Russian officers as training aides. Like everything else connected with political propaganda, this enterprise, too, had been improvised, and its size bore not the slightest relation to the importance of the task.

Ropp's senior-ranking Russian colleague, General Blagoveshchensky, became head of the Dabendorf camp's Russian administration, while Ropp ran the training program. Officially, he was supposed to make sure that the courses were ideologically "sound." Actually, however, he and the other German liaison officers concentrated on shielding the camp from outside interference so that the training could proceed along Russian nationalist lines. Strikfeldt was head of the propaganda section, and Cavalry Captain Eduard von Dellingshausen was his deputy. In no sense was Dabendorf a continuation of the Wuhlheide experiment, but, instead, a new creation of the OKW's Propaganda Department and the OKH. The Propaganda Ministry had been deliberately excluded from involvement.

The camp began operations officially on March 1, 1943. Members of existing volunteer units from front-line areas predominated in the first class. On their arrival in Dabendorf they were officially released from prisoner status and sworn in by General Malyshkin. They wore German uniforms with the insignia of the Russian Liberation Army, the ROA. (This insignia, which had been approved the previous month for all Russian volunteer formations, served merely psychological ends, since such a liberation army under a single command enjoyed just as little reality now as in the past.)

A Russian artist, A. N. Rodzevich, had been commissioned to design the insignia. He first drew nine sketches, all with the old Russian colors—white, blue, and red—which were submitted to the Reich Ministry for the Occupied Eastern Territories. They were returned after Rosenberg had personally crossed them all out—prompting a bitter comment by Vlasov: "I would really like to leave it that way: the Russian flag crossed out by the Germans because they fear it." [6]

Malyshkin then suggested using the St. Andrew's cross, and the sketch finally approved by Rosenberg featured a blue St. Andrew's cross on a white field. Rosenberg probably did not know that a banner bearing this cross had been the war flag of the Tsarist navy.

Vlasov grasped the potentialities of the Dabendorf undertaking and attributed a growing understanding to the German leadership. He was still unaware that Dabendorf was in fact a camouflaged operation, and that if the Führer's headquarters were to discover its true aims and intentions, his German guardians and friends, not to mention the participating Russians, would all be arrested.

A short time later, he met Lieutenant General Fedor Ivanovich Trukhin,[7] who had come from Wustrau—a camp under the Eastern Ministry's control—as one of a group of qualified men recruited by Strikfeldt for service as instructors in Dabendorf. Trukhin was a man of great intelligence and culture, with a combination of personal qualities and knowledgeability that

---

[6] A. N. Rodzevich: "On the ROA Insignia," MiD, p. 174.
[7] Information on Trukhin has been supplied by: Dellingshausen, unpub. ms.; Kazantsev, op. cit., pp. 218 ff.; Vladimir Pozdnyakov: "Major General Fedor Ivanovich Trukhin," Borba, Nos. 9/10, 1949; Zaitsev, Kromiadi, and Bormann, interviews; and G. von der Ropp, letter to author.

made him a uniquely gifted teacher. He came from an aristocratic Russian family and had joined the Russian Revolution while a young officer. After graduating from the military academy, he advanced rapidly. Trukhin had been chief of staff of the Baltic Military Region at the beginning of the war and had fallen, wounded, into German captivity in the summer of 1941. He had declared his opposition to Stalin, made contact with the NTS in the Wustrau camp, and soon risen to its circle of leaders. Joining Vlasov and the liberation movement was for him a matter of course. Trukhin was generally well liked, although he impressed people as taciturn and reserved. His quiet confidence was of great help to others during this period of nerve-wracking tension. However, he rapidly lost faith in the competence of the German leadership and was pessimistic about the future of those active in the liberation movement. Nevertheless, he continued his work without betraying his real feelings. For him it was a question of conscience, and of faith that what had become a firm conviction among many young Russians would eventually be translated into reality.

The first class in Dabendorf ended on March 22, 1943, with Vlasov presiding over the graduation ceremonies. He cherished the hope that Dabendorf would serve as an ideological center for the Russian liberation movement and as a center for selecting and training capable leaders. An editorial staff headed by Zykov was also assembled in Dabendorf. Publication of the Russian newspaper *Klich* ("The Call") was suspended, and it was replaced by the papers *Zarya* ("Dawn"), for the POW's and slave laborers, and *Dobrovolyets* ("The Volunteer"), for the volunteer units. In their first issues, which together had a total run of 600,000 copies, there appeared the Smolensk Proclamation. Subsequently, *Zarya* had an average run of 100,000–120,000, and *Dobrovolyets* one of about 20,000 until the fall of 1944, when it grew to 40,000–60,000.

Prisoners' statements and monitored orders revealed that the Soviet government had sternly forbidden all conversation on the subject of the Russian Liberation Army and had instructed political commissars to keep a special watch for Vlasov leaflets. After an initial silence of months, Soviet army newspapers described Vlasov as a "Trotskyite, one of Tukhachevsky's collaborators, and an agent who had worked for the Germans and Japanese before the war." And while they cited German colonializing ambitions and atrocities, the papers made no mention of the liberation movement and army.[8] By this measuring rod the Vlasov operation seemed very promising. Yet, no official approval or support was forthcoming from the German leadership.

Vlasov therefore refused the request of Grote and Strikfeldt that he visit the rear area of Army Group North. After Vlasov's success with Army Group Center, Field Marshal Küchler and Colonel General Lindemann had pressed to have him tour their area and stood ready to assume full responsibility for his presence. Vlasov asserted that he would return again with empty hands, that he still could not point to a single positive decision by the German leadership. Once again, however, his objections were overcome with the argument that success would cause additional pressure on the Führer's headquarters.

And so, on April 19, 1943, he began his second tour of the occupied eastern territories, accompanied by Captain von Dellingshausen and by his adjutant, Captain Antonov, who had deserted at Stalingrad after reading one of Vlasov's leaflets.[9] In Riga, their first stop, the local propaganda unit received Vlasov with great ado, giving him, despite a prior warning from Grote, a big build-up. The Russian journal *Novy Put* ("New Road") extolled him as the future liberator of Russia.[1] Vlasov's visit to the editorial offices of the Russian paper *Za Rodinu* ("For the Fatherland") is described by a staff member:

About forty POW's worked on the editorial staff, among them professors, artists, journalists, teachers, and also former

[8] Dallin, op. cit., p. 586.
[9] Details on this tour were provided by: E. von Dellingshausen, interview and unpub. ms.; N. von Grote, letter to author; and interviews with R. Antonov, G. Klein, and W. Strik-Strikfeldt.
[1] *Novy Put*, No. 10, 1943.

officers. The mood was bad. No one believed any longer in a change of German policy, all the less so in view of the disgraceful treatment of staff members. A German private named Knop had ordered the entire staff to help in loading propaganda material. The cartoonist Boris Savalov, graduate of an art academy and an outstanding artist, arrived five minutes late because he had wanted to finish a drawing, and for this, Knop worked him over with his belt and with kicks. This incident made it obvious to everyone how defenseless they were as Russians, how they were treated by their ally— they, the volunteers who freely worked for an anti-Bolshevik newspaper. Several staff members insisted that the Germans had substituted another man for Vlasov, that Vlasov himself had died in the battle of the Volkhov. Two former officers of the Second Shock Army were present who had seen Vlasov at the time. They would be able to say whether it was he or not. Accordingly the tension was great when he entered the room.

Everyone was immediately struck by the calm assurance of his bearing. He sketched his career, explained the reasons for his decision against the Stalin regime, and indicated the possibilities and aims of the movement. When he finished, those present asked questions. Above all, they wanted to know whether the Germans would permit a national mass movement. Vlasov replied that the Germans would have to if they did not wish to suffer ruin. When somebody asserted that the Germans were their most important allies whether they liked it or not, Vlasov answered that the millions on the other side of the front were the most important allies and, pointing to a drawing of a senseless attack by Polish horse cavalry against German tanks, declared: "We must do everything to avoid ending in the same situation as these brave Polish lancers." [2]

[2] The author has in his possession an eyewitness report by V. Verbin on Vlasov's visit.

Even this group of intellectuals had no doubts about the possibility of overthrowing Stalin; but they did have profound doubts as to whether the Germans would allow Vlasov to act freely.

Vlasov's next stop was in Pskov, where he stayed from April 24 to May 3. He was given an official reception in which community leaders and representatives of the various German government branches, of the autonomous Russian administration, and of the Church all participated. Vlasov also visited the editorial offices of the local Russian newspaper, where the members of the so-called "Initiative Group" were presented to him. It had been formed in the winter of 1942 to recruit supporters through active propaganda for the liberation struggle against Stalin. Among its members was Khromenko, the newspaper's editor-in-chief, while the group's main spokesman was a man named Bozhenko, who later became a captain in the ROA. Continuing his tour, Vlasov visited various other towns and cities, among them Mazlogoztizy, Gdov, Plyussa, Luga, Ziverskaya, and Volozovo, where he spoke to Russian volunteers and the population at large. Thousands streamed in to see and hear him.

Despite all these encouraging signs, however, Vlasov remained bitterly and profoundly distressed by the attitude of the German leadership. A conversation in Plyussa with his interpreter, Gert Klein, revealed this only too clearly. On orders from the Administrative Section of the Army Group Rear Area, Klein had accompanied Vlasov as an observer since the latter's arrival in Pskov. He had won Vlasov's confidence by calling his attention to efforts to improve the living conditions of the populace and by his open criticism of *Ost* policy. Vlasov was particularly impressed by the establishment of schools. (He did not know that schools for the Russian population had actually been forbidden by higher authority and that the Administrative Section had allowed textbooks to be printed at its own expense and with the silent consent of the Army Group commander.)

In his own quarters, at the end of a strenuous day—which had included an alcohol-drenched dinner in the field commander's company—Vlasov unburdened himself to Klein. Dropping the optimistic front he felt compelled to adopt publicly for the sake of the cause, he frankly expressed his deep anxiety over the attitude of the German leadership. His impressions on this tour had further strengthened his view that the efforts already being made everywhere by the populace afforded an ample basis for a unified liberation movement and the creation of a large and powerful national army. Simply place the existing volunteer units under his command, and an army of more than half a million men would result.

But the Germans distrusted him. He could not see Hitler. The officers he knew were most certainly sincere, but apparently they did not wield enough influence. He had always felt great respect for the Germans—they were great organizers and good soldiers —but he could not understand Hitler or National Socialism. Perhaps old émigrés were advising Hitler, and they distrusted him because he was a revolutionary. All those with him were revolutionaries and naturally did not want any restoration of Tsarism and former conditions. They simply wished to realize what the Revolution had promised. Only with this aim could the people be won.

What was needed was the establishment of a Russian opposition government, along with an official statement from the highest authorities that Germany wanted to liberate, not conquer; the transfer of civil administration in the occupied territories to the Russian inhabitants; deployment of the ROA on a sector of the front; a sifting of deserters and prisoners by the ROA; and the transfer of anti-Stalinist propaganda operations to the organs of the liberation movement. Such measures would prove quickly— and enormously—successful.

Only in this way was success possible, only in this way could Germany avoid defeat, because a huge country like Russia could not be occupied against the will of the population. The help of the Russians was needed to overthrow Stalin. Germany had no alternative other than defeat. He was at a loss to understand why these realities were not recognized. Now, while enormous areas of Russia were occupied, it was not too late, even though much precious time had been squandered. But soon it might be too late, and then Germany would not go under alone—the end would also be at hand for him and his supporters. The hardest thing to bear was standing idly by until the German leadership learned its lesson. Perhaps the coming reverses at the fronts would teach it to them. He could only hope it would not be too late by then.[3]

Vlasov's speech in the municipal theater on April 30 represented the high point of his stay in Pskov. Tickets were distributed in the surrounding villages as well as in the city itself. The auditorium, with a seating capacity of two thousand, was overcrowded a full hour before the meeting was to start, with hundreds left waiting outside. When Vlasov entered the hall, he received a standing ovation.

A Russian was speaking to Russians on Russian problems. Hitler was not mentioned once, although the German people was greeted as an equal partner. The goal was unambiguous and clear: the liberation of the Fatherland from Bolshevism, the creation of a free, democratic Russia. This was what these people had hoped for, and they were ready to fight for it.

This agitation for national goals inevitably aroused the advocates of Nazi colonialization and of the idea that Slavs were subhuman. As a pretext for protest they seized upon a remark made by Vlasov in Gatchina to the staff of the German Eighteenth Army. Impressed by their cordial reception, he expressed the hope that he might reciprocate the courtesy someday in Moscow. This quite natural sentiment was described as arrogance. It was an intolerable provocation for this Slav to impudently invite Germans as guests of an independent Russian government.

It is not surprising, therefore, that—at the very time when Vlasov had inspired many of his countrymen with enthusiasm, when the more sensible Wehrmacht leaders in the east were

[3] G. Klein, interview.

awaiting a change in Hitler's *Ost* policy—Keitel demanded to
know from the Propaganda Department how it was possible for
Vlasov to flout the express will of the Führer and make political
statements which revealed that unjustified and impermissible
hopes had been stirred in him. He demanded the exact text of
Vlasov's statement and threatened sharp countermeasures should
it be confirmed that Vlasov had behaved publicly like a "future
Russian leader." His remark in Gatchina could not be hushed
up; it was already known, and had to be reported. The next day,
Keitel issued an order to all the authorities involved, including
the commanders of army groups and armies. It was typical of
the spirit prevailing at the Führer's headquarters and read as
follows:

> In view of the absolutely shameless statements of the
> Russian war prisoner General Vlasov, on a trip to Army
> Group North, which occurred without the Führer's knowl-
> edge and without my knowledge, it is ordered that General
> Vlasov be immediately returned under special guard to a
> prisoner-of-war camp, which he is not to leave again for any
> reason. The Führer no longer wishes to hear Vlasov's name in
> any connection except propaganda operations in whose im-
> plementation the name but not the person of General Vlasov
> will be needed. Should General Vlasov appear once more in
> public, he is to be handed over to the Secret State Police
> [Gestapo] and rendered harmless.[4]

The order was a blow for everybody who supported Vlasov
and favored a change in *Ost* policy. Gehlen and Stauffenberg
pulled all the strings at their command to keep Vlasov in Berlin
and succeeded conditionally: He would now be "in custody."
Strikfeldt managed to find a small villa on the Kiebitzweg in the
Dahlem section of Berlin where Vlasov was to be taken on his
return.

[4] Quoted in Thorwald, op. cit., p. 219.

Vlasov—buoyed up by the success of his trip and ignorant of the fate threatening him and his plans—arrived in Berlin on May 10. He was taken to the Kiebitzweg house, where Malyshkin welcomed him as he entered. From now on, he was to live there with Malyshkin, his adjutant Antonov, a cook, and a Russian bodyguard assigned from Dabendorf. There were two bedrooms with baths on the upper floor, and a study and dining room below. The relative luxuriousness of these new quarters impressed Vlasov as a good sign. For the moment he was unaware of the true meaning of this move: that he had been politically shelved.

Shortly afterward, Strikfeldt discovered, in Sergei Fröhlich, a reliable German liaison man, who joined the Kiebitzweg household as "major domo." Fröhlich had a Russian mother and spoke fluent Russian. He had volunteered for this assignment and succeeded in getting it through the good offices of SA Colonel Girgensohn.

Meanwhile, the Wehrmacht circles supporting Vlasov were reluctant to submit to Keitel's order. A conference took place on May 14 in which Count Schenckendorff, Gersdorff, Tresckow, Gehlen, and Schmidt von Altenstadt participated. They decided to arrange, through the intercession of General Wagner and Colonel von Freytag-Loringhoven, a meeting between representatives of the General Staff and Rosenberg's plenipotentiaries for the purpose of preparing a joint plea to Hitler. Since Keitel had barred the army's channel to Hitler, they could only reach him through Rosenberg.

Rosenberg, despite many misgivings, agreed to the conference, which took place on May 25, 1943, in Mauerwald, the Army General Staff Headquarters. Dr. Bräutigam, Professor von Mende, and Dr. Knüpffer represented the Ministry for the Occupied Eastern Territories, while the General Staff was represented by twenty officers led by General Wagner, General Hellmich, and Gehlen. Rising in front of Wagner was a mountain of memoranda, complaints, and entreaties from all the

armies, calling for the initiation of a positive *Ost* policy. On top
lay a summary of all the arguments, written by Tresckow and
signed by Field Marshal von Kluge. It started clearly and plainly
that the war was lost without an immediate reorientation of *Ost*
policy.

It turned out, however, that Rosenberg's representatives
lacked authority to make decisions. The one result of the increasingly heated debate was Bräutigam's promise to submit the
views of the General Staff to Rosenberg and do his best to get
a positive response.[5] Schmidt von Altenstadt summed up the
feelings of the General Staff officers: "The gods strike blind
those whom they would destroy!" Rosenberg finally yielded to
Bräutigam's pleas and agreed to see Hitler together with Jodl
or Keitel.

Meanwhile, Keitel had heard of the conference and the
criticism of his conduct by the General Staff officers. Obviously
intent on stopping, once and for all, any further initiatives of
this kind, he goaded Hitler into taking a position against Vlasov. A briefing for Hitler on June 8 gave him his opportunity.

To begin with, he "reported" that leaflet No. 13, besides
offering the usual inducements, had promised Russian defectors
a chance to join a Russian liberation army. This had to be
corrected. Hitler immediately pounced on this point and went
off into one of his long monologues. Agreeing with Keitel, he
said there could be as much propaganda activity as desired,

> on condition that not the slightest practical consequences
> result from it and above all, that those engaged in it shun
> the state of mind which I, unfortunately, have already found
> spreading among some gentlemen. Even Kluge has displayed
> signs of it a few times. . . . I can only say here that we will
> never build a Russian army, that is a phantasm of the first
> order. Before I ever do that, it will be much simpler to bring

[5] Dallin's statement (op. cit., p. 588 fn.) that Wagner did not take
part in the conference is incorrect, according to the diary of Herre
and a letter by him to the author.

the Russians as workers to Germany. . . . Most important of all, we would be giving up the war goals established from the outset. . . .[6]

Despite Stalingrad, despite the reversals on all fronts, Hitler insisted on keeping unchanged his war aims, which excluded Russian independence and its corollary, a Russian army. He could not grasp how unattainable these aims were under existing circumstances. General Kurt Zeitzler, the army's chief of staff, expressed accord with Hitler's views and recommended that Hitler personally explain them once and for all to the commanders of the Army Groups. Satisfied, Keitel said at the end of the meeting: "Now I see. It's petty self-deception. People are hoping to lighten their burdens and don't realize the kind of trouble they're creating for themselves." He informed Rosenberg that the Führer had categorically banned any further activity by Vlasov in the occupied territories. Nor was there to be any thought of keeping promises already made to Vlasov. The meeting requested with the Führer was unnecessary.

Hitler's decision completely destroyed the first large-scale campaign to effect a fundamental change in the *Ost* policy. The majority of officers serving in the east had assumed that no reasonable person could seriously challenge their arguments. But this only showed how poorly they understood Hitler's frame of mind and the spirit of National Socialism.[7]

[6] Shorthand report of conference in Helmut Heiber: *Lagebesprechungen im Führerhauptquartier* ("Briefings at the Führer's Headquarters") dtv-Dokumente, Stuttgart, 1963, pp. 109 ff.

[7] Dallin's statement that "Nobody asked himself even for a moment whether the situation was at all reversible" (op. cit., p. 582) is inaccurate. The Russians, who knew the situation best, as well as their German supporters, were unquestionably convinced that a radical change of course at this time could still lead to the overthrow of the Stalin regime. Dallin, who had no opportunity to study these matters at first hand, fails to take into account the fact that most of the memoranda on which he bases his judgments had to be written in an Aesopian language which concealed the writers' actual ideas or feelings. For example, it was unthinkable to attempt to justify a change in *Ost* policy on other than military grounds. Any reference to moral scruples would have been counterproductive, injuring the

The case of Captain Theodor Oberländer illustrates how brutally the Nazi leadership reacted to any criticism of its policy. On June 22, 1943, the second anniversary of the Soviet-German War, Captain Oberländer, commander of several Caucasian volunteer units, had written a memorandum stating that the situation in the east was approaching the point of decision. Unless Germany's *Ost* policy changed, the decision would go against the Germans: "There are moments in history which come only once. Generations thereafter may exert themselves to the utmost, but Providence does not give again what she was ready to proffer just a short time before."

Oberländer sent his memorandum to all the important authorities, including Keitel, Rosenberg, and Himmler, with no suspicion of the disaster he had created for himself. Eight days later the army dismissed him, and had it not been for the intercession of Minister of State K. H. Frank in Prague, he would have been sent to a concentration camp. Instead, he was assigned to help wounded SS officers prepare for the state law examination.[8] Keitel and Himmler described the memorandum as an "underhanded attempt to bore away at the official 'marching orders' the Führer unequivocally and irrevocably laid down on June 8."

Wehrmacht opponents of the *Ost* policy had to recognize that for the time being, Hitler's verdict had nullified their plans. And yet, this was the very time when the publication of the Smolensk Proclamation and Vlasov's public appearances were making their full impact. The population and volunteer

---

cause and endangering the writer. To simply deduce an opportunistic attitude on the part of the writer from the text easily leads to false conclusions. For many of the men involved, the political outlook of Vlasov and hundreds of thousands of his countrymen represented far more than a military or political episode. They saw in it, rather, a situation fraught with great potential for Europe's future, having nothing in common with the political illiteracy of National Socialism. They saw Hitler's overthrow as a logical consequence of Stalin's ouster.

[8] T. Oberländer, interview; H. Raschhofer, letter to author.

formations were waiting impatiently for further steps. Only the top army leaders knew of Hitler's negative decision, and they kept it from Vlasov as well, so that he continued to expect progress. He told the German journalist Melitta Wiedemann that at last he was at peace with his conscience because he knew the majority of the people thought and felt as he did.[9]

Vlasov's residence on the Kiebitzweg became known through many secret channels, and a swelling stream of visitors found their way there—soldiers on leave, conscripted Eastern workers, old émigrés, and Germans. The letters to Vlasov multiplied to the point where Strikfeldt had to assign him an army post office number and set up a private office for him. Life on the Kiebitzweg settled down to a normal routine, and there ensued a period of waiting—for decisions that were not being made. For Vlasov this period was bearable only because Strikfeldt and like-minded officers were working tirelessly to establish new connections that might be of service to the cause.

Meanwhile, the development of the Russian liberation movement continued without the knowledge of the Führer's headquarters. The propaganda section at Dabendorf became the most important instrument of this activity. Without sponsorship by any official German agencies, but protected by the German cadres attached to it, a political and ideological center of the Russian liberation movement evolved with surprising swiftness. The first training course had been more or less improvised; but the second course, begun on March 23, 1943, followed a systematic plan and had about a thousand "students" enrolled.

Playing a key role in this progress was the group transferred, under Trukhin's leadership, from Wustrau to Dabendorf. Trukhin replaced Blagoveshchensky as Russian camp commandant. He filled Dabendorf with a new spirit, and his dynamism communicated itself to the entire staff. Next to him, the camp's

[9] Melitta Wiedemann, letter to author.

outstanding figure was Alexander Nikolayevich Zaitsev, who took charge of ideological instruction as chief lecturer and instilled in his classes clear and sound ideas on the structure of a future Russia. Zaitsev, a young, talented scientist, had been captured in 1941. He had come into contact with NTS representatives in Wustrau and, realizing that political goals could not be achieved without organization, had joined the group.

His lectures were on a very high level and convinced his auditors most of all because of their emphatically nationalistic viewpoint and the frank, occasionally sharp and ironic, criticism of German *Ost* policy. His unsparing criticism of Communism, however, caused a spiritual crisis in many attending the course. Until then they had possessed an ideology on which they could fix their faith, hope, and labors—even if Stalin had corrupted it. Now they confronted a vacuum. Not until the last part of the course did they understand what was being offered them. Almost without exception, Zaitsev won them over and they became supporters of the liberation movement. In some cases, Soviet agents revealed themselves and went over to Vlasov.

The proclaimed goal was a national, free, and democratic, though not unconditionally capitalist, Russia. Sincere friendship with the German people, not to be identified with National Socialism, seemed logical—especially since Russian and German culture had been very closely linked during the nineteenth century, and many Germans with whom these Russians were allied were opponents of the *Ost* policy and friends of the Russian people.

When the Germans raised their battle flag on the highest mountain of the Caucasus, the Elbrus, Zaitsev remarked that this achievement had far more significance for mountain climbing than for military strategy. In a lecture on a future Russian state he declared:

Freedom of speech and press is one of the foundations of a state governed by law. It provides the possibility of keeping control over what happens in the country. It is the guarantee that sinister intrigues, whether engaged in by those who hold power or ordinary citizens, will not escape denunciation and punishment. Where genuine freedom of speech and press exist, a totalitarian regime is inconceivable under which all sorts of adventurers rise to power and a seminary dropout or a corporal stands at the head of the state.[1]

The Gestapo twice wanted to arrest Zaitsev, and it took hard work to stop it. On the first occasion he was accused of condemning the annihilation of the Jews, praising Marxism, and expressing the idea that the Germans could not win the war without the Russian nationalists. Zaitsev defended himself skillfully during the interrogation: He had simply said that the liquidation of the Jews made a negative impression on Orthodox Christian Russians, which accorded with the facts. He had to discuss the successes of Marxism in Russia because he could not convince his listeners if he denied the good elements in it. This time the Gestapo settled for the admonition that the Germans did not need the Russians to win, and permitted him to continue his activities.

The Jewish question did not represent a problem for most of the Russians. They were accustomed to a multinational state. Those who expressed anti-Semitic feelings usually justified them by pointing to the high percentage of Jews among the Communist leaders.

Gestapo arrest threatened Zaitsev a second time because of his anti-German statements and membership in the NTS. This time, too, the worst was averted thanks to a very clever report by Baron von der Ropp which was transmitted by Helmut von Kleist, the intelligence officer.[2]

It was possible for people like Zaitsev to propagate their ideas in the Third Reich without serious consequences only because of the German liaison officers. Von der Ropp, the Ger-

---

[1] Kazantsev, op. cit., p. 219; A. Zaitsev and G. von der Ropp, interviews.
[2] The text of this report is in the author's possession.

man educational director; his deputies, Ragozhin and Kerkovius; the camp commandant, Captain Peterson; Strikfeldt's deputy, Baron von Dellingshausen; and the intelligence officer, Baron von Kleist, were all more concerned with protecting the Russians from the SS Security Service and the Gestapo than with their official task of exposing subversive activities by Communist agents. When von der Ropp once showed up unexpectedly during a discussion in which German actions were being criticized, a Russian shouted: "Careful! A German officer!" Von der Ropp covered his shoulder straps with his hands and said: "There is no German officer here! You can speak freely."

Like the other officers, he knew that such discussions had nothing to do with treason or pro-Communism, but that the Russians felt increasingly disillusioned and betrayed by the Germans. The pamphlet *Der Untermensch* ("The Subhuman"), commissioned by Himmler and published in the spring of 1943, played no small part in this reaction. Among other things, it stated: "The *Untermensch*, a creation of nature that seems fully like man . . . is, however, completely different, a horrible creature, a try at man that has failed—having manlike features, but intellectually, spiritually, lower than any beast." [3]

At times the Russians gave vent openly to their quite understandable indignation. The Russian Count Lamsdorff, for example, presented himself thus to a high German staff officer of the Central Sector: "*Untermensch* Captain Count Lamsdorff reporting!" [4] When one of Vlasov's orderlies slammed a door shut, Vlasov turned to the German officers in the room: "Your pardon, an *Untermensch!*"

Dabendorf developed into a center opposed to National Socialism and Hitler's plans. Under the protection of the Wehrmacht, aims were pursued which, had they been presented

---

[3] This pamphlet was issued on Himmler's authority by the publishing division of the SS Main Office in 1943. The author was SS Captain König.

[4] Lamsdorff, interview.

openly, would have led to the immediate arrest not only of the Russians but of the Germans active in their cause. The Gestapo and the SS Security Service, of course, kept on searching for evidence against Vlasov and his collaborators. Gestapo chief Heinrich Müller made no secret of the fact that he would be delighted to liquidate all of them. But time and again the Wehrmacht managed to avert the danger. And by 1944 it had the support even of a group inside the SS Security Service, which had come to recognize the danger of Hitler's *Ost* policy. In addition, Dabendorf became the birthplace of a Russian officer corps stamped with a new and distinct character of its own. Even when these officers returned to their original units, they remained members of a tightly knit political organization. A kind of secret service gradually emerged which fed Vlasov and his aides a steady stream of information.

Although Dabendorf could not actually be called the germ cell of the Russian liberation movement—which had cropped up spontaneously and in a variety of forms since the beginning of the eastern campaign—it was unquestionably the organizational spearhead. At any time the existing volunteer units, the Russian local militias, and the organs of Russian autonomous administration could have been placed under Dabendorf's control. The freedom with which everything could be discussed inspired the Russians to call Dabendorf the "free republic." Many of those taking the training course were initially distrustful. But the honesty and fraternal spirit with which all questions were discussed won them over, too.

Vlasov knew exactly what was happening in Dabendorf—Trukhin and Zaitsev thrashed out all the problems with him. The first thirty-three issues of *Zarya* and *Dobrovolyets* were practically free of German censorship, and Zykov fully exploited this opportunity to express nationalist ideas. He stressed the fact that the allies of the Russians were not German underlings, and that these were no longer German newspapers for the Russians, but newspapers of the Russians.

This situation, however, lasted only a short time. All the editors were called before Colonel Martin after the thirty-third issue and accused of having exceeded their authority. Zykov replied: "You can, of course, regard us as provocateurs and Soviet agents and not believe us, but perhaps you will consider why we really fight you on different questions, even though we earn your displeasure by doing so. If we were agents, it would be simpler to say 'yes' and pursue our sinister plans quietly." [5] Martin explained that he had to follow his orders; the arrest warrant lay in front of him and he was having trouble holding it off. Zykov obviously had not yet grasped the fact that to advocate Russian nationalism and Russian equality was in Nazi eyes a crime fully comparable to the activity of a Soviet agent. Censorship was subsequently strengthened. Demands were made for anti-Semitic and anti-Western statements. Editorial supervision was placed in the hands of Sonderführer Werner Bormann.

After the confrontation with Martin the Russians conferred on whether to continue their work under the given circumstances. Zykov, ordinarily a man of quick decision, seemed irresolute. But finally he advised further collaboration. The only hope lay in waiting for the course of events to impose its own logic.[6] But the more time slipped away, the more depressed the circle around Vlasov became, and the greater their disgust with the German leadership. Zykov gave succinct expression to the Russians' pessimistic view of their prospects: "I don't estimate our personal chances to be very good, even though I believe the Stalin regime will fall: thirty per cent that the Germans liquidate us; thirty per cent that we fall into Stalin's hands; thirty per cent that the Americans and English hang us, despite our

---

[5] Kitayev, op. cit., p. 6.
[6] Information on the Dabendorf camp was supplied by: von der Ropp, interview and letters to the author; Peterson, Bormann, Kleist, Grote, and Zaitsev, interviews; Dellingshausen, unpub. ms.; Kazantsev, op. cit., p. 219; "Shkola Politicheskikh Boitsov" ("School of Political Combat"), *Zarya*, No. 89, November 5, 1944; R. Antonov: "Wuhl-heide-Dabendorf," in *S Narodom—Za Narod*, No. 5, 1965.

respect for them; I allow only a ten per cent chance that we come out of this with a whole skin." [7]

It was about this time that Vlasov learned of the arrest and death of his wife. How this news reached him is not known.

In a diary entry dated June 28, 1943, Herre noted the mood prevailing among the friends of the liberation movement: "To abandon the hope that the military situation will yet compel the top leadership to reason means to truly doubt the existence of reason. It is now our task to find means of preventing the volunteers from the east from falling back into a void and to support Vlasov and his circle so that he doesn't fall apart."

Although Hitler's decision excluded any basic change in political aims, several steps could still be taken organizationally to strengthen the eastern volunteers. Stauffenberg managed to get Zeitzler, the chief of staff, to approve a service directive on the Hiwis which Freytag-Loringhoven had drafted. Some time later the members of the volunteer formations also acquired a uniform status under another directive. General Hellmich, who had been appointed chief of Eastern Troops in December 1942, assigned "commanders of Eastern Troops" as advisers to the various army commanders. A "school for indigenous officers, officer-candidates, and interpreters" was set up in Mariampol with a Russian, Major General Assberg, as commandant. Laborious statistical work—understandably, units often did not report the full total of their Hiwis—established that in June 1943 there were more than 600,000 Hiwis and approximately 200,000 members of volunteer units—a reserve from which a liberation army could be mobilized whenever approval was forthcoming.[8]

[7] Kitayev, op. cit., p. 6.
[8] General Zeitzler reported a figure of 220,000 Hiwis in his briefing of June 8, 1943 (cf. H. Heiber: *Lagebesprechungen im Führerhauptquartier* ["Briefings in the Führer's Headquarters"], dtv-Dokumente, 1963, p. 109), but may have wished to give Hitler as low a figure as possible. He had not yet received the findings of the Foreign Armies East Department at this time. ([There were 47,000

Strikfeldt kept a tireless lookout for people he thought might be helpful in influencing developments in the desired direction. One such was the writer Edwin E. Dwinger, who had participated in the eastern invasion as a war correspondent and had been converted by his experiences into an opponent of *Ost* policy. Another was Günter Kaufmann, editor-in-chief of the Hitler Youth magazine, *Will and Power*. Influenced by former Hitler Youth leaders serving on the eastern front, Kaufmann had published a special issue of the magazine on the Russian question, containing both the Smolensk Proclamation and an article by Dwinger entitled "The Individual Russian—the Means to Overcoming Bolshevism." This had no influence, however, on official policy. Himmler and Rosenberg banned their reprint in other publications.

Kaufmann did manage to interest Baldur von Schirach—the former Reich youth leader, and then governor of Vienna—in eastern problems, and arranged for Vlasov to visit Vienna. Vlasov was received there with full honors. He stayed at the Hotel Bristol as Schirach's guest and had free use of the latter's car for sightseeing trips.

Schirach was no champion of *Ost* policy or the theory of the Slavic *Untermensch*. When he received an order from Keitel directing that Russian POW's be allowed just one meal a day and be made to sleep on the ground, he ripped it up and ordained adequate food and lodging and decent treatment for the Russians within his jurisdiction. He had disapproved of the attack on the Soviet Union and saw in it not only an injustice but also a possible cause of defeat. Schirach still considered a

---

Hiwis deployed just to protect rail lines in the area of Army Group North (Heiber, p. 121). According to an incomplete table of the Eastern Ministry of January 24, 1945 (cited by Heiber, p. 118 fn.), 600,000 members of "Eastern peoples" served in armed units. This figure, however, does not include the Hiwis, the Cossack formations, or the Russian, Ukrainian, and White Russian SS units. Therefore, the estimate of about one million men belonging to the various peoples of Russia who took up arms against the Stalin regime may be correct.

separate peace with Stalin possible and desirable—even if it meant handing over all the Russian volunteers on the German side.

Ignorant of the psychological situation in the Soviet Union and the occupied eastern territories, he did not accept Vlasov's thesis that Stalin could be overthrown through cooperation with the Russian people. At bottom he considered Vlasov a traitor, and though he treated his Russian guest courteously, Schirach maintained an inner reserve toward him. If he urged Hitler to approve a Vlasov army, it was only because the military situation was critical and he thought such a step might bring an improvement.[9] Vlasov and Strikfeldt did not sense Schirach's reservations, believing they had convinced him of the correctness of their position. His courteous attitude had impressed Vlasov and further strengthened his hopes for the final success of his efforts.[1]

During this period of anxiety and expectation, Sergei Ivanov brought a new hope: After the failure of the Ossintorf experiment he had submitted his plans to the Reich Security Main Office (RSHA), in the belief that the SD had more power and political opportunities than the army. He had, in fact, been offered command of a Russian brigade attached to the SD, which with competent aides he was to develop into the first ROA unit. He had immediately brought his old associates Kromiadi, Sakharov, and Lamsdorff into the picture, and with SD approval had visited Vlasov in order to undertake this step in his name. After some consideration, Vlasov agreed. For him it was a means of testing whether the SD had actually received new authority from either Himmler or Hitler's headquarters. However, he insisted on one condition: that Zhilenkov assume leadership of this new unit.

The SD brigade was stationed near Pskov and called itself

---

[9] Baldur von Schirach, interview and letter to author.
[1] Strik-Strikfeldt, interview.

the Druzhina ("Bodyguard"). It was commanded by a former officer on the Soviet General Staff, Lieutenant Colonel Radionov, who used the pseudonym of Gil. This brigade was the only large Russian-led unit the SD had organized—and, in the end, the only one betrayed by its commander into partisan hands.

The SD had created its own intelligence service before the war to compete with Admiral Canaris's military network.[2] During the eastern campaign the SD established a special organization called Operation Zeppelin, which was independent of military intelligence (Abwehr I) and whose aim was to smuggle agents into the Soviet hinterland. The Druzhina Brigade was organized as a reservoir for such agents and, to test its reliability, was assigned the task of fighting partisans.

The brigade had originated as the so-called "Russian National Union," which had been founded in the Suvalky POW camp in the winter of 1941–2 to fight Bolshevism. The group was of approximately battalion size. After being taken over by the SD and given its new name, it was ordered to set out for Stary Bykhov in the summer of 1942. The unit was originally led by a number of high-ranking Russian staff officers, among them Major General Bogdanov, former commander of the Forty-seventh Rifle Division; the aforementioned Lieutenant Colonel Radionov; Lieutenant Colonel Orlov; Major Yukhnov; and Major Andrusenko. Its motto was "For Russia."

A second Druzhina unit came into existence somewhat later. Its core, consisting of 135 men, was recruited on December 11, 1942, in Stalag 319A, by Major Blazhevich and the camp leaders, Alelekov and Makarenko; the group was subsequently sent to Gaidov near Lublin. Both units were transferred in March 1943 to the Glubokoye area in White Russia and were

[2] Cf. George H. Stein: *Geschichte der Waffen-SS*, Droste Verlag, Düsseldorf, 1967 (also, *The Waffen SS*, Cornell University Press, Ithaca, 1966), and Heinz Höhne: *Der Orden unter dem Totenkopf* ("Decorations under the Death's Head"), Sigbert Mohn Verlag, Gütersloh, 1967.

merged under the name of "SS Druzhina Brigade," although there was no connection with the SS.

It was about this time that there began a series of incidents which led to the political demoralization of the unit. In February 1943 a group of fifty brigade members visited Berlin. Although they were impressed by the standard of living and by German efficiency, contacts with inmates of the Oranienbaum Concentration Camp and with conscripted women workers from the east brought to light the disgraceful treatment of these people by the Germans. In addition, under Blazhevich's influence, Gil-Radionov formed a leadership group that began to terrorize the unit, suppressing and persecuting all elements it disliked. At this time, Blazhevich had already made contact with Soviet intelligence during a series of trips to Latvia, and his obvious aim was the gradual demoralization of the unit. Gil, a coward and opportunist, became steadily more dependent on him. Officers resisting their tactics were either demoted or shot. As for the SD, it gave Gil a completely free hand. The SD liaison officer, SS Major Appel, a former SA leader, confined himself to teaching the Russian officers how to conduct themselves in an officers club.

In May 1943 the Druzhina joined German units in a large-scale operation against partisans. Its performance gave no cause for criticism, and there were no defectors. An intensive nationalistic propaganda campaign was then initiated, and the unit was described as part of the Russian liberation army. With volunteer enlistments it grew to about three thousand men.

The group around Gil spent much of their time drinking, chasing women, and playing cards. Gil increasingly neglected his duties as commander, and dissatisfaction with his leadership spread among many of the brigade's officers. This situation led the RSHA in Berlin to consider replacements in the unit's leadership. However, the local SD authorities disagreed. And Gil stated that as soon as a liberation army had been approved, he would place the unit in its entirety under Vlasov's command.

As for Zhilenkov, Gil disposed of him by placing him in charge of a three-hundred-man training detachment.

The local SD headquarters left it at that and turned Zhilenkov and his group over to SS Major Otto Kraus, who had organized the northern high command of Operation Zeppelin in Pskov. Kraus had completely different responsibilities and lacked the means to cope with a large Russian unit. Moreover, it became apparent that the operation had not received political sanction. So as not to disappoint the Russians, and in the hope that a basic change might occur in the reasonably near future, Kraus expressed his willingness to form a unit of five hundred men. It was designated the First Guard Brigade of the ROA and was stationed in the small village of Stremutka, about nine miles from Pskov. This was the first military formation to maintain regular contact with Vlasov.

The appearance of the brigade caused tremendous excitement. The population had, of course, heard of a liberation army but had not been quite ready to believe in its existence. But there the unit was, and it stimulated the speculation that elsewhere additional detachments were being organized which would later all be united into one great army. The soldiers behaved in exemplary fashion, and good relations with the population were quickly established. Squads were sent into the villages to help with the harvest. The staff received many letters of thanks.[3]

On June 22, 1943, the second anniversary of the start of the Soviet-German War, a German military parade was held in Pskov. To everyone's surprise the parade was led by a company of the Guard Brigade. The effect was sensational, and the conviction grew that a liberation army was really in the making.

Meanwhile, however, the situation in the Druzhina was coming to a head. Zhilenkov's arrival had plainly strengthened the suspicions of Gil and his cohorts that the SD wanted to replace them because of their conduct. Blazhevich now made direct contact with the partisans. At the beginning of August

[3] S Narodom—Za Narod, No. 5, p. 15.

the Soviet leadership authorized the Zhelezniak Partisan Brigade to enter into negotiations with Gil for the defection of his entire unit. To prevent suspicion from being cast on himself, Gil sent on this mission his intelligence chief, Major General Bogdanov, who knew nothing of Gil's true intentions. In the talks, Bogdanov categorically rejected desertion and was prepared only to halt operations against the partisans as long as the latter reciprocated with respect to the brigade, the German units, and the population. The negotiations were fruitless. At this point, Gil took a personal hand. The partisans promised him an amnesty if the brigade defected with all its weapons, joined in fighting the Germans, and turned over Bogdanov as well as the émigré Captain Count Mirsky. Gil accepted these conditions.

On August 13, 1943, the partisans surrounded the Druzhina. Gil sounded the alarm and then, together with his friends, shot in the back many of those officers and soldiers who they assumed would not join in the betrayal. Those who died included Bogdanov, Colonel Orlov, all the regimental commanders except one who followed Gil, and all the battalion commanders. The SD liaison group was also slaughtered. Next, the Kruglevshchina railroad station was occupied and the line to Polotsk was cut. Glubokoye was attacked, but this assault was thrown back. The defecting elements of the Druzhina Brigade then retreated into the forest with the partisans.

Some of the soldiers and officers who had been caught in the surprise attack returned to Glubokoye. Thirty surviving officers and five hundred enlisted men gradually trickled back. That part of the Druzhina which had gone over to the partisans was renamed the First Anti-Fascist Brigade by the Soviets, and Stalin decorated Gil with the Order of the Red Star. The brigade suffered heavy casualties in a series of engagements, as did its former comrades on the other side who also fought in these encounters. In the winter of 1943–4 the brigade's surviving three hundred men were encircled near the Zyabki railroad station and annihilated. Gil himself was shot by one of his former officers with the parting words: "A dog's death for a dog." [4]

By the end of August 1943 it had already become clear that the SD had neither the will nor the ability to build a large liberation army. All its promises had merely served the purpose of attracting capable people to Operation Zeppelin. Kraus, who no longer wanted any part of this maneuver, requested that the Zhilenkov group be relieved. So, poorer by one more hope, they returned to Berlin. Only Lamsdorff stayed on with the First Guard Brigade, which continued to function on a modest scale.

In the meantime, Vlasov had been confronted in Berlin with the problem of the post-World War I émigrés. Zykov and Zhilenko, fearful of negative repercussions in Russia, rejected official ties with these people. Vlasov, however, was willing to cooperate with them, provided they did not propose the restoration of pre-Revolutionary conditions. The links between the Paris émigrés and the Western Powers might be useful in getting the West to recognize the liberation movement. Initially the majority of the émigrés, especially the older generation, wanted no part of Vlasov. To them he was one of Stalin's collaborators and a revolutionary upstart. But gradually the idea gained ground that the liberation movement desired to create a new, democratic—albeit not Tsarist—Russia which the old émigrés could also accept.

The driving force in this connection was the young director of the Russian Office for Confidential Affairs in France, Yurii Sergeyevich Zherebkov, a grandson of General Alexei Zherebkov, the former adjutant general to Tsar Nicholas II. Yurii Zherebkov had met Vlasov in February 1943, during a visit to Berlin, and immediately recognized that with this man, com-

---

[4] The origins and fate of the Druzhina are described by N. Klimenko: "Pravda o Druzhine" ("The Truth About the Druzhina"), Suvorovets (Buenos Aires), Nos. 17 and 20–23, 1950; Sofia Varshavskaya: "Otnosityelno Druzhiny" ("Concerning the Druzhina"), S Narodom—Za Narod, vol. 5, 1965; Kromiadi and Lamsdorff, interviews; O. Kraus, letter to author.

pletely new perspectives opened up for the Russian cause. He
began supporting Vlasov's activities and publicized the liberation
movement in the Russian-language émigré newspaper he edited,
Parizhskiye Vestnik ("Paris Bulletin"). He returned to Berlin
at the beginning of June to report to Vlasov and propose a
personal appearance for him in Paris. Vlasov was willing, but
doubted the Germans would permit him to visit Paris. To send
him there in the face of Keitel's unequivocal order would mean
a death sentence for both Vlasov himself and the liberation
movement. Pressed by Grote and Strikfeldt, Martin finally
agreed to let Malyshkin go if Zherebkov gained the approval of
the Paris military commandant.

So it was that on July 24, 1943, an emotionally charged
meeting took place in the Salle Wagram hall in the heart of
Paris. Four thousand people crowded into the main auditorium,
while another two thousand listened in another room via loudspeakers. Representatives of the French and German authorities,
diplomatic missions still in Paris, and foreign correspondents
were present. The audience gave Malyshkin an ovation lasting
several minutes when he appeared on the platform. He was the
first former Soviet general to come to Paris. The difficult years
in alien surroundings, the longing for the far-off Fatherland,
the hope for a return, as well as the bitterness generated by
humiliation at the hands of the German leaders—these all found
expression in a national demonstration that exceeded anything
in the émigrés' previous experience.

The meeting seemed to present a dramatic means of informing the West of the aims of the liberation movement and
opening the way to its recognition as a political force. Malyshkin not only spoke freely but voiced sentiments that were
extremely dangerous both for him and for the entire liberation
movement. Just a few weeks earlier, Hitler had strictly banned
all nationalistic political activity by Vlasov and his associates.

Consequences were soon forthcoming. The very next day the
Paris military commandant summoned Zherebkov to tell him
that statements had been made which the German leadership

considered intolerable, and that he could expect serious difficulties. To protect Vlasov and the movement from danger, Zherebkov and Malyshkin immediately doctored the stenographic record, either eliminating or toning down all nationalistic and anti-German remarks.[5]

Zherebkov managed to persuade Colonel Schmidtke, head of the commandant's propaganda section, to accept his text as the original one, even though Schmidtke had already received hostile accounts of Malyshkin's anti-German statements. In addition, Zherebkov conferred with the head of the security police and SD in France, Dr. Knochen, and the German consul general, Dr. Quiring, both secret opponents of *Ost* policy; these officials thereupon transmitted positive reports to their Berlin superiors. The SD interrogated Malyshkin on his return to Berlin, but he stuck to the revised version of the stenographic record. And so the danger was averted. Zherebkov, however, received orders not to organize any more meetings and to stay away from Berlin.[6]

The realization that precious, irreplaceable time was flowing by tormented Vlasov relentlessly. Once, during an evening card game, he exploded indignantly: "I can't understand it! I know Stalin, his methods, his weak spots, I know exactly what has to be done—and here I sit playing preference!" [7]

[5] A corrected version of the text was published in *Parizhskiye Vestnik*, No. 59, on July 31, 1943. The émigré press (for example, *S Narodom—Za Narod*, vol. 3, November 1964) has since expressed doubts that Malyshkin ever actually made such anti-Semitic statements as this version contains. Their assumption is that these remarks were inserted afterward by Zherebkov in order to satisfy the German authorities. But according to a letter to the author from Zherebkov himself, this speculation is not correct. It is possible that Malyshkin employed these anti-Semitic statements as a camouflage, but also that they expressed his own beliefs. Dellingshausen, Strik-Strikfeldt, and Zaitsev (interviews), as well as von der Ropp (letter to author), affirm that all of Vlasov's colleagues, including Malyshkin, were horrified by the Nazis' destruction of the Jews.

[6] Zherebkov: *Russian Days in Paris*, unpub. ms.; Grote, interview.

[7] S. Fröhlich, unpub. rept., p. 2, Institute for Contemporary History (IfZ), Munich.

How could he possibly fathom what was happening when the power struggles were an impenetrable jungle even to his German friends? He saw a dictatorship, but it seemed grotesque compared to Stalin's. He saw influential officials, but they had conflicting opinions. There was no uniform policy, no system. " 'Blood and Soil'—but that isn't an ideology," he once observed.

The Soviet state was built on different, and apparently unshakable, foundations. Like every Soviet citizen, he had passed through a rigorous training which still influenced his thinking, even though he had repudiated Communism. Like many Russians, he had ascribed to Germany an ideological foundation stronger than Communism. At first, he found it simply inconceivable that no system existed, that the men at the top did not even have a common plan, that while Hitler's orders were obeyed, sources of influence and authority worked against each other.

Vlasov sometimes expressed his criticism quite bluntly: "A strange country, where you can't learn anything about enemy doctrine because the Gestapo's fat behind is sitting on it. You can read everything in our country, though with destructive commentaries." Another time he said: "I like your order, your discipline, but you lack generosity. You can't even supply me with clothes. How will you beat Stalin?" [8] Only very gradually did he discover the true nature of the German reality. In this he was helped by frequent conversations with Theodor Krause, whom he had met through Strikfeldt. Krause, a German from St. Petersburg, and a departmental head in the press section of OKW, served as a sort of intermediary between Russian and German culture.

Vlasov did not believe that any counterideology was needed to challenge the Soviets. What was required was simply to advocate the opposite of what the Soviet regime embodied: justice, private property, individual security, freedom from op-

[8] T. Krause, unpub. rept., p. 1, IfZ, and letter to author.

pression; in short, what the people yearned for. National Socialism was neither desired nor suitable, particularly since Vlasov
recognized that it basically meant a drive for power, violence,
and the oppression of others. As happened with other Russians,
his original high esteem for German efficiency and achievements gave way to growing distaste and disillusionment, to a
reluctant use of German resources because no one else was
fighting Stalin. These feelings were intensified by the fact that
Vlasov's sometimes naïve sense of justice was repeatedly outraged.

In September 1943 an incident occurred which threatened to
destroy everything accomplished thus far. Zeitzler called in
General Hellmich on September 15 and revealed to him that
several Eastern battalions had defected. The Führer had immediately ordered all volunteer units disarmed, starting with a
group of eighty thousand men who were now to be shipped
to France for work in the coal mines. He expected a report on
the execution of his command within forty-eight hours. Zeitzler
dismissed Hellmich's objections that he knew of no such instances, that the contrary was true, and that the unreliability
rate was not more than one per cent despite the hard fighting
during the general German retreat. The Führer had issued an
order and he, Zeitzler, was fed up with taking abuse time after
time because of those damned volunteers.

Hellmich's staff feverishly gathered information on the real
state of affairs. They found that there was not a single indication of unreliability among the Eastern volunteers attached
either to Army Group North or to Army Group South. In the
latter, a number of units had more than stood the test. Only
a Cossack battalion and part of a construction battalion had
deserted on the southern wing of Army Group Center, and
both these units had been inadequately equipped for the tasks
assigned them. In sum, even in the face of the tremendous
strain of the retreat, talk of general undependability was al-

together groundless. Hitler had obviously been looking for a scapegoat in his rage over the bad situation at the front.

Hellmich asked Herre[9] to go to Zeitzler with a detailed report. Although every possible step had to be taken to prevent execution of this absurd order, Hellmich himself did not feel suited for such tasks. He was a soldier, accustomed to obeying orders. Political negotiations, contradicting superiors—it wasn't his style. Herre brought Zeitzler proof that not more than 1,300 volunteers and Hiwis had deserted; that is, a mere 0.17 per cent of the volunteers on the German side. He pointed out that the disarming of eighty thousand men would have disastrous consequences of which the Führer's headquarters apparently had not the slightest idea. For the Russians, being disarmed would be a disgrace, and working in the coal mines a humiliating punishment. They had joined the struggle voluntarily and conducted themselves bravely and irreproachably. Disarming them would lead exactly to what they were being falsely accused of—unreliability. Moreover, such an action would inevitably have a tremendous impact on the attitude of the six million Eastern workers.

Zeitzler at last gave in, but explained that Hitler's instructions still had to be carried out as far as possible. When Herre told him that only three to five thousand men could be supplied at most, and that even then, selecting them would be very difficult, Zeitzler flared up: "Are you mad? Do you seriously believe the Führer will go along with anything like this?"[1] Herre replied that the Führer would *have* to go along—anything else would lead to catastrophe. Zeitzler finally agreed to make another appeal to Hitler; but he demanded a list beforehand of those units whose disarming would, in the opinion of the chief of Eastern Troops, not do grave harm. The decision came three days later: Hitler reluctantly agreed to the disarming of only

[9] Herre had been transferred from Foreign Armies East to the post of operations officer on Hellmich's staff.
[1] Herre, diary.

those formations picked by Hellmich. What at first appeared a victory for reason, however, proved to be the opposite shortly thereafter—when the Führer's headquarters ordered all volunteer units transferred to the western front.

Hitler ignored the fact that these volunteers wanted to fight to liberate their country, that they were not mercenaries indifferent to their enemy. If this decision were not to instigate revolts, a reasonably plausible justification for it would have to be found. No one at the Führer's headquarters, however, seemed to give the matter a moment's thought.

At this time an incident occurred which demonstrated how questionable the selection of five thousand allegedly unreliable volunteers had been. Strugi Krasnye, a small town on the Luga-Gatchina rail line where seventy Germans were stationed, was attacked by some six or seven hundred partisans. The situation seemed hopeless. With half the German garrison already fallen, however, the unit's commander managed to reach the railroad station a couple of miles from town, where stood a train carrying an "unreliable" and disarmed Turkic battalion. The commander armed the battalion from a weapons depot near the station, led it in an attack from the rear on the partisans, and defeated them. Over one hundred partisans were killed.[2]

A few units under SS jurisdiction were exempted from the transfer. One was the Kaminsky Brigade, which turned to fighting partisans in the Lepel area after the retreat from Lokot. Kaminsky had tried to establish an autonomous area there as well, but he was no longer operating on familiar, native ground, and German assurances that they would soon be returning lost credibility from day to day. Demoralization was slowly setting in.

A Cossack division organized by Stauffenberg at the end of April was shifted to Yugoslavia, rather than the western front, to fight Tito's partisans. The core of this division consisted of two units: the Kononov Regiment from Mogilev, led by Lieutenant Colonel Jungschulz, which had seen a good deal of

---

[2] Klein, interpreter in Section VII of Rear Area of Army Group North, interview.

action during the summer of 1942 in the Mozdok-Achikulak area; and a battalion, led by Lieutenant Colonel von Wolff, from the Poltava region. The division's commander, Colonel (later Lieutenant General) Helmut von Pannwitz, was a man of outstanding military and human qualities, who quickly won the trust of the Cossacks.

The division completed training in September and two weeks later was fighting in Croatia. Another Russian unit was already deployed in Yugoslavia—the fifteen-thousand-man "Russian Security Corps," under General Steifon. The corps consisted exclusively of Russian émigrés of the First World War period who had volunteered in order to fight on the eastern front but who found themselves fighting against Tito instead.

The Cossacks enjoyed a rather exceptional position because Rosenberg had planned to give them an autonomous region, "Cossackia," and had approved a Cossack administration under the old Tsarist general P. N. Krasnov. Tens of thousands of Cossacks retreated with the Germans; they and their families trekked westward in enormous columns. The largest migration was that led by Ataman (Headman) Sergei Pavlov, who on his own initiative had organized a Cossack unit after the Red Army had withdrawn, and had called a meeting in Novocherkassk of representatives of various Cossack villages. This assembly had decided to propose the formation of a great Cossack army to the Germans. Fifteen thousand people, half of them bearing arms, took part in the trek led by General Domanov following Pavlov's death. After months of marching, this force was finally directed into the Tolmezzo area in northern Italy.

A replacement-training regiment of ten to fifteen thousand men for Pannwitz's Cossack division was organized in Mokhovo. Its commander was the former Tsarist general A. G. Shkuro, a legendary Civil War hero who had been awarded the Order of the Bath by King George V of England.

A meeting took place at the end of September between Krasnov and Vlasov. But it had no practical results, since Vlasov's hands were still tied. Krasnov declared his willingness to cooperate with Vlasov, but refused to place himself under the latter's command. He maintained this position to the end, though the great mass of Cossacks wanted to be incorporated into a grand liberation army.[3]

The transfer of the Cossacks from the eastern front was completed without serious difficulties. But it soon became clear that the Russian volunteer units were not at all ready to follow German orders blindly. They stubbornly pressed their demands to see Vlasov. Insubordination and mutiny were in the air. In this situation, General Jodl remembered Vlasov, whom the Wehrmacht had "watched over like a new-laid egg." Now Vlasov could show whether he truly exercised the influence of which there was such constant talk. He demanded that Vlasov write an open letter explaining to the volunteer units that the transfer was necessary.

Strikfeldt, after all that had happened, at first refused to exact this from Vlasov—who was, moreover, then in a state of great indignation and despair. For it had at last become plain to him that the German leaders had never desired anything but mercenaries. He vowed to find ways of publicly denouncing this betrayal, and demanded to be sent back as a prisoner to a camp. It took Strikfeldt days to calm Vlasov down. He pointed out that given Hitler's frame of mind, any new incident could end with the volunteer units being disarmed. At least as things stood, the substance had been saved. Meanwhile, perhaps the deteriorating situation at the front might force a change in Hitler's attitude.

Finally, Grote—with the aim of restoring calm so that the organization of a liberation army could proceed—drafted an

---

[3] The attitude of the Cossacks during the eastern campaign and of Pannwitz's corps is reported on by: H. D. von Kalben: *Zur Geschichte des XV Kosaken-Kavallerie-Korps* ("On the History of the Fifteenth Cossack Cavalry Corps"), *Deutsches Soldaten-Jahrbuch* ("German Soldiers Yearbook"), 1963–4–5; E. Kern: *General von Pannwitz und seine Kosaken* ("General von Pannwitz and His Cossacks"), Plesseverlag, Göttingen, 1964; K. Cherkassov: op. cit.; H. Stöckl: *Die Entstehung des Kosakentums* ("The Origin of the Cossacks"), Historische Zeitschrift, 1953.

General Andrey Andreyevich Vlasov

Vlasov in China with interpreter Sun Kuei-chi

Vlasov and Maria Voronova following their capture, 1942

Vassily Malyshkin

Wilfried Strik-Strikfeldt

Mileti A. Zykov and Georgi N. Zhilenkov

Kaminsky in Lokot, 1942

Zhilenkov, Kromiadi, and Boyarsky in Pskov, 1943

Fedor I. Trukhin

Official conference in Prague.
Left to right: General Toussaint, SS General Lorenz, Vlasov

With the first division in Münsingen.
Sakharov, Bunyachenko, Vlasov

open letter in which the transfer was described as a temporary measure caused by the situation at the front. It seemed extremely unlikely, however, that Jodl would agree to Grote's formulation. But the unexpected happened: Jodl approved.

This brought a surprising improvement in Vlasov's mood. He believed that Jodl's approval of the open letter meant as well his approval of the announced organization of a liberation army; for, despite his unhappy experiences, it was inconceivable to Vlasov that a top-ranking German officer could act dishonestly. The Germans around him did not disabuse him on this point. They felt they must do everything to keep Vlasov and the Eastern troops ready for possible action someday.[4]

Strikfeldt requested permission for Vlasov to visit the volunteer units. But Jodl refused, for reasons that made his attitude clear. On the margin of Strikfeldt's written request, he wrote: "No. Purpose fulfilled with 'open letter.' No intention of repeating the mistake of the Dabendorf propagandists magnified a hundredfold. Dabendorf an anti-German nest. It should be broken up." Actually the outlook in Dabendorf was not anti-German as such; but there was unquestionably overt opposition to National Socialism.

In a speech in October 1943, to top officers of the Waffen-SS and the army, Himmler said:

> . . . High hopes have been placed in this General Vlasov. But these hopes were not as justified as many assumed. I believe they resulted from a false estimate of the Slavs. Every Slav, every Russian general will, if we can induce him to talk, if we appeal to his vanity, start to chatter in a manner that is incredible to us Germans. . . . Herr Vlasov—and it doesn't surprise me—engaged in propaganda in Germany itself and, I must say, on many occasions lectured us Germans in a grotesque fashion. I saw great harm in that. We can make propaganda directed abroad and employ whatever means we please. . . . Every means is legitimate which these

[4] Strik-Strikfeldt, letter to author.

savage peoples place at our disposal and which results in a
Russian dying instead of a German. This is proper and
answerable before God and men. But something happened
that we did not desire: With the arrogance peculiar to the
Russian, the Slav, Herr Vlasov began to tell stories. He said:
Germany has never been able to defeat Russia, only we Russians can defeat Russia. This proposition, gentlemen, is very
dangerous. . . . The morning, noon, and evening prayer of
the German army must be: We are superior to every enemy in this world. If a Russian comes, a deserter at that—
the day before yesterday a butcher's apprentice, perhaps, and
yesterday made a general by Stalin—and with Slavic pre-
sumption delivers lectures and then slips in the sentence that
Russia can only be conquered by Russians, then I have
something to say: The man proves what a swine he is by
virtue of this sentence alone. . . .

Everything that we shall now have to suffer during the
coming winter, during which we shall certainly have to kill
and slaughter another two or three million Russians—all
these things are merely passing phases. . . . For us the end
of this war means an open road to the east, the creation of
the Germanic Reich. . . . This means we extend the fron-
tiers of the German nation by three hundred miles to the
east. This means peace, gentlemen, it means the end of the
war, it means the marvelous future we have envisaged.[5]

Himmler's speech was known in the Kiebitzweg three days
later. Generally, Strikfeldt was in the habit of frankly discussing
all difficulties with Vlasov; but this was one time he would have
preferred not to have had to deal with such a prime example of
Nazi arrogance. Several times in these weeks of disillusionment
and bitterness, Vlasov had been close to giving up altogether.
Long conversations with Malyshkin, Trukhin, Zhilenkov, and
Zykov finally brought all of them to the decision to go along for
the sake of the volunteers, POW's, and conscripted laborers

[5] Text quoted in Thorwald, op. cit., p. 304.

from the east. The opportunities to remedy abuses and ease conditions continued to multiply, and Dabendorf played an expanding role in this process. The graduates of the courses there reported their impressions of the prison and labor camps, so that Vlasov was kept informed; then, through Grote and Strikfeldt, abuses could at least be mitigated, if not always eliminated.

Moreover, an independent, quasi-legal intelligence service had grown up which supplied information on events in the Russian volunteer units and the occupied eastern territories. A rupture with the Germans, however dishonorably they might have acted, would not only have threatened everything already achieved, but would also have meant the end of the Russian liberation movement. Astonishingly, despite the German leadership and all the obstacles they had thrown in its path, a politically significant movement had already become an established fact. Its core consisted of the Dabendorf graduates; seven former Soviet generals; some sixty colonels; and several thousand lower-ranking officers, scientists, engineers, and members of other professions. They did not all share the same political views; but all wanted Russia liberated from the Stalin regime.

A book outlining policies and programs for ROA members was published at this time, which summed up the common goals:

The ROA is first of all a Russian army, that is, one which is national in nature, aim, and spirit. The prime goal of its struggle is the creation of a national Russian state. It is a liberation army which seeks to free the people from the present regime. However, it does not seek to restore the pre-Revolutionary state of affairs, but to build a new Russia based on new principles. It is not only an instrument of struggle but a political force as well, a part of the liberation movement of the peoples of Russia.[6]

[6] This work—*Voin ROA, Etika, Oblik, Povedeniye,* ROA Propaganda Press, 1944—is in the author's possession.

Vlasov and his supporters hoped their friends in the Wehrmacht would succeed. They considered the overthrow of Hitler possible and began to think of making contacts with the West. Discussions were held on what would happen if Hitler were to give Vlasov a free hand under pressure of the situation at the front but then, at a later stage, if Stalin fell, were to continue to pursue his expansionist plans. They understood that a conflict with Germany would in this case be unavoidable, and they counted on support from the Western Powers in such a situation. Since the Allies had supported a Communist Russia against Hitler, they most certainly would back one that was non-Communist. In any case, Hitler's downfall seemed inevitable.

A long period of waiting in vain for decisions extended through 1943 and nearly half of 1944. Nevertheless, some accomplishments were realized. Twenty new field hospitals were established for the volunteer soldiers. A Russian nurse corps, with its own uniforms and training school, was organized. Rest-and-recreation facilities, nursing homes for disabled soldiers, rehabilitation camps, and libraries were approved, and the right to the Iron Cross decoration was granted. Russian propaganda personnel, including some women, were assigned to all the larger front-line units.[7]

General Ernst Köstring, who replaced Hellmich as commander of the volunteer units on January 1, 1944, had contributed more than a little to these successes. Köstring had grown up in Moscow, spoke Russian, and had served as a military attaché in Moscow. He saw what was wrong with the *Ost* policy, but no longer believed in the possibility of changing it. Still, he was determined to do what he could to aid the Russians' national aspirations.

Meanwhile, the idea of a Russian liberation movement had begun to exercise a strong attraction for numerous Germans.

---

[7] An informative, albeit subjective, picture of the employment of women in propaganda activity is given by Maria de Smeth: *Roter Kaviar, Hauptmann Maria* ("Red Caviar, Captain Maria"), Verlag Welsermühl, Wels, 1965.

Many of them contacted Vlasov, and there was no lack of efforts—vain though they were—to help him. An always welcome guest to the house on the Kiebitzweg was Colonel von Freytag-Loringhoven, the Russian-speaking intelligence officer of Army Group B, who inspired new hope in Vlasov by his hints concerning changes in the near future. Since he could converse with Vlasov without an interpreter, Freytag-Loringhoven spoke more frankly to him than he might otherwise have done. What he had meant became fully clear when he committed suicide just after the failure of the July 20 plot against Hitler.

Despite the visits and demonstrations of sympathy, this period of senseless waiting was wearing Vlasov down. He drank, he got through the evenings playing cards. Malyshkin and Kromiadi (on his return from Pskov, the latter had replaced Kalugin as Vlasov's secretary) were his constant companions. Before strangers he concealed his anxieties and attempted to maintain a façade of serenity, to continually radiate strength of conviction. His natural charm—a faculty he could bring into play at will—was still much in evidence, and he could be gay and lively in the company of friends. But alongside this fleeting vivacity there grew a gloomy and oppressive hopelessness, a foreboding sense that it was now "too late." Once, when visiting Melitta Wiedemann, he remarked to her Russian servant girl: "If you manage to get back home, Nadya, don't forget me. Tell your friends that our intentions toward our people were honorable." [8]

Maria Voronova, whose whereabouts Vlasov had tried unsuccessfully to ascertain, appeared unexpectedly in Berlin in the spring of 1944. She had contacted Fröhlich in Riga, where he was spending his leave. Now she took over management of the small, womanless household. At first, she said very little about what had happened to her in the interim; but a few days after her arrival she confessed to Vlasov that partisans in Lithuania had sent her to poison him.

[8] Wiedemann, letter to author.

It was about this time that Vlasov met two men who were to be numbered among his most loyal colleagues: Colonels Meandrov and Maltsev. Meandrov was a calm, serious man, and a fanatical nationalist; Maltsev, impulsive and quick, was a brilliant speaker. In the thirties he had served as commander of the Central Asian Air Force. He had been imprisoned for two years after the Tukhachevsky Affair and had remained voluntarily in Yalta as director of an air force hospital when the Germans conquered the Crimea. With German approval, he had organized an eastern squadron of Russian fliers who dropped propaganda material and agents behind Soviet lines. In addition, he visited the labor and POW camps to recruit for the liberation movement. He was usually accompanied by two of his officers, Antelevsky and Bychov—both "Heroes of the Soviet Union" and both fanatical foes of Stalin.

Shkuro, the Cossack general, visited Vlasov in the spring of 1944. They discussed placing Pannwitz's Cossacks under Vlasov's command as soon as the organization of a Russian liberation army became feasible. The two men also agreed on the inadvisability of any former Tsarist general (such as Shkuro himself) assuming command of the Cossack units, since this would give Soviet propagandists a welcome opportunity to claim that the liberation army aimed to restore the pre-Revolutionary order. Like most Cossacks, Shkuro looked upon himself as a Russian and considered Rosenberg's plan for an autonomous "Cossackia" a joke. Through Shkuro, Vlasov resumed relations with Kononov, whom he had not seen since his visit to Mogilev.

In June 1944, Pannwitz's division was raised to the status of a corps, becoming the Fifteenth Cossack Corps, and reached a strength of more than twenty thousand men. The next month, Pannwitz visited General Gottlob Berger, head of the SS Main Office, and proposed to him that the Cossack Corps be placed under nominal SS jurisdiction. This would enable the corps to receive more weapons, as well as to sidestep the local police and administrative officials, whose perpetual quarrelsomeness was causing the Cossacks difficulties. Berger agreed to this. The corps's German officers remained members of the Wehrmacht, and there was no change in the unit's uniforms.

Vlasov had also learned of developments in White Russia, where, at the beginning of 1944, the green light had been given for the establishment of a White Russian Rada ("parliament") in Minsk. Professor Ostrovsky had become president of the Rada.

The Rada had issued a call for the creation of an army, and though a German victory could hardly be expected any longer, about thirty thousand men had volunteered. There was also hope in White Russia of support from the Western Powers after the demise of National Socialism. It was even considered possible that the Wehrmacht, which the population of the occupied territories had supported, would make common cause with the Western Powers against Stalin after Hitler's overthrow.[9]

In January 1944 seventy-two volunteer battalions finally arrived in France. Since Vlasov was not allowed to visit these units, it was Zhilenkov who traveled to France, accompanied by Fröhlich. The situation they found was anything but good. Most of the German liaison officers, as well as the regimental commanders to whom the battalions had been assigned, had never dealt with Eastern volunteers or served in the east, and their attitude toward the volunteer units was unfavorable. Moreover, these units, whom Hitler considered too unreliable to use in the rear areas in Russia, were now on their way to the front lines at the Atlantic Wall. Representations made to the commander in chief in the west by Major Walther Hansen, operations officer of the volunteer units, brought some improvement; but the situation was far from resolved. Hope for the creation of a Russian liberation army was all that held the men together.[1]

---

[9] D. Kozmovich, interview.
[1] Details on the situation of the volunteer units in France are given by Walther Hansen: *Tagebuchaufzeichnungen* ("Diary Notes"), IfZ; and Fröhlich, interview.

About this same time, General Trukhin visited the volunteer units on the Italian front, accompanied by Captain von Dellingshausen and by his adjutant, Romashkin. The trip had been undertaken at the request of Field Marshal Albert Kesselring because some Russians had deserted and a slump in fighting morale had been noted. After dining with Kesselring and twenty other high-ranking officers, Trukhin traveled by night in Kesselring's car to the front near Monte Cassino and Nettuno. It turned out that most of the German commanders of the Russian battalions fighting there didn't know a word of Russian and didn't understand how to deal with the Russians. The weapons and clothing of the volunteers were inferior to those of the German units, and the Russians were indignant over their second-class treatment. Moreover, they objected strongly to being compelled to fight on a front to which they were indifferent. Yet, despite all these negative factors, only twenty-two men had deserted. The one battalion which did have a Russian-speaking commander, and whose company and platoon leaders were also Russian, had distinguished itself.

Trukhin made speeches, visited the most advanced fighting positions, consoled the soldiers with the prospect of soon joining a great Russian liberation army, and told them that as of May 1, Russian workers in the Reich would no longer have to wear the discriminatory *Ost* insignia. In a final talk, Kesselring promised better equipment and treatment for these battalions and emphasized that the main problem was the lack of a basic decision on the Russian question. He pledged that he would personally intervene in Berlin in favor of such a decision. Before Trukhin departed, he was received in Rome by General von Mackensen, who displayed an understanding of the Russian problem.[2]

Kazantsev appeared in the Kiebitzweg in June. He gave Vlasov important news about the occupied areas and, in addition, information on conditions in a number of German agencies where NTS members were employed. The situation of the

[2] Dellingshausen, letter to author.

NTS was becoming increasingly precarious. It had initiated an intensive anti-German propaganda campaign among the Russians in the winter of 1942–3, and the Gestapo, moreover, was suspicious of the NTS's collaboration with Wehrmacht opponents of the *Ost* policy.

Kazantsev brought an offer from Baidalakov, head of the NTS, for Vlasov to avail himself of a connection with the Western Powers which the organization had established through a Swiss intermediary. Vlasov, however, declined the offer. As long as the Western Allies considered Hitler Enemy Number One, and Stalin was carrying the main brunt of the war, they would hardly be ready to give Stalin's enemies assurances to be made good at a later date unless the latter immediately attacked Hitler—a step that would inevitably lead to the destruction of the liberation movement.[3]

Soon after this conversation there appeared a new and ominous warning signal for the NTS, in the dismissal of several of its members, for no apparent reason, from their jobs with German government agencies. Only Dr. Vladimir Poremsky, an NTS leader, was told the truth—by Dr. Knüpffer, his superior in the Eastern Ministry. Knüpffer informed Poremsky that he was dismissing him because Poremsky would sooner or later be arrested, and Knüpffer did not want this to happen in his office. He did promise, however, not to reveal Poremsky's dismissal. Shortly afterwards, the ax fell: Hundreds of NTS members were thrown into jail or concentration camps. Only those who had been able to keep their membership a secret—among them Zaitsev, Trukhin, and Kazantsev—were spared.

[3] Kazantsev, op. cit., pp. 167 ff.

V

TOO LITTLE
AND TOO LATE

Kazantsev urged Vlasov to speak up for the arrested men; but
the latter's chances of winning a hearing were slight. Besides, he
had to avoid endangering his own plans—which suddenly, to
everyone's surprise, received support from almost the last quarter Vlasov and his friends would have imagined: the Waffen-
SS and Himmler.

Neither the Waffen-SS nor the SS's Main Office for State
Security (RSHA), which also operated under Himmler's jurisdiction, was as monolithic as it outwardly appeared. Many commanders of SS units serving in the east had learned from their
experience at the front and in the occupied areas how irrational
the *Ost* policy was; there were opponents of the official program
in the RSHA as well, people who had firsthand knowledge of its
consequences. Although Gestapo chief Müller unswervingly supported the official thesis of the Slavic *Untermensch*, there were

in the Security Service (SD) a number of young intellectuals whose wide knowledge of the situation caused them to realize the untenability of the official line.

Among them was the director of the Foreign Intelligence Service, Walter Schellenberg, and the director of the Internal Intelligence Service, Otto Ohlendorf. Ohlendorf was an outspoken foe of the tactics of Erich Koch, Reichskommissar for the Ukraine, which—as Ohlendorf said—created resistance and revolt far more effectively than the enemy. Ohlendorf also voiced the sharpest criticism of domestic political measures, particularly Hitler's habit of ignoring existing organizations when assigning new tasks and handing them over to special representatives. As a result, the state apparatus was paralyzed by the proliferation of innumerable agencies, staffed mainly by incompetent people working side by side and against each other—a veritable caricature of a totalitarian dictatorship.[1]

Since the beginning of the war there had also been opponents of the Ost policy among SS majors and captains who tried through their official activities to exert an influence on events. While lacking authority to make policy, they did gradually become a political factor. Among them were men who had not found an alternative to the Nazi Party and were profoundly depressed by what was happening. Although, officially, the SD was not allowed to spy on party organs—this was the limit set to Himmler's power—the latter knew all about the corruption, incompetence, and megalomania of most party leaders.

The disaffected elements had enough experience in internal party maneuvering to know where and how to get something done. They understood thoroughly that an objective could only be achieved by detours and by masking real intentions. Proposals could be submitted only on the grounds of sheer expediency in the interests of German war strategy, of the German "final victory." Any direct action faced certain failure because

[1] F. Kersten: *Totenkopf und Treue* ("Death's Head and Loyalty"), Mölich-Verlag, Hamburg, 1953, p. 247.

it brought National Socialist principles into question and was incompatible with Hitler's war aims. It was, in addition, extremely dangerous.

Within the SD it was the Internal Intelligence Service's Office IIIb, headed by SS Colonel Hans Ehlich, which had particular responsibility with regard to nationality questions in the occupied areas and to problems of foreign workers in the Reich; and it was this office that continually and steadily reported on the consequences of the *Ost* policy. This activity was intensified when, at the end of 1943, SS Major Friedrich Buchardt became head of Departmental Section IIIb2, with responsibility for political intelligence among the Eastern peoples living in the occupied territories.

Buchardt, a Russian-speaking Balt, had had certain lessons driven home to him during various operations in the area administered by Army Group Center. He had already, at that time, pointed out that without a sound plan, success would be impossible, and that Vlasov's name meant more to deserters, POW's, and the civilian population than German officialdom was ready to admit.

When Buchardt assumed his new post, Ohlendorf assured him that he could strike out in new directions in *Ost* policy, provided he took the necessary precautions. He could also recruit his Baltic countrymen for this work. Balts were employed in almost all the eastern agencies because of their knowledge of the requisite languages, and many kept in touch with Buchardt. A group sharing the same viewpoint crystallized, using Buchardt's office as an information clearinghouse and base of operations. The group buttressed its suggestions with reports processed by its own members, all of which indicated the need for political decisions. The key objective was to win over one person with sufficient power and influence to gain Hitler's approval in some form.

As in the past, the unconditional enemies of all Russian national aspirations included the top party officials, led by

Reichsleiter Martin Bormann (Hitler's party secretary); the Gestapo; and Rosenberg and the ethnic nationality groups he supported, who labeled any encouragement of Vlasov as betrayal of the Germans. In addition, there were those who, while they did favor better treatment for the Russians, wanted the way kept open for an agreement with Stalin, as in 1939.

For this same reason the Japanese also opposed Vlasov and tried to block his program by any means available. They attempted to flatter Himmler by playing up his photo in their press.[2] In February 1944, Japanese Ambassador Oshima proposed a separate peace with the Soviet Union; but Himmler torpedoed this scheme.[3]

Himmler certainly was among Vlasov's enemies; still, it seemed that he could be approached. And while outwardly he gave unconditional support to Hitler's blueprint for the east, he had tried experiments—such as the creation of Estonian, Latvian, Caucasian, and even Russian SS units—which indicated some doubt concerning the effectiveness of the *Ost* policy. There seemed a certain logic in suggesting a Vlasov *Aktion* to Himmler as a kind of insurance in case of a German defeat. The possibility of influencing him at least remained open, given his ambivalent and vacillating character and his penchant for embracing absurd ideas. For example, he seriously ordered various agencies to investigate the feasibility of settling Cossacks in military villages on the rim of European Russia as a protective wall against Asia. Again, in the spring of 1943 he expressed the intention of liquidating the Orthodox Church during a new German advance into Russia because it strengthened Russian nationalism, and of introducing Buddhism in order to "pacify" the Russians! And a short time later he instructed the Gestapo to search in the concentration camps for sectarian "Bible seek-

---

[2] Friedrich Buchardt: "Die Behandlung des russischen Problems durch das nationalsozialistische Regime" ("Treatment of the Russian Problem by the National Socialist Regime"), unpub. ms., p. 231.

[3] Gottlob Berger, interview.

ers" whose pacifism might reduce the military effectiveness of the Russians and paralyze their will to fight.[4] New opportunities opened up when Himmler requested a Russian-speaking SD officer, and Buchardt suggested a countryman of his, Captain von Radecky. Suitable, up-to-date reports were subsequently channeled through this man to Himmler, from which the latter could deduce that things could not continue as they were.

The Gestapo, meanwhile, sensed that something was in the wind. They noted the Russians' increased self-confidence and received reports of anti-German statements. However, since these were not enough to offset the protection afforded by the Wehrmacht, the Gestapo decided to proceed against Vlasov on the basis of political-ideological evidence. It therefore asked Office III of the SD to hand over the Vlasov file for evaluation. Buchardt and Ehlich advised Ohlendorf not to deliver the file because it dealt with intelligence, not police matters. Ohlendorf, though no friend of Gestapo chief Müller, knew Himmler's attitude and had no wish to be drawn into a power struggle with the Gestapo. Still, he did manage to withhold the file, using a series of pretexts. With no time to lose, Buchardt's group, via Radecky, fired off a new and more comprehensive report to Himmler, which espoused the need for a positive shift in *Ost* policy as soon as possible on the following grounds:

(1) Some 700,000 members of Eastern peoples, under arms as volunteers on the German side, would only remain loyal to the Reich and maintain their fighting spirit if they were given political objectives for which they could fight. The purely negative slogan of struggle against Bolshevism no longer sufficed.

(2) The propaganda operations Himmler desired could not be successful unless they proposed such objectives.

(3) The Eastern workers, so important to the armaments industry, also had to be given objectives, so that they would work in their own interest. Coercion and compulsion were yielding dwindling results, and these workers, numbering in the millions, could easily become a disruptive factor in the economy.

[4] Buchardt, op. cit., p. 212.

It was also recommended that Vlasov be received informally and his proposals heard out.

The decisive turn in Vlasov's favor was finally achieved, not through the efforts of the SD, but through those of an individual acting on his own: Colonel Gunter d'Alquen of the Waffen-SS. D'Alquen belonged to a group of young intellectuals who before 1933 believed in National Socialism as the only alternative to the rising tide of Communism—with the emphasis placed chiefly on "Socialism," as a reaction to the bourgeoisie's "burden of sin." He was twenty-three years old when the Nazis seized power, and just a few years later was chief editor of the SS magazine, *The Black Corps*.

At the start of the eastern campaign he was commander of a war-correspondents battalion, with Himmler's complete support. The unit was later assigned propaganda duties and expanded to regimental strength. Journalists and propagandists of different nationalities worked together in it for the SS concept of a "new Europe." At thirty-four, d'Alquen was one of the youngest colonels in the Waffen-SS.

He and his colleagues were not professional soldiers and operated in unorthodox fashion. The scope of Himmler's ambitions became clear to them much sooner than to many others, and they did not hesitate to criticize the corruption of the party leaders. Once, when Grote visited their unit on a service mission, he observed at first hand their impassioned and uncompromising opposition to the "gold pheasants." [5] At first, Grote believed he was being deliberately provoked. They spoke of wanting a "better" National Socialism and expatiated greatly on the theme of "Just wait till we get home!"

D'Alquen, being a Rhinelander, had few concrete notions of conditions in the east at the beginning of the war. Communism was associated in his mind with what he had learned in street fighting with the Reds in Germany. The first mutilated Soviet

[5] A nickname given to Nazi Party functionaries because of their gold-brown uniforms.

corpses he saw as a war correspondent did nothing to correct this viewpoint. He did not see, or did not wish to see, the crimes committed by the Germans.

However, interrogation of many Soviet war prisoners, contacts with the Russian population, and conversations with Waffen-SS commanders, who measured the *Ost* policy against the realities they encountered—all played a part in opening up new perspectives for him. As far back as 1941 a Waffen-SS corps commander named Bittrich had declared: "The things Heinrich says are sheer nonsense! Things will go badly if we don't drastically change our ways." SS Generals Krüger, Hausser, and Steiner were equally vociferous. Steiner called Himmler a fool in front of fifteen high-ranking officers[6]; and in June 1943 he permitted his friend Count von der Schulenburg, former deputy police commissioner of Berlin, to say, "We shall have to kill Hitler before he destroys Germany completely"—without contradicting him or denouncing him to the authorities.[7]

These SS officers had no respect at all for Himmler; but neither did they have any political influence. Consequently, knowing that d'Alquen, who was under Himmler's direct command, was a man not easily shocked by frank talk, they poured out their doubts to him. All of this gradually led d'Alquen to realize that the entire *Ost* blueprint of National Socialism was wrong. When he spoke over radio on the first anniversary of the eastern campaign, he felt the discrepancy between what he said and what he thought. He began channeling reports to Himmler which repeatedly implied that the realities were considerably at variance with what the leadership imagined. He could go much further in this respect than others, since Himmler liked him and bragged of his reports in Hitler's presence. D'Alquen exploited this situation.

As indicated previously, Hitler in June 1943 flatly forbade the Wehrmacht to make political use of Vlasov and the liber-

[6] Gunter d'Alquen, interview.
[7] Höhne, op. cit., p. 475.

ation movement. D'Alquen, unaware of this ban, ventured for the first time to tell Himmler in a sweeping report the thinking of SS commanders as well as what he himself had learned at first hand, and then drove home the essential points: The *Ost* policy was wrong, and was driving the Russians back into the arms of Bolshevism; only a basic change could bring victory. Himmler, however, simply would not tolerate anything that might undermine the aims and beliefs of National Socialism.

In November, d'Alquen began a propaganda operation in Major General Steiner's area. He authorized thousands of interrogations and evaluated and reported on them, stressing the negative effects of misconceived political aims on the Russians. After an interlude on the Italian front, where he mounted another propaganda campaign against General Anders's Polish units, he was ordered back to the eastern front. Himmler was demanding a new, large-scale propaganda effort. And once more d'Alquen insisted that decisive victories could be achieved only through a drastic change in *Ost* policy and the employment of Vlasov and the Russian liberation army. He saw no other way.

Himmler was no longer as disapproving as in the past; but he didn't want to hear Vlasov's name again. Otherwise, he gave d'Alquen a surprisingly free hand—just let him look for other Russian generals. D'Alquen immediately visited Grote in Berlin, reported on the state of affairs, and asked him to name leading figures who might replace Vlasov. More could not be accomplished at the moment. Grote suggested Zykov and Zhilenkov. Zykov was an outstanding personality, but the Gestapo had him under surveillance, believing him to be a Jew and a Marxist. This did not bother d'Alquen—the caliber of people was what mattered to him.

The very next day a discussion took place at d'Alquen's home in Wannsee in which Zykov, Zhilenkov, Strikfeldt, and Dellingshausen participated. Zykov immediately declared himself a Russian nationalist, harshly criticized the mistakes which had been made, and demanded complete independence in organizing the propaganda operation as a condition of cooperation. D'Alquen replied that he knew what opportunities had been missed, and how the Russians had been treated. Although he could not promise to succeed in spurring a basic change, he pledged to make an honest try and believed that the undertaking now at hand gave them a new chance. The Russians, impressed by d'Alquen's frankness, agreed to cooperate after conferring with Vlasov. Perhaps the SS would succeed where the Wehrmacht had failed.

The campaign was scheduled to begin two days later. But something now occurred that showed dramatically the defenselessness of the Russians under Wehrmacht protection, and the kind of methods one Nazi agency used against another: Zykov was missing when d'Alquen and his group prepared to depart; he had vanished without a trace.

It was not only to the Gestapo that Zykov was suspect; he also had enemies in Dabendorf. It was feared that his Marxist politics might cause the movement harm, and a group of Russians had for this reason asked Vlasov to remove him. Vlasov, however, had refused. Although he did not always agree with Zykov's views, he prized highly the latter's great intelligence and patriotism.

Zykov did not conceal the fact that he was embittered and terribly disillusioned with the Germans, and he was continually involved in conflicts with them. Particularly provoking to him was the ban on the very notion of a Russian nation. This "speech regulation" went so far that, for example, in an article on the anniversary of Pushkin's death the word "Russia" could not be mentioned. Zykov lived with an ex-actress, Zinaida Petrovna Andrich, the daughter of a Tsarist general, whom he had met in Belgrade—a slender, attractive woman who was devoted to him. Their small home in Kalkberge, about eighteen miles north of Berlin, was an island of cultivation and refinement, and they entertained frequently.

The evening before Zykov's scheduled departure, his adjutant and most trusted aide, a man named Nozhin, was with him at his home. While they were at supper, Zykov was called to the phone, which was located in a bakery several hundred yards away. Nozhin accompanied him. Neither of them returned from this errand.

At 5 a.m., Miss Andrich notified Captain von Dellingshausen, who immediately called Gestapo headquarters. The officers on duty were obviously not very interested—since no gasoline was available, a man would be sent out by train sometime that day. An official later picked up Dellingshausen in his car and drove to Gestapo headquarters, where an investigation had as yet turned up very little. Neighbors had seen Zykov and Nozhin talking excitedly to three men, and then they had all driven off in an auto. A search of the neighboring woods proved fruitless.

Months later, a Gestapo official hinted to Dellingshausen of the involvement of his organization in this affair. But where Zykov and Nozhin were taken, where and how they died, has remained a mystery.[8] Vlasov gave Miss Andrich shelter in his house on the Kiebitzweg. Eventually, when all the investigations had failed to produce results, she returned to Belgrade. D'Alquen, whose inquiries had been equally fruitless, had to travel to the front without Zykov. Zhilenkov took over leadership of the Russian group.

The propaganda operation got under way at the end of June under the code name "Scorpion East." D'Alquen dispersed his staff among the various divisions and established his headquarters in Zymna Voda, not far from Lvov. Most of the propaganda guidelines had been worked out by Zhilenkov. It became increasingly clear, however, that nothing could replace Vlasov's name. D'Alquen, his hands tied by Himmler, proposed that Zhilenkov become leader of the liberation movement. But Zhilenkov rejected the idea: As a former Communist Party functionary, he could never hope to have Vlasov's magnetism.

On July 11 the Soviets began their summer offensive in the

[8] Dellingshausen, Kromiadi, and Fröhlich, interviews.

Army Group South sector. That same night, d'Alquen's aide, Robert Krötz, profoundly affected by a talk with Zhilenkov, implored d'Alquen to fly back to Himmler and make emphatically clear that the one chance for victory lay in an honest pact with Vlasov and a radical change in the whole Ost policy; everything else was pointless and would end in ruin.[9] D'Alquen, oppressed by the same thoughts, quickly decided to return, without giving notice to Himmler, who was staying in Salzburg.

Himmler received him coldly. Not until the next day, during a trip to East Prussia, did he have time for d'Alquen, who described the situation bluntly. When Himmler began to consider all the inevitable consequences this would have for Nazi ideology, d'Alquen countered that it was now a question of victory or defeat and for that reason consequences could be weighed later.

His discussion with Himmler lasted more than an hour. The SS Reichsführer plainly wanted to avoid bringing Vlasov to the fore, both because of Hitler's attitude and because of his own derogatory remarks. Finally, he yielded. "I've known you a long time," he said to d'Alquen at the end of the conversation, "and you have always been a realist. I don't suspect you of being a pro-Russian fanatic like those Balts and some army snobs. For heaven's sake, contact Vlasov and report to me." [1] That same evening, d'Alquen flew to the front to pick up Zhilenkov; they were back in Berlin on July 15.

Twenty-four hours later d'Alquen and Vlasov met. Vlasov was reserved, but spoke with a candor and self-confidence that impressed d'Alquen: He had given up all hope of finding one reasonable German leader; but if Himmler really was able—and willing—to take the requisite, long-overdue measures, then something decisive could still be accomplished. Vlasov demanded the unification of all scattered volunteer units under his command, the subordination of the nationality committees, the sole right

[9] Robert Krötz, letter to author.
[1] D'Alquen, interview.

to work among the POW's and Russian laborers in the Reich, the transfer of all propaganda activities under his authority, and the creation of a political and intellectual Russian center which would be allowed to issue a proclamation stating the aims of the Russian liberation movement to the world.

D'Alquen promised to do his best. On July 17 he delivered an almost rapturous report to Himmler. Himmler said that in the interim he had talked to the Führer and would see Vlasov at his headquarters on July 21, and that he was considering naming him a marshal. D'Alquen pointed out that it would be undesirable from the propaganda standpoint for the Germans to promote Vlasov—an objection which convinced Himmler to drop the idea. However, the proposal showed how unfamiliar he was with the problems involved.

In Berlin again, d'Alquen informed Vlasov of his conversation with Himmler, requested him to prepare for the meeting, and then flew back to the front.[2] Vlasov recognized that d'Alquen's intentions were honest, and despite all the humiliations he had suffered, he was ready to talk to Himmler. It would, he realized, require the most intensive efforts to convince the world that he and those with him were not traitors but fighters waging a political struggle against a regime the Russian people had never ratified.

The background materials and papers for the conversation were feverishly assembled. But shortly before Vlasov and Strikfeldt were set to leave, Himmler informed them by telegram that the discussion would have to be postponed because of unforeseen complications. He would set a new date. That same evening, the Propaganda Department learned of the abortive revolt against Hitler. It became known that General Wagner, Stauffenberg, Schmidt von Altenstadt, Roenne, Tresckow, and Freytag-Loringhoven had all taken part in the plot. Fears arose that

[2] Reports on d'Alquen's role by: Dallin, op. cit., p. 618; Buchardt, op. cit., pp. 254 ff.; d'Alquen, Krötz, and Strik-Strikfeldt, interviews; Erhard Kroeger, letter to author.

the Gestapo would exploit the affair in order to eliminate Vlasov and his supporters as well—but these anxieties proved groundless. A call from Lieutenant General Berger, the director of the SS Main Office, inviting Vlasov and his aides to dinner, pointed instead to a rise in Vlasov's stock.

After the failure of the July 20 plot the most ardent champions of the Russian liberation movement were ousted from the Wehrmacht; now the only chance lay with Himmler, and only time would reveal how sincere he really was: Such were Vlasov's thoughts as he started out for Berger's. By chance, SS Colonel Erhard Kroeger had arrived from Denmark and reported to Berger that same day on official business. When their talk had been concluded, Berger asked Kroeger whether he would be willing to interpret that evening. He had invited General Vlasov to dinner at Himmler's request, but did not wholly trust the Wehrmacht interpreter.

In the evening, Berger presented his guest Vlasov with a gift, the book *Tsushima*, by Frank Thiess, without realizing how tactless this was. Vlasov thanked him and said cryptically that Tsushima had been an unlucky battle for Russia and he would drink a toast to greater success in the next battle. He explained to Berger that he was ready for any serious action against Stalin, but would no longer allow himself to be used simply as a front for propaganda.

Berger was a rather inarticulate man, inwardly unsure of himself, and not very adroit politically. He had, nonetheless, considerable personal courage and spoke his mind plainly, even to Himmler. He had seen combat all through the First World War, had been decorated, and had returned home with the rank of captain—after which he had scratched out a living as a gymnastics teacher. He had transferred his loyalties from the Stahlhelm to the SS, whose troops he had trained for combat,[3] and owed his career to this fact, as well as to his ability to get along

[3] The Waffen-SS grew from 100,000 men in mid-1940 to about 900,000 at the end of 1944. Cf. Höhne, op. cit., p. 140.

with Himmler. He had risen to SS general and chief of the SS Main Office in just a few years.

Kroeger strongly advised him to give a positive report and join Himmler in preparing a Vlasov operation. Should Himmler agree, Kroeger asked to be placed in charge of its political and administrative implementation. Berger reported to Himmler the next morning and received approval to begin the *Aktion* with Kroeger in charge. The latter immediately began to assemble his staff.[4] Kroeger was thus still under Berger's authority.[5]

Before being assigned to the Waffen-SS, Kroeger had belonged to the SD, which made matters easier—particularly since the head of the RSHA, Ernst Kaltenbrunner, had a low opinion of Berger and believed that with the latter supervising the Vlasov operation, it would fail. Berger's relations with the SD had, in fact, never been good. He described Reinhard Heydrich, Kaltenbrunner's predecessor, as power-hungry and completely unscrupulous.

Kroeger pressed Berger to convince Himmler to receive Vlasov as soon as possible, so that a binding agreement could be worked out. Schellenberg was also working to this end. Himmler, however, was allegedly busy with other matters. The news of Vlasov's improved standing spread rapidly, and representatives of other Slavic peoples, especially the Bulgarians, Slovaks, Czechs, and Serbs, tried to get in touch with him. While certainly opposed to National Socialism, they desired at the same time the overthrow of the Stalin regime, from which they could expect nothing good.

At this same time, Finnish Marshal Carl Mannerheim let it

---

[4] Kroeger, letter to author; Berger, interview.

[5] The assertions of Dallin (op. cit., p. 626) and Thorwald (op. cit., pp. 336 ff.), that Kroeger was placed under the authority of Dr. Arlt, director of Head Office East in the SS Main Office, are incorrect. Nor did Kroeger see Berger on Arlt's recommendation—Arlt and Berger did not even know each other. Dr. Arlt, who accepted Rosenberg's political program with respect to the east, did try to get Kroeger put under his authority: Buchardt and Berger, interviews; Kroeger, letter to author.

be known semi-officially, through one of his generals, that the separate peace he was planning with the Soviet Union was a consequence of his disappointment in Germany's *Ost* policy. He was a Finnish patriot, but as a former Russian Guard officer he felt bound by strong ties to the Russian people. His final decision depended on whether the German government, late as it was, would embark on a sweeping change in its *Ost* policy. An SD query to Himmler on Mannerheim's position remained unanswered.[6]

To spare Vlasov the turmoil of the preparation period, it was suggested to him that he withdraw to a rest home. There he could prepare himself for the impending meeting with Himmler. He protested that he did not need a rest and was tired of doing nothing, but finally yielded and traveled in mid-August with Strikfeldt and Fröhlich to Ruhpolding. Adeleide Bielenberg, the young widow of a doctor, had established a rest home for destitute families of fallen soldiers in the old Zell monastery near Ruhpolding, and she had been asked to accommodate Vlasov and his personal staff.

Frau Bielenberg also lived in the monastery, so that personal contacts inevitably occurred. There were discussions and musical performances, and for the first time since his capture, Vlasov enjoyed the cultivated atmosphere of a refined household. It is not surprising that Frau Bielenberg, a good-looking woman, aroused a more than fleeting interest in him, and that, in turn, the mysterious Russian general, with his plans and possibilities, increasingly fascinated her. Vlasov sang Russian melodies to guitar accompaniment, told stories of his life, and was more communicative than he had been in a long time. The tensions of his life in Berlin dissolved. Thus began, in the weeks before the last effort, a love affair—an experience all the more intense for Vlasov since the dangers ahead never completely vanished from his mind.[7]

[6] Buchardt, op. cit., p. 230.
[7] Adeleide Bielenberg, Dellingshausen, and Fröhlich, interviews.

At the beginning of September 1944, Malyshkin returned from France, where he had vainly sought to determine the fate of the volunteer units which had been caught in the German retreat after the Allied invasion. It was still impossible to discover how many had survived the retreat and how great the losses had been. The Americans announced twenty thousand prisoners. There had been practically no deserters, chiefly because of these men's still-existing hope of becoming part of a liberation army. Allied propaganda had made its own contribution, however, by promising to send Russian deserters immediately back to their homeland—the one thing they feared most.[8]

The long-awaited call came on September 9: Himmler would receive Vlasov on the 16th. On the night of September 15, Vlasov left from Berlin's Stettin Station on the regular courier train. He was accompanied by d'Alquen, Strikfeldt, and, as representative of the SD, Colonel Hans Ehlich. Kroeger joined them in Posen, where he had been informed of the meeting while on a weekend pass.

Aboard the train, d'Alquen once more discussed with Vlasov the main points to be brought up with Himmler. He stressed the fact that since July 20, Himmler had become commander in chief of the Replacement Army and therefore had the power to organize new troop units on a large scale as well as the authority to institute a radical change in Ost policy. D'Alquen advised Vlasov to cite frankly the errors committed and the opportunities missed and then to advance proposals for the immediate future. He wanted Vlasov, whom he had described to Himmler as a remarkable personality, to live up to this description and make the desired impression. He was convinced that this meeting, if successful, could initiate a historic turn and decisively influence the course of the war.

They reached Himmler's headquarters at 9 a.m., and the dis-

---

[8] The impact of the Allied invasion on the volunteer units in France is reported by Hansen, op. cit.

cussion began in his offices an hour later. At Himmler's request, Strikfeldt did not participate. He was regarded as a Russophile and unreliable from the Nazi point of view. Those present were Vlasov, d'Alquen, Ehlich, and Kroeger, the last-named acting as interpreter.[9] D'Alquen, as initiator of the meeting, formally introduced Vlasov, and Himmler greeted him with a handshake. They all sat down at a large, round table.

Himmler opened the discussion with a declaration: He was informed about Vlasov's past, activity, and plans. He regretted the lateness of this conference, but believed it was not too late. Decisions of this kind required time for examination. He personally was slow to make up his mind, but once he agreed to something, he felt solidly bound by it. He knew the mistakes the Germans had committed and therefore requested Vlasov to be brutally frank. Vlasov should not construe the postponement of the meeting as an act of distrust. He asked for an understanding of the difficulties which had arisen after July 20.

Vlasov, addressing Himmler as "Herr Minister," thanked him for the invitation. He then pointed out that this meeting between Himmler, the strongest man in the German military leadership, and himself, the first general to defeat a German army in this war, already constituted a program. He stated that he was the son of a peasant, loved his country, and for that very reason hated the Stalin regime. Despite all its recent successes, the Bolshevik system was doomed to destruction if it could be hit in its most vulnerable spots. Cooperation between the Russian liberation movement and the Germans on the basis of absolute equality was the condition. He would be interested to learn Himmler's attitude in principle on this issue, particularly his estimate of the pamphlet Der Untermensch.

Himmler dodged the question skillfully. He said that both sides must carefully avoid generalizations. The pamphlet had

[9] Contrary to the statements of Thorwald (op. cit., p. 379) and Dallin (op. cit., p. 632), Berger did not participate in this meeting, according to Kroeger (interview) and Berger himself (letter to author).

described the human type under the Communist system, which threatened Russia as much as Germany. This conference proved that it did not apply to the Russian people as a whole. Every nation had its share of subhumans, except that in the Soviet Union they held power, while in Germany he had put them into concentration camps. He wanted to help Vlasov accomplish this overturn in Russia, too. He wished to know whether Vlasov believed the Russian people would welcome the general as a liberator if he did just this.

Vlasov did not limit himself to the immediate situation. Among other things, he said that Stalin's so-called Patriotic War, with which the latter wanted to save the Communist system, had previously been anything but nationally oriented. Before the German attack of June 1941, Stalin had scheduled an advance into southeastern Europe, aimed at Rumania, Bulgaria, and the Dardanelles, for the beginning of 1942. This plan had been based on the Leninist theory of capitalist war, according to which, in a war between capitalist powers, the Soviet Union had to attack the side which emerged victorious—Germany in this case. The German attack had not been expected so early and had therefore disrupted the uncompleted assembling of Soviet armed might. This explained, in part, the great initial German victories. While he recognized the magnificent achievements of the German soldiers, he was compelled to say that the war, as the Germans were waging it, could not be won. The Soviets could be beaten only with political, not military means. But the Germans had conducted the war along the old imperialist lines, as a war of naked conquest.

Stalin had expected, and feared, that the Germans would take the opposite tack. He had clearly expressed both his surprise and his satisfaction at this spectacle and thereupon had raised the cry of the "Patriotic War." Had the Germans come as liberators instead of conquerors, the Stalin government would have collapsed long ago. But Vlasov remained convinced that even today the mass of the Russian people could be mobilized against Stalin's dictatorship if a large Russian liberation army were to appear; the Germans themselves would no longer be believed if they raised liberation slogans. For this reason the immediate formation of such an army was his most insistent demand. He possessed the authority to lead it, since he was no obscure émigré operating in a vacuum, but one of the best-known generals of the Red Army, whose name was familiar to every soldier and officer. He had not deserted to the Germans but had been captured in a hopeless situation.

In the solitude of the Volkhov-Kessel forest and in later conversations with fellow prisoners he had come to recognize that Stalin represented a misfortune for Russia and that he could be overthrown with the help of the Russian people. This is why he expressed his readiness to collaborate with the Germans, especially since he had become acquainted with many Germans who approved of his plans. He would not enumerate the countless disappointments he had experienced since then.

Without flinching, Himmler listened to remarks that previously would have caused him to explode in anger. Vlasov's allusions to his victory near Moscow, the doctrine of the Slavic *Untermensch*, the Germans' political mistakes, the impossibility of defeating Russia militarily, and finally, the assertion that only Russia's liberation from the Stalin regime could still save Germany, were arguments no one had dared present so sharply to Himmler. That Vlasov voiced them at this hour showed his self-confidence and inner independence.

Himmler asked for Vlasov's estimate of the military situation. Vlasov explained that the Soviet system, like every rigid social structure, had its weaknesses and was vulnerable to the effects of the unexpected. The appearance of strong Russian national forces now would come as a surprise to Stalin. Germany contained the manpower for a Russian army of more than a million men, most of it already existing in the form of small armed units. If they were united, and simultaneously, an alliance of equals were concluded between the Germans and a provisional

Russian national government, this might prove to be a turning point.

Himmler referred to the difficulties of providing armaments, particularly heavy weapons, and the consequences of rapidly withdrawing Russian units already in combat, since there was a shortage of German manpower. However, he promised the creation of an army corps and other units. He had spoken with Hitler and Jodl. Vlasov could now consider himself commander in chief of a Russian liberation army with the rank of colonel general, possessing disciplinary authority and the right to appoint officers up to the rank of colonel. He was to submit his proposals for higher command posts to the German Army Personnel Office.

Vlasov, who was in possession of very precise and accurate statistics, insisted once again that all Russian units be released from German control and placed under his command. He also demanded that the ban on negotiations with Rosenberg's separatist minority representatives be lifted and that all these groups be subordinated to his authority. He stated his willingness to accept a federal structure for Russia as the basis of negotiations. The ultimate form of the Russian state would eventually be settled by a popular plebiscite. At present, separatist tendencies were providing the Soviets with their richest propaganda opportunities in the political struggle. It would be best to set up a single German agency with the power to settle all questions quickly and finally.

The conversation then turned to Russian workers in Germany, whom Vlasov regarded as a great reservoir of manpower. Himmler objected that the armaments industry would suffer if they were released from their work. However, he conceded that very few acts of sabotage had been committed, considering the wretched conditions under which they unfortunately had to live. He would welcome the political activization of these people by Vlasov.

Vlasov proposed that they be placed under a Russian government. They would surely work harder and more willingly under Russian administration and discipline. Himmler countered by saying it would be better if Vlasov restricted himself to positive measures, such as increasing rations, improving living conditions, etc. In that way he would become even more popular. Vlasov agreed to this.

Himmler closed with the assurance that he saw no obstacles to acting on the points discussed very soon. Once the liberation army had been organized and a Russian countergovernment set up, Vlasov would be presented to Hitler in an official state ceremony. Himmler confirmed Kroeger in his post as political representative, with additional authority on questions of practical coordination. Kroeger was to work closely with the SS Main Office on economic questions, and there was, as well, to be close cooperation with d'Alquen on all problems of psychological warfare.

After the conference was concluded, all present sat down to a meal which was accompanied by relaxed conversation. Himmler asked about Vlasov's career, about his activity in China and the battle for Moscow, displaying special interest in the improvisations adopted by the Soviets. When he asked why Tukhachevsky's conspiracy had failed, Vlasov replied that Tukhachevsky had committed the same error as Hitler's enemies— he had not taken the masses into account. Vlasov left at 3 p.m. Himmler then spoke briefly with d'Alquen and Ehlich. He was evidently impressed by Vlasov and assured them that he would keep his promises to him. Still, Vlasov was a Russian, and one had to be careful. He asked d'Alquen to keep his eyes open and immediately report any unexpected developments.[1]

---

[1] D'Alquen wrote a memorandum on the meeting between Himmler and Vlasov in 1947. Since d'Alquen believed at the time that this meeting would lead to a decisive turn of events, his recollection of it is probably quite accurate. His description is in fact confirmed in all points in letters to the author by Kroeger and Ehlich. D'Alquen, Kroeger, and Ehlich all agree that there was no mention of a withdrawal from the Crimea. Berger, too, recalls no such statement by Himmler at any time. Therefore, the unsigned note from Berger's

★

At first, Vlasov was optimistic. He and his colleagues believed the most urgent task to be the creation of a large army and a quasi-governmental body representing the liberation movement —one which would give them a basis for negotiating with the Western Powers after the predictable demise of National Socialism. Those Germans involved in the Vlasov enterprise acted promptly and energetically. At Himmler's request, d'Alquen visited Gestapo chief Müller—who, it was feared, might seek to obstruct the new policy—and informed him of Himmler's decisions. D'Alquen said that all this would also have consequences for the Gestapo and that Himmler asked him to make the appropriate preparations. Knowing d'Alquen's special position, Müller told him he disapproved of the whole scheme, but if Himmler had ordered it, he would have to obey. Next, d'Alquen spoke to Kaltenbrunner, who listened skeptically at first, but then said: "Now I see things differently; this certainly has enormous implications!" And at the end he remarked: "I can almost share your optimism as I listen to you."[2]

D'Alquen fell seriously ill at the beginning of November and was incapacitated until February 1945. This meant the loss of one of the major driving forces behind the whole enterprise. Not even he, however, could have pushed through the necessary changes, and, in retrospect, d'Alquen's optimism is hard to understand. Still, the German armaments industry was operating full blast at the time, and, on the basis of his knowledge of the psychological situation on the Soviet side, d'Alquen thought that the appearance at the front of a large army led by Vlasov would have a crucial impact.

While d'Alquen was negotiating with Müller and Kaltenbrunner and beginning to reorient the propaganda operations of his regiment, Buchardt was engaged in creating a unified RSHA

---

documents mentioned by Dallin cannot have been composed after the Himmler-Vlasov discussion. Obviously, it was an earlier draft that was subsequently discarded.

[2] D'Alquen, interview.

staff, drawn from all SS/SD offices, for liaison with Vlasov. This
new group had the independent status of an *Einsatzkommando*
("task force"). It was called Special Task Force East and took
its place beside the Waffen-SS liaison staff headed by Kroeger.
A bitter quarrel subsequently erupted among the interested departmental chiefs—Schilling, Ohlendorf, and Müller—over the
appointment of a director for this new liaison group. But ultimately, as initiator of the project, Buchardt was named its
head.[3]

For Vlasov's circle the identity of the director was of crucial
significance. The more the Russians came to believe that Himmler and Hitler were once again playing them false, the more
frequently they vented anti-German sentiments; if these were reported by the SD, the entire project could well be brought to an
abrupt end. One favorable factor was the smooth cooperation
between Buchardt and Kroeger, who had been friends for years
and shared the same views on the Reich's *Ost* policy. But this
was hardly surprising, given the strained relations between the
RSHA and Berger.

Berger's irritable and unpredictable nature was shown by his
reaction to the report that an ROA noncom had indulged in
some angry remarks about the perfidious Germans in the waiting
room of a Berlin railroad station. He had allegedly threatened:
"Just wait until we have our army; we'll cut them to pieces!"
Berger immediately wanted to report the incident to Himmler
and close up the whole "Vlasov shop." Kroeger had a hard time
calming him down, but finally convinced him that the outburst
of an NCO who had lost his head was hardly significant.

Despite Himmler's promises, no decision on a change in *Ost*
policy had actually been made as yet. Nor was it clear just how
well informed Hitler was about what was going on. The consequence was general uncertainty, which prevented Kroeger from
carrying through the requisite political and administrative measures. The situation was further complicated by the growing
chaos at the top, with one Nazi leader often countermanding

[3] Buchardt, letter to author.

the instructions of another. Then, too, there was the incredible inertia of the civil and military bureaucracy, which proved incapable of coping with matters which did not fit into the usual routine.

Gauleiter Erich Koch forbade any mention of the Vlasov undertaking in East Prussia and demanded the disarming of all Eastern units on East Prussian soil. Himmler made no move to intervene. Rosenberg—still obsessed with his partition policy, and believing that he alone was in charge of the Vlasov operation—complained to Himmler and Bormann after having summoned Kroeger and reprimanded him for meddling in his ministry's affairs.

Himmler's attitude had not really undergone any fundamental change, as was shown by his annoyed comment to Berger that if the Vlasov business was going to cause so much irritation at the start, then he would drop the whole affair.[4] His shallowness and opportunism were revealed even more clearly when he called in General Köstring for a discussion of the steps that had to be taken. Kroeger had previously, over Berger's opposition, won Himmler's approval for entrusting the supervision of Vlasov's army to the Wehrmacht, rather than the SS. Kroeger felt that the Wehrmacht had better personnel and technical resources and that, moreover, the SS would be a burden to the liberation movement both politically and propagandistically.[5] Himmler's agreement to this proposal was all the more surprising since he, like all the other Nazi leaders, distrusted the Wehrmacht more than ever after July 20. "The army's intentions were not good," he had said on August 3 in a briefing of Gauleiters in Posen.

Himmler had not had the slightest notion of the number of Eastern volunteers. When Köstring told him that the total came to 800,000–900,000, he was dismayed. Nobody had informed him of this; it was certainly alarming! Instead of viewing it as evidence of how ready the Russians were to cooperate with the

[4] Buchardt, op. cit., p. 245.
[5] Kroeger, letter to author.

Germans, he reacted with fright. Two divisions were to be set up first, then more; but he must talk to the Führer. However, the problem as a whole, with all its ramifications, was never discussed or thought through.

To determine the general extent of Hitler's concern with the Vlasov project, Köstring proposed to the OKW that it place all dispersed volunteer formations under Vlasov's nominal command. The response was illuminating: Jodl stated he had no intention of organizing Germany's executioners, while Keitel said he had been insulted by Hitler too often in this affair, and would not lift a finger for Vlasov.[6]

Hitler had reluctantly agreed to the creation of several Russian divisions and the proclamation of a Liberation Committee. But he had never intended to enter into an honest partnership with Vlasov—as was demonstrated by a headquarters briefing on January 27, 1945. When Guderian mentioned that in the aftermath of clashes between Russian and German soldiers, Vlasov wished to submit records of interrogation, Hitler said: "Vlasov is a nobody." The following dialogue then ensued:

> *Göring:* The Vlasov people are so hated on the other side that they are punished when captured.
> *Hitler:* Don't say that, they still desert.
> *Göring:* That's the only thing they can do: desert; they're not capable of anything better.
> *Guderian:* Shall the organization of the division in Münsingen be speeded up?
> *Hitler:* Yes, finish it up.
> *Fegelein:* The Reichsführer [Himmler] wants to be given command of both divisions.
> *Hitler:* Vlasov is not to be given command.
> *Göring:* That's all they can do, desert. But then they don't gobble up any more food. . . .[7]

[6] Herre, interview.
[7] Heiber, op. cit., p. 318.

Such was the ignorance and primitivism with which leaders of the Reich spoke about a cardinal problem of the war. During the entire Russian campaign there was not a single Eastern expert on Hitler's operations staff.

Meanwhile, in Dahlem and Dabendorf, where after Vlasov's meeting with Himmler the Russians still believed in the latter's power and good intentions, the organization of the "Committee for the Liberation of the Peoples of Russia" (KONR) was under way. Four main departments were created first: the administrative department headed by Malyshkin, who was also Vlasov's deputy; the civilian department, to protect the interests of the conscripted eastern workers and POW's, with General Zakutny as director; the propaganda department, headed by Zhilenkov; and the General Staff of KONR's armed forces, with Trukhin as chief and Boyarsky as his deputy. The commanders for the first two divisions and the officers school were chosen. To provide a political foundation, the text of a proclamation stating the aims of the liberation movement was drafted. It was to be promulgated amidst the pomp of a state ceremony in Prague, which had been selected for this purpose because it was deemed necessary to have the ceremony staged in a Slavic city.

Great care was lavished on the proclamation. A former associate of Zykov's, Kovalchuk, wrote the introduction, Zaitsev the main body, and Nareikis the conclusion. After Vlasov and his closest aides had approved the draft, it was submitted to the relevant German authorities, Rosenberg being bypassed in the process. The text—whose political importance everyone recognized—was designed to say everything that had to be said, yet without offering opponents any opportunity for direct attack.

Still, despite its being written under a dictatorship, the proclamation emerged as a firmly democratic document. Its key demands, commitments, and aims included: overthrow of the Soviet regime and realization of the goals of the February (1917) Revolution, which the Soviets had betrayed; conclusion of an honorable peace with Germany that effectively excluded a colonialistic policy or domination by the latter; acceptance of German military aid under conditions that did not violate Russian honor and independence; and condemnation of all despotism and oppression of foreign peoples. In truth—although National Socialism was never explicitly mentioned—it was not just against the Soviet regime that the proclamation was directed.

Himmler returned the draft with the comment that it was too long. He also deplored the absence of an unequivocal stand on the Jewish Question and the Western Powers. Kroeger urged Himmler to let the text go through as it was, since the Russians surely knew best the psychology of their countrymen and how most effectively to address them. Vlasov categorically refused to include an anti-Jewish passage. However, to safeguard the proclamation, a formulation was chosen which alluded not only to the fight against Stalin, but to that against his Western allies. The final version was then submitted to Hitler by the Foreign Office representative, Sonnleithner.

Hitler, however, refused to give his approval. Himmler had said nothing about the proclamation, and the Führer wanted to talk to him about it. Clearly, there had at no time been any discussion of a major change in *Ost* policy; Himmler had described the entire program as simply a tactical maneuver. Here, as before, those favoring a policy change were constrained to proceed outwardly in terms of a tactical and propagandistic operation until the desired consequences occurred automatically, "unintentionally," so to speak.

Hitler finally agreed to let the proclamation be announced in Prague, but insisted on a small gathering. As a result, most of the German notables invited declined to attend. Only SS General Lorenz participated at the meeting as a formal representative of the German government.[8]

Meanwhile, Vlasov's initial optimism was reverting to disillusionment. For Himmler had hardly kept a single one of his promises. Instead of the ten divisions pledged, only one was in

[8] Buchardt, op. cit., p. 273.

process of formation by mid-October, and it had proved impossible to secure the release of the volunteer units serving with the Wehrmacht.

Failure also marked the plan to institute collaboration with the representatives of the nationalities and place under Vlasov's command the 162nd Turkic Division, the Ukrainian Division, and the Cossack Corps. Backed by Rosenberg, the representatives of the nationality groups refused to accept Vlasov's authority. They justified their attitude on the ground that they were fighting for the independence of their peoples, whereas Vlasov embodied the old Russian imperialism. Vlasov viewed their stance as self-centered and shortsighted, since the manifesto guaranteed "equality of all the peoples of Russia, their right to national development, self-determination, and, if called for, full state sovereignty." One condition was stipulated with regard to this last step: The people themselves would have to ratify such decisions *after* the overthrow of the Soviet system. In Vlasov's words: "You cannot beat Stalin with outspread fingers, only with a clenched fist." The majority of volunteers and Eastern workers did not share the extreme and unrealistic view of the nationalities, but saw in KONR their natural and most effective representative—as is attested by petitions they drew up, as well as SD reports.

Greater than ordinary tensions prevailed in relations with the western Ukrainians from the former Polish Galicia. These people, who constituted five to six per cent of the world's 35,000,000 Ukrainians, were Catholics, whereas most other Ukrainians were of the Orthodox faith. The westerners were far more fanatical nationalists than their brethren in the Soviet Union. They believed that the Great Russians enthusiastically supported Stalin for having made Russia even larger than the Tsars did, and felt that cooperation with Vlasov would not win the sympathy of the Russian people and would lose that of the non-Russian peoples. This attitude coincided with Rosenberg's views, and with his help they tried in every possible way to block the Vlasov operation. The western-Ukrainian leader Bandera even traveled to Yugoslavia to visit the Cossack Corps there and delivered speeches against Vlasov until Pannwitz stopped him, threatening him with arrest if he continued his activity in the area.[9]

Ohlendorf and Schellenberg applied pressure in an attempt to smooth out all these ethnic differences. They finally arranged a meeting between Vlasov and one of the most militant representatives of the Caucasians, a man named Khedia; but this proved unavailing. Khedia declared: "I prefer Stalin in front of me to Vlasov behind me." [1] Vlasov thought it pointless to try to force cooperation and abandoned his efforts to come to terms.[2]

But it was not only on the nationalities question that Himmler failed to keep his promises. The commitment to grant Russian POW's the same status as that enjoyed by captured soldiers from other countries was only partially fulfilled. The Propaganda Ministry's Office for Eastern Propaganda was not placed, as had been expected, under KONR's jurisdiction; it received control only of the Russian press operating in Germany. After the proclamation had been promulgated in Prague, KONR began publishing *Volya Naroda* ("The People's Will") as its main organ.

Strikfeldt said goodbye to Vlasov in mid-October. He was no longer wanted as Vlasov's adviser once the SS liaison staff under Kroeger had been established, and he had been assigned by Gehlen to write the history of German *Ost* policy and the Vlasov *Aktion*. He did not find the leave-taking easy. Strikfeldt had worked with Vlasov for two years, and their official relationship had early ripened into one of friendship. Now he had to

---

[9] Berger, interview.
[1] Kroeger, interview.
[2] There is a copious literature on the nationalities problem. Sources given by M. Shatov: *Bibliographiya Osvoboditelnovo Dvizheniya Narodov Rossii* ("Bibliography on the Liberation Movement of the Peoples of Russia"), All-Slavic Publishing House, New York, 1961; Dallin, op. cit., pp. 620 ff., with sources; Buchardt, op. cit., pp. 270 ff.; G. Fischer: *Soviet Opposition to Stalin*, Harvard University Press, 1952, pp. 62 ff.

leave Vlasov at the moment when it had become clear that their common efforts had come to naught, that the goal could no longer be achieved in conjunction with the Germans. He advised Vlasov to protest the new demonstration of German duplicity by resigning after the manifesto had been proclaimed. Such a step, visible to all, would be an effective repudiation of the Nazi *Ost* policy. What remained to be done subsequently could be entrusted to Trukhin. Vlasov sought time for reflection; but after conferring with his Russian associates, he rejected Strikfeldt's suggestion the next day. He did not want to abandon those who, more than ever, placed their hopes in him. He also feared the unfavorable effects of such an act on the condition of the Russian workers and the creation of the liberation army.

November 14, 1944, was picked as the date for the proclamation of the KONR manifesto. The special train carrying Vlasov and his most important KNOR colleagues, guests of honor, and the press arrived in Prague the night before, and Vlasov and his associates spent the night in the sleeping car on a siding.

The ceremony that unfolded was of a type normally reserved for high-ranking state visitors. The *"Untermenschen"* had suddenly become respected allies. At the station, Vlasov was welcomed by the commandant of the military district, General Toussaint, and a German honor guard presented arms. The reception given by Minister of State Frank in Czernin Palace, the banquet he had arranged for a small circle of German and Russian officers—everything went off in a well-organized and impressive fashion.

The solemn reading of the manifesto took place at 3 p.m. in the famous Spanish Hall of Hradcany Castle. High-ranking Wehrmacht and SS officers, delegates of the Reich authorities, representatives of states allied with the Third Reich, and those of several neutral countries were present, as well as representatives of the Bohemia-Moravia Protectorate and the press. Many who a few months earlier had rejected any contact with the "*Untermenschen*" now participated eagerly.

When Vlasov—flanked by Frank and the representative of the Reich, SS General Lorenz—entered the hall, all present rose. Frank greeted Vlasov and the Liberation Committee members in the name of the city of Prague and the Ministry of State. Next, Lorenz spoke on behalf of the Reich, describing Vlasov as a "friend and ally in the fight against Bolshevism." Vlasov thanked them and then turned to the main business at hand: the reading of the manifesto. After the preamble, with its criticism of the Soviet regime and a review of the successive attempts to achieve freedom, Vlasov raised his voice as he proclaimed the program for which he had fought so hard:

In the light of these facts the representatives of the peoples of Russia have, in the full consciousness of their responsibility before their peoples, before history and posterity, founded the Liberation Committee of the Peoples of Russia with the aim of organizing the common struggle against Bolshevism. The Liberation Committee of the Peoples of Russia sets itself the following goals:

(a) Overthrow of Stalin's tyranny, liberation of the peoples of Russia from the Bolshevik system, and restoration of the rights won by the peoples of Russia in the popular revolution of 1917.

(b) Ending of the war and conclusion of an honorable peace.

(c) Construction of a new, free national statehood without Bolshevism and exploiters.

The following principles shall govern the new statehood of the peoples of Russia:

(1) Equality of all the peoples of Russia, their right to national development, self-determination, and, if called for, full state sovereignty.

(2) Organization of the nation's activities so that all state interests are subordinated to the task of increasing prosperity and developing the nation.

(3) Maintenance of peace and establishment of friendly relations with all countries, as well as promotion of international cooperation.

(4) Comprehensive government measures to strengthen the family and marriage; equal rights for women.

(5) Abolition of forced labor and guarantee of the right to free employment so as to ensure material prosperity for the entire working population.

(6) Liquidation of the collective farms, the land to be transferred to the peasants as their private property without payment; freedom to cultivate the soil as each sees fit; freedom to dispose of the products of one's labor; elimination of compulsory deliveries and cancellation of all indebtedness to the Soviet government.

(7) Inviolability of private property acquired through work; restoration of private trade and handicrafts; guarantees of the right and opportunity to participate in the country's economic life.

(8) Creation of opportunities for the intelligentsia to work freely on behalf of the nation's welfare.

(9) Ensuring of social justice and protection from every form of exploitation for all working people, regardless of their origin or former activities.

(10) Guarantee of the right to free education, medical aid, vacations, and old-age pensions for all.

(11) Abolition of the system of terror and violence; an end of forced resettlement and mass deportations; guarantees of freedom of religion and conscience, speech, assembly, and press; guarantees of the inviolability of person, property, and home; equality of all before the law; the impartial and open administration of justice by an independent judiciary.

(12) Release of all political prisoners and the return home from prisons and camps of all those persecuted because of their struggle against Stalinism; no retaliation against or persecution of those who cease the struggle

for Stalin and Bolshevism, whether they shall have fought out of conviction or under compulsion.

(13) Restoration of national wealth destroyed during the war—cities, villages, factories, and utilities—at government expense.

(14) Government support for war invalids and their families.

The manifesto closed with a summons to the struggle against Stalin's dictatorship.[3] Not a single word of it referred to Hitler or National Socialism. Since the document represented the beliefs of men all too familiar with Stalin's regime, its democratic character is hardly surprising. What *is* surprising is that it was allowed to stand. A possible explanation may be the desire at that time of several Nazi leaders to promote a clash between the Western Powers and the Soviet Union.

The basic importance of the proclamation lay in the historical sanction it could lend the liberation movement. For until this moment, Vlasov and his supporters had never been allowed to proclaim openly the goals, motives, and scope of their movement, and the uninformed outside world had necessarily had to regard them as traitors. Now the manifesto made it clear that they were pursuing their own political aims, in contrast to the quislings of other countries, who wished to adopt the Nazi system.

After the ceremony, Frank gave a banquet for fifty guests in Czernin Palace. The Russians were in a good mood. Toasts were drunk, and then Vlasov rose and paid warm tribute to his friend and adviser, Strik-Strikfeldt, who had been seated inconspicuously in a back row during the meeting. Later, the Russians sang the ballad of Stenka Razin, the Cossack leader who had enjoyed freedom to the full and paid for it with his head on

---

[3] The text of the manifesto, with a facsimile of the signatures, was published in S Narodom—Za Narod, No. 4, December, 1964. On the Prague Proclamation, cf. M. Shatov: *Bibliographiya ODNR v Gody Vtoroi Mirovoi Voiny* ("Bibliography on the ODNR During the Second World War"), New York, 1961, Columbia University.

the executioner's block. At last, at 2 a.m., Vlasov and his KONR associates drove to the station, where a special coach had been coupled to the night train for Berlin.

The proclamation was carried in the first number of KONR's new organ, *Volya Naroda*, which appeared in a large edition on November 15. At the same time, leaflets with the proclamation text were dropped on Soviet territory.

A meeting was held on November 18 in the large auditorium of Berlin's Europa House, attended by some 1,500 people, most of them members of delegations from labor and POW camps. In a long speech, Vlasov explained the aims of the liberation movement and concluded by reading the proclamation. Of the other speakers, the audience was particularly responsive to the priest Kizilyov, who stressed the democratic principles of the manifesto, and to Lieutenant Dmitriyev, who exclaimed in closing: "We are not, and have no intention of ever becoming, mercenaries of the Germans. We are fighting for an independent Russia without Bolshevism and oppressors." An ovation lasting several minutes greeted these words, and many of those present wept. The meeting ended with the singing of the hymn *Kol Slaven*.

On November 19 a service of prayer for the victory of the liberation fighters was conducted in Berlin's Russian Cathedral by the head of the Russian Church Outside of Russia, Metropolitan Anastasy, and the metropolitan for Berlin and Germany, Seraphim. Afterwards Vlasov received Anastasy in Dahlem for a discussion that lasted several hours. In welcoming the metropolitan, he observed the custom of asking the churchman's blessing—Vlasov recognized the Church and its rites, although he was not a believer in any orthodox sense. On November 20, ROA propagandists held meetings with POW's and Eastern workers to inform them of KONR and the manifesto. Over the next few days, 470 collective telegrams arrived from various worker groups, as well as thousands of individual letters, in which, altogether, more than thirty thousand men volunteered for the

ROA. Contributions of money, jewelry, even marriage rings poured in to help pay for building the army.[4]

At a time when the collapse of the Third Reich was in sight, tens of thousands of people pledged their support to the liberation movement. The dishonesty of the German leadership aside, it is quite inaccurate to describe the Prague proclamation and the rallies for KONR as "farce," or mere "sound and fury."[5] The Russians were ready to make every sacrifice for liberation from the Stalin regime. They saw themselves threatened once again by the steadily approaching juggernaut of Stalin's forces, and their urgent need was to close ranks as tightly as possible. They had now a representative body in the form of KONR and an instrument of power, ROA, as a means of protection from the Germans' arbitrary behavior. They believed the Western democracies would understand the political character of their struggle for freedom. They considered the Western alliance with Stalin a matter of expediency and felt that it would inevitably break up as soon as the collapse of Hitler's Reich was achieved and Stalin's international revolutionary ambitions became clear once more. This faith in the Western Powers may seem naïve in retrospect; but so, also, was the faith of better-informed men in the West in "good old Uncle Joe."

The tension that had tormented Vlasov in the previous weeks eased once the Prague proclamation was a reality. Up until the last minute he had feared a ban. As he told Melitta Wiedemann: "Now it has happened, and nobody can change it. If Fate has condemned us to death, we will die. But the seed of truth lies in the soil; it will shoot up and bear fruit."[6] Exhausted by the long struggle against the blindness and arrogance of the German leaders, Vlasov no longer expected very much for him-

---

[4] Kromiadi, Dellingshausen, Tenzorov, Zherebkov, and Antonov, interviews; G. Trukhin: "Vooruzhenniye Sily Osvoboditelnovo Dvizheniya" ("The Armed Forces of the Liberation Movement"), *Volya Naroda*, No. 2, November 18, 1944.

[5] Dallin, op. cit., p. 649.

[6] Wiedemann, letter to author.

self. What now remained was the creation of as large an army as possible to forestall further German encroachments and to demonstrate the palpable existence of a political liberation movement. Survival depended on the emergence of a political force which would be recognized as such by the Western Powers.

For the use of the ROA in the final phase of the war—whose end was generally not expected until the autumn of 1945—two plans were now under discussion: a breakout on the eastern front to join with the Ukrainian Insurgent Army (UPA); or, alternatively, unification with the Cossack Corps, the Russian Corps, and Mihailovich's forces in Yugoslavia.

Through Rosenberg's intervention, two Ukrainian nationalist leaders, Bandera and Melnik, had been released from prison at the end of September 1944. Vlasov made contact with them and proposed cooperation with the UPA. Bandera, however, explained that after such a long imprisonment he lacked the authority to act and wished to do so only in conjunction with the Supreme Liberation Council, which had emerged as the chief political force in UPA-held territory. The repressive policy of Reichskommissar Koch had driven the UPA into a struggle against the Germans; but now that the Red Army had reconquered the Ukraine, the insurgents had resumed the fight against the Soviets. The UPA had been strengthened by surviving elements of the SS Galician Division, which had been decimated near Brody in July 1944.

At this point the Wehrmacht began supplying the UPA with arms. Captain Witzel, chief of Army Group A's Reconnaissance Command at the front, flew over the front lines to the UPA to size up the situation, and saw for himself its considerable military strength.

The Ukrainians smuggled across the front lines a representative of the Liberation Council who negotiated with Bandera and the German authorities, conducting himself with great self-assurance. He claimed that large parts of the Ukraine, with the exception of the cities and main lines of communication, were in the hands of the UPA, which expected Western support after the German collapse. The UPA, he said, was ready to cooperate with Vlasov if the latter would recognize the Liberation Council as the representative body of a free and independent Ukraine.[7]

Vlasov rejected such recognition of independence and referred the Ukrainians to the relevant provisions of the manifesto. He declared, however, that—once the first three ROA divisions were organized, and were joined together with the Cossack Corps, the Steifon Corps, the Second Ukrainian Division, and Maltsev's air force group, a total of about 100,000 men—he would seriously consider a frontal breakthrough to initiate the revolutionary struggle jointly with the UPA, whose strength was estimated at 50,000 troops. In this event, sizable elements of the Red Army were counted on to desert, and the Western Powers, it was hoped, would come through with support.

To discover whether the NTS was also ready to participate in this plan, Vlasov sent Meandrov to negotiate with the imprisoned NTS leaders in Berlin. Vlasov's efforts to win their release had been unproductive, but talk of shooting them had been dropped, and the Gestapo even allowed Meandrov to conduct his negotiations without supervision. The NTS leaders considered the success of the plan doubtful at this late date, but were willing to go along, since they saw no other alternative.[8]

The plan, however, was dropped when the Red Army advanced to the Oder River in mid-January. Discussion then turned to the deployment of all available forces in Yugoslavia. The ROA, in concert with the Cossack Corps, the Steifon Corps, and Draža Mihailovich's forces, would strive to prevent Tito and his Communists from seizing power. Support by the Western allies was hoped for after the Third Reich collapsed. It seemed inconceivable that England, where King Peter lived in exile, would surrender Yugoslavia to Communism. However, the swift pace of events in the final phase of the war blocked this plan as well.

Frantic activity had gripped Dabendorf and Berlin after the

[7] Buchardt, op. cit., pp. 277 ff.
[8] V. Poremsky, interview.

Prague proclamation. Overnight Vlasov's headquarters had become a political center where planning and activity went on independently of the Third Reich's policies, and in part against them. Germans, Russians, foreigners came out of curiosity or sympathy, or in the expectation that something new of political significance was in the wind.

The director general of the Bank of Dresden offered Vlasov a credit of one million marks. Unofficial representatives of the Bulgarians, Serbs, Slovaks, Hungarians, and the Baltic States indicated that the Prague manifesto contained a political program which they could accept. It was clear that a struggle for a non-Bolshevik Russia would evoke a strong response among these peoples.

To emphasize Vlasov's international importance, Kroeger arranged for Zhilenkov to visit the Slovak capital of Bratislava as Vlasov's representative and to lecture on the liberation movement before the German-Slovak Society there. Slovak President Tiso accorded Zhilenkov an official reception; ministers showered him with gifts and exchanged fraternal Slavic kisses with him.

Although officially a sovereign state, Slovakia had been completely dependent on Germany since the abortive uprising of August 1944. All the more remarkable, therefore, were the questions asked of Zhilenkov and the frankness with which he responded to them. At a reception for foreign correspondents in Bratislava, the following were among the questions put to him:

Q. What is KONR's attitude toward the Western Powers?
A. The ROA will fight only against the Soviet regime. We have no hostility toward the Western Powers. The units fighting in the West are not under Vlasov's command.
Q. What is KONR's attitude on the Jewish Question?
A. There is no special Jewish Question in Russia that needs a solution.
Q. What payment has KONR promised the Germans for their help?
A. We did not negotiate about any payment. Besides, it is

obvious that we would not make any agreement that in any way violated Russia's honor.

Q. For what reasons had Zhilenkov, a prominent Communist, gone over to the German side?

A. He had never gone over to the German side, but with many others who shared his views, had begun the struggle against a government that suppressed freedom in Russia. As a former high official he knew better than most the faults of the Stalin regime.[9]

After this trip, Himmler instructed Kroeger to break off Vlasov's contacts with the outside world. Approval was denied for a pan-Slavic congress, planned for February 1945 in Bratislava, with Vlasov as chairman. While Vlasov was trying to accelerate the creation of the ROA divisions and win control of the Cossack Corps and other combat-ready units, the struggle within German official circles continued. Rosenberg persisted in attempting to torpedo the Vlasov program. The Gestapo warned against the danger of KONR's switching to the side of the Western Powers, and Taubert, head of the Eastern Department in the Propaganda Ministry, summarized the objections of all KONR opponents: "The Vlasov movement does not feel inwardly bound, for better or worse, to Germany. It has strong Anglophile sympathies and is playing with the idea of a possible change of course. The Vlasov movement is not National Socialist. It is significant that it does not fight Jewry, that the Jewish Question is not recognized as such at all." [1]

These comments were accurate, but they were voiced by the advocates of the Nazi *Ost* program, which called for the subjugation and oppression of Russia. The Germans supporting Vlasov out of conviction rather than opportunism did so because

---

[9] Buchardt, op. cit., pp. 294 ff. Buchardt accompanied Zhilenkov.

[1] W. Taubert: *Tätigkeit im deutsch-sowietischen Krieg* ("Activity in the German-Soviet War"), December, 1944, quoted by A. Dallin, op. cit., pp. 665 f.

he was neither a traitor nor a mercenary. At long last, Vlasov's supporters and the Great Russian line won in the struggle for a new *Ost* blueprint. Rosenberg was outmaneuvered and confronted with a *fait accompli*. But he continued trying—a few months before Germany's total collapse—to impose his ideas. He denounced Vlasov's "subversive intentions" and "the preparation of a Great Russian dictatorship with the help of unknown fatheads"; if KONR alleged that the struggle against Stalinism had to be waged under a unified command, "the Vlasov Committee overlooked the fact that such unity could only be secured through the German High Command"; he bluntly described the formation of national departments in KONR as "deliberate provocation"; he criticized the SS for having sanctioned a fatal course without having informed him. Rosenberg no longer had access to the Führer; if someone didn't tell the Führer what was happening, then, thirty years after the German victory and Vlasov's installation as the Great Russian ruler, "a centralized power might confront our children," simply because "some authorities had not understood the logic of events." [2] When Gustav Hilger became the Foreign Office official in charge of KONR, Rosenberg suspected him of "pro-Bolshevik sympathies" and charged that Hilger was a friend of one of the worst German-haters, Emil Ludwig-Cohn, whom he had allegedly visited in Switzerland. "I do not believe," he concluded, "that Hilger of all people is the man to handle Eastern problems in the National Socialist state." [3]

Vlasov heard only fragmentary rumors of such conflicts among the different factions. He wanted nothing to do with Rosenberg and his "colonial ministry," as he called it. When no agreement could be reached with the nationality groups Rosenberg supported, KONR established its own departments for the different nationalities.

[2] Quoted by Dallin, op. cit., pp. 655 f.
[3] Rosenberg to Ribbentrop, January 20, 1945; Dallin, op. cit., p. 667 fn.

★

The organization of two divisions in a relatively short time was due primarily to the efforts of General Staff Colonel Heinz Herre. Herre had been brought back by Köstring from Italy, where he had commanded the 232nd Infantry Division. Arriving in Berlin on November 8, he went to Potsdam to report to Köstring, whom he found considerably aged and in a pessimistic frame of mind. Although haunted by the sense that it was now "too late," Köstring still wanted to do as much as possible to create a Russian army—even if it was only, as he put it, "in some way to save these forces for a future that lies beyond our defeat." [4]

Herre put together in Berlin a small staff familiar with Russian problems. As his operations officer he picked Major Keiling, who had been awarded the Iron Cross while commanding the 621st Russian Artillery Battalion. Herre saw very quickly that the difficulties were far greater than he had imagined. Animosity, lack of understanding, and obstructiveness were the rule, and despite Himmler's orders he had to fight for every troop allocation.[5] The first and second divisions, to be called the 600th and 650th Infantry Divisions (Russian), were set to be organized on the drill grounds of Münsingen and Heuberg, respectively, in the Swabian Alps. However, the Wehrmacht was willing to transfer, to make up these units, only the remnants of sundry formations that had been more or less destroyed in combat, keeping intact battle-tested units which it felt were indispensable.

Two larger groups that had been under Waffen-SS command formed the core of the first division: the remnants of the White Russian SS Sigling Division, which had been decimated in France, and five thousand men of the Kaminsky Brigade. There

---

[4] Herre, diary.
[5] Information on the organization of the divisions supplied by Herre's war diary and by the commander of the Second Regiment of the first division, V. Artyemyev: *Die erste Wlassow-Division* ("The First Vlasov Division"). The manuscript of this unpublished work, written in 1946, is now in the author's possession.

were no problems in integrating the White Russians, but the incorporation of the Kaminsky Brigade presented greater difficulties. The earlier liberation force, RONA, had been organized in the Lokot area with peasant recruits who had had little or no military training, and with soldiers and officers of the Red Army who after the siege of Bryansk had joined the Kaminsky Brigade instead of going into POW camps. The shortage of senior officers had been alleviated by promotions from the ranks, and the military experiences of the new appointees had sufficed for the struggle against the partisans. But now a review commission decided that only a few had received the degree of training appropriate to their ranks. Even Kaminsky's successor, "Colonel" Belai, had been only a first lieutenant in the Red Army. Few of the officers, therefore, were accepted. The Kaminsky people were understandably depressed. After Kaminsky had been shot, his followers had felt betrayed by everybody; they had hoped to find a new sense of purpose in the ROA.

The brigade, indeed, had suffered disillusionment and disappointment since the retreat from the autonomous district of Lokot, where RONA had been more or less independent and isolated. In Lepel, however, its members had come face to face with the real attitude of the German leadership. They had suffered degrading treatment at the hands of German administrators and had learned the truth about conditions in the labor and POW camps. Doubt and demoralization had spread. A Russian ethnic German teacher serving as an interpreter had shot himself after protesting that everything had turned out to be completely different than he had expected and that he was ashamed to be a German. A captain had similarly killed himself after seeing the conditions in the POW and labor camps in Germany.

RONA's situation was especially complicated because those members who came from the Lokot area had brought their families with them—which meant that more than fifty thousand people had to be provided for. Under these circumstances, Kaminsky had accepted the proposal of the police and SS chief in Gottberg that he place himself under SS command. He had hoped that this would result in improved living conditions for the families and better equipment for his men, whose uniforms were thread-bare and weapons inadequate.

Himmler had awarded Kaminsky the Iron Cross, First Class, and appointed him an SS colonel. The unit was renamed the Twenty-ninth Division of the Waffen-SS, RONA (Russian). Only a small contingent, however, had received new uniforms. (Those who did, immediately removed the German markings and replaced them with RONA's insignia.) When Lepel, in turn, had to be given up in the summer of 1944, many of the families refused to retreat any further with the Germans. Still, the with-drawal involved fifteen thousand soldiers and about twenty thousand civilians. The plan to move the civilians into Hungary collapsed, and the brigade remained in Upper Silesia.

There Kaminsky received orders to help the Germans crush the 1944 Warsaw Uprising. At first, he refused, just as previously in Gottberg he had refused to fight Polish partisans, explaining that he was fighting Bolshevism, not the Poles.[6] He had won his point in Gottberg, but this time he finally gave in after Himmler had personally sent him a surprisingly polite telegram: "Await your help in this affair." So as not to break up the families of his people again, he recruited bachelors, mostly young men, and sent off a 1,700-man regiment under the command of Major Frolov. Because they were still clad in Soviet uniforms, they wore yellow armbands. The right to pillage was explicitly granted, since Hitler had ordered Warsaw razed to the ground.

The regiment served in Warsaw from August 5 to August 26, 1944. The luxuriousness of the dwellings abandoned by the inhabitants of the fashionable Ochota district dazzled the young peasant soldiers, who made generous use of the right to plunder. Kaminsky himself spent ten days in Warsaw and attempted to claim a part of the booty, particularly jewelry, for his unit and its members. This proved his undoing. The regiment was withdrawn from combat, and Kaminsky, after a heated verbal exchange, was ordered arrested in Lodz by SS General Bach-Zelewski. He was

[6] R. Redlich, interview.

brought before an SS court-martial, quickly sentenced, and shot. The execution was treated as a secret government affair and hushed up. No one dared inform the brigade. The report was spread, instead, that Kaminsky had been shot by Polish partisans while on the way to Hungary. Because Kaminsky's officers were dissatisfied with this explanation and wanted to visit the site of the alleged attack, his car was driven into a ditch, riddled with bullets, and smeared with goose blood. The Germans rejected the demand of Kaminsky's officers that they be allowed to retaliate against the population in order to recover the corpse of their commander. Bach-Zelewski expressed his condolences to the officers, and then the civilian dependents and most of the married men were put to work on farms in Pomerania. About five thousand of the brigade's men signed up with the first Vlasov division.[7]

The staff of the first division arrived in Münsingen November 12. On Köstring's recommendation, Vlasov had promoted Colonel Sergei Kuzmich Bunyachenko to major general and appointed him commander. Bunyachenko, a peasant's son from the Ukraine in his early forties, and a member of the Communist Party since 1919, had risen rapidly in the Soviet army. In 1939 he was in command of a Far East division in Vladivostok, and his last post had been as a member of Timoshenko's staff. He had deserted to the Germans at the start of the war and taken over command of a volunteer unit, first on the eastern front and then in France. He was an unwavering enemy of both the Stalin regime and National Socialism—a man of great will power, straightforward, short-tempered, sometimes crude, a man who understood his craft. His chief of staff was Lieutenant Colonel Nikolayev, a former General Staff officer of the Red Army, and a capable, intelligent, and flexible man who negotiated diplomatically where Bunyachenko flared up.

Most of the division's officers came from Dabendorf, where

[7] On the Kaminsky Brigade, see also Chap. IV, pp. 78 ff. Also, Buchardt, op. cit., pp. 113 ff.; E. von Krannhals: *Der Warschauer Aufstand* ("The Warsaw Uprising"), Verlag für Wehrwesen, Frankfurt, 1962.

secret lists with the names of suitable officers in all Russian units had been kept for a long time. Lieutenant Colonels Arkhipov, Artyemyev, Alexandrov, and Zhukovsky became regimental commanders. Differences cropped up concerning the commander of the reconnaissance detachment—Major Kostyenko, a former Kaminsky officer—between Herre, who thought him unqualified, and Bunyachenko, who insisted on keeping him. Herre had not yet grown accustomed to seeing the Russians exercise sole responsibility for the ROA. Having been compelled for years to bow to German authority, the Russians took satisfaction in ignoring his objections.

In the succeeding few weeks, Bunyachenko showed what he was capable of. He subjected the hastily assembled troops to his strict discipline and in return received their good will. Bunyachenko overwhelmed Herre with reproaches when anything went wrong, when weapons and equipment failed to arrive. He suspected that the delays and foul-ups were intentional; that the Germans didn't trust him and really wanted to block the creation of the ROA.

Herre worked to the point of exhaustion to overcome all obstacles. It almost seemed like a miracle to him when the division became a reality at the beginning of February and the second division in neighboring Heuberg also started to take shape. Colonel G. A. Zveryev was appointed commander of the second division and simultaneously promoted to major general.

Zveryev, a worker's son, was a capable officer, who had risen to the post of division commander during the Finnish War. At the start of the eastern campaign his division had been smashed and he himself wounded. Dressed in civilian clothes, he had succeeded in making his way back to Red Army lines—only to find himself immediately arrested on suspicion of espionage and, after months of interrogation, demoted to major and ordered to central Asia. Not until 1942 did he return to the front again as a division commander.

The Germans took him prisoner in March 1943 during the siege of Kharkov. Along with about a thousand other officers, he was first interned in Dnepropetrovsk. Political discussions immediately began on Vlasov's liberation movement, word of which had been spread by German leaflets at the beginning of the year. Seven hundred and eighty officers signed a petition in which they asked to be enrolled in the liberation army, with Zveryev's name heading the list. The group was promptly sent to Limburg; most remained there, but eight officers went on to Dabendorf.

At the behest of Himmler—who had taken personal command of Army Group Vistula on January 24, 1945—a Russian light-armored detachment was to provide, in the first days of February, a "sample demonstration" of the Russians' readiness for combat. Neither Vlasov nor Bunyachenko was happy with this mission, since their goal was to form and train a strong army as quickly as possible; to have it prematurely split up was the last thing they wished. Finally, however, a 150-man detachment led by Sakharov and Count Lamsdorff was organized with volunteers from the first division and the propaganda company, and was sent off by Vlasov. The detachment went into combat against a Soviet bridgehead in Neulowin and then in Pomerania, fought with great bravery, and captured prisoners. The exploits of the unit were mentioned in Wehrmacht reports, and they impressed Himmler, who sent Sakharov a gold watch. Sakharov and Lamsdorff subsequently joined a Russian regiment brought from Denmark, with which they took over a sector of the front. The light-armored unit returned to Münsingen.[8]

Meanwhile, Vlasov and KONR had made some progress despite all difficulties. The condition of Russian workers in Germany had improved; there were KONR spokesmen in many camps in a position to remedy abuses. At the beginning of January, Himmler had ordered that henceforth anyone who beat Russians was to be sent to a concentration camp. (Equal treatment with German workers, however, was not attained until March 1, 1945.)

KONR wished to determine the exact number of POW's and

[8] Lamsdorff, interview; Buchardt, op. cit., p. 315.

of Eastern workers and for this purpose contacted the head of the Statistical Section of OKH, Colonel Passow. He came up with a figure of 6–7 million for Eastern laborers, but only 1.2 million for war prisoners—although the total number of captured soldiers and deserters was supposed to be almost 6 million. He explained the discrepancy by asserting that this last figure was exaggerated, since almost one million had joined the German army as Hiwis and volunteer soldiers, several hundred thousand Ukrainians had been released, hundreds of thousands had fled from the camps and transports, and the rest had died in the camps, a majority in the first winter.[9]

On January 17 the German Foreign Office and KONR signed a financial agreement under which the Reich granted KONR unlimited, interest-free credit without any strings attached. The funds were to be repaid after Russia's liberation. This pact, the first written agreement between the Reich and KONR, meant that the latter was now recognized under international law as the representative of the liberation movement. The German negotiators included, most notably, State Secretary von Steengracht of the Foreign Office and State Secretary Reinhard of the Finance Ministry; on the Russian side were Vlasov, Malyshkin, Professor Andreyev, head of KONR's Financial Department, and his deputy, Schlippe, and Zherebkov, KONR's liaison to the Foreign Office.[1]

While they were dining together following the successful conclusion of the negotiations, Steengracht received word of the start of the new Red Army offensive on the Vistula. The Russian attack eventually came to a halt once again at the Oder; but it was now clear that the German collapse would occur even before autumn. Vlasov and his officers worked all the more feverishly to organize the few divisions that could still be armed. On January 28, authority over the ROA was transferred to

[9] Cf. *Borba*: "The Struggle for the Rights of the Eastern Workers," No. 14, 1945, p. 25.
[1] Zherebkov, unpub. rept.

KONR, with Vlasov as commander in chief, and the ROA thus ceased to be controlled by the German High Command. Several days later, Trukhin and Boyarsky led the headquarters staff in a shift to Heuberg, where the second division had reached its required strength of about fifteen thousand men, although it was not yet fully armed. Colonel Neryanin was appointed chief of staff.

On February 2, in Karinhall, Hermann Göring received Vlasov together with Maltsev and Kroeger, at the request of Air Force General Aschenbrenner, who had jurisdiction over the Russian air force unit commanded by Maltsev. Aschenbrenner, a former air force attaché in Moscow, had done everything possible to make the unit combat-ready. Now Göring was being asked to approve its placement under Vlasov's command. Göring admitted he didn't know much about Russian problems and readily agreed to the transfer of authority. He also acknowledged that mistakes had been made in the treatment of Eastern workers: He had believed the Russians were used to being beaten, but now realized he had erred. His conversation then lapsed into trivia, touching on such topics as the ROA insignia, which he suggested should be worn on the chest instead of the sleeve. In addition, he displayed interest in Red Army medals and marks of rank, and wanted to know why Stalin called himself Generalissimo. Vlasov replied that because of a swollen ego he wanted to set himself apart from all the other generals. The Reichsmarschall accepted this explanation, apparently without detecting any other implications.[2]

Kroeger met with Pannwitz in Berlin in this period. The Cossack Corps had not only fought well against Tito's partisans, but on December 26, 1944, had been sent into battle against the Red Army near Pitomaka and had smashed a Soviet bridgehead and taken a large number of prisoners. Kroeger urged that the Cossack Corps join the liberation movement and place itself under Vlasov's authority. At the outset,

[2] Kroeger, letter to author.

175

at least, Pannwitz would remain commander. Pannwitz confirmed the fact that the Cossacks wished to unite with Vlasov's movement, and he himself had nothing in principle against Vlasov as top commander. But the change-over failed to come about because of the protests of Rosenberg and Krasnov and the continuing hesitation of Himmler.[3]

Despite all his duties and burdens, Vlasov found time to maintain warm personal relationships with his friends and colleagues. Dellingshausen recalls that once, after a heavy bombing attack on Berlin about this time, Vlasov appeared at his house at 5 a.m. He had come to make sure nothing had happened and to see if he could be of any help. He was relieved to find everything all right and said that he was going on to inquire about some other friends. He had walked the long distance from Dahlem to Charlottenburg.[4]

The increasingly dangerous situation prompted KONR to move its headquarters to Karlsbad on February 6. The reception there, however, was not at all friendly. Konrad Henlein, Gauleiter of the Sudetenland, objected violently; he did not want Vlasov or any other Russians in his region. He told Buchardt that if Vlasov did not leave the Hotel Richmond in a few hours, the "Russians would really get hurt," that he would have Nazi strong-arm squads drive them out of the Sudeten.[5]

To be sure, these threats were not taken seriously; KONR ignored Henlein's objections and stayed in Karlsbad. But the Gauleiter's attitude was typical of most Nazi officials. The old antagonism between the party and the SS was unmistakable. Bormann's fears that he would be outmaneuvered by Himmler and the SS with regard to *Ost* policy had led in January to a plan to install in the party chancellory an Eastern expert who would set guidelines for government and party officials to follow. For this post he proposed Erich Koch's closest associate,

[3] Kroeger, letter to author.
[4] Dellingshausen, interview.
[5] Buchardt, op. cit., p. 304.

176

Dargel, a rabid champion of the enslavement policy and an enemy of the Vlasov project. But the plan died stillborn because of the objections of Himmler, as well as of Ribbentrop and even Rosenberg, who feared for the existence of his own ministry.[6]

By mid-February, Herre and Bunyachenko had brought the seemingly impossible to pass: The first division stood fully armed and trained. On February 16, with a full-dress parade to mark the occasion, General Köstring formally transferred it to Vlasov's command. Vlasov was visibly moved when Bunyachenko reported to him as commander of the parading division. It did not amount to much, considering what might have been; but still it was his own, a well-armed force under his sole command, which could no longer be used arbitrarily to further German interests.

After the parade the Russian officers and their German guests gathered in the officers club. There Vlasov made a speech in which he referred to the difficulties that had impeded the formation of a liberation army. He also described his conversation with Himmler, to whom he had said that he and his supporters would try to forget what had happened in the past, but that henceforth no insult or humiliation would be forgotten. Vlasov concluded with the words: "The flag of liberation will one day be planted in our homeland, if not by us, then by our brothers. Many of us will not live to see that day, but it will come."

These words betrayed strong overtones of the pessimism that the Russians felt in far greater measure than the Germans—who could not conceive the possibility that the Western Powers might turn over hundreds of thousands of his enemies to Stalin, or that Rumania, Bulgaria, Hungary, Czechoslovakia, Yugoslavia, and Poland would be abandoned to Communism. But the Russians knew Stalin.

After Vlasov had reviewed the still-forming second division in Heuberg, he returned to Karlsbad. There, on February 27,

[6] Buchardt, op. cit., p. 303.

a meeting of KONR took place, at which Vlasov reported on the success of the light-armored detachment and the transfer of the first division to his direct authority.

At this point, however, Forostivky, the mayor of Kiev during the occupation, took the floor and addressed Kroeger and the other Germans in a very sharp tone:

> I have nothing to lose; I am a candidate for death. My name is on the list of those who have been condemned to death by the Soviets for collaboration with the Germans. This is why I can speak the truth here. I personally sent 45,000 of our best young people to work in Germany, sixty per cent of whom went voluntarily, because I believed that by their work they could serve our cause, the struggle against Bolshevism. What have you done to them? You have made slaves of them and do not want to treat them decently even now. We received you as liberators. You deceived us. We waited for three years, hoping that the voice of reason would triumph. Now it is too late—for you and perhaps for us as well.[7]

Kroeger remained silent. He now had to take responsibility for what he personally had opposed. The catastrophe which was already casting its shadow ahead could no longer be averted.

Soon afterward, Vlasov visited Maltsev's air force, now also under his command, in Neuern. It had grown to four thousand men and consisted of a fighter squadron, a light bomber squadron, two other squadrons, an antiaircraft regiment, a paratrooper battalion, and a training unit with a school for pilots in Eger. The initiator of the Russian pilot group, as well as of a Latvian-Estonian unit, had been First Lieutenant Gert Buschmann, an Estonian now serving as General Aschenbrenner's adjutant.[8]

[7] Kitayev, op. cit., p. 11; Kroeger, interview.
[8] Gert Buschmann, interview.

★

When Vlasov returned to Karlsbad, he found a combat order from Himmler for the first division and immediately hurried off to Münsingen. The division was fully equipped and supplied, and its men believed that they would no longer be playthings of the Germans, that only Vlasov could now give them orders. Bunyachenko was therefore all the more dismayed when, on March 2, Herre brought the order to link up for action with Army Group Vistula, which was under Himmler's personal command.

This represented a clear breach of the agreement stipulating that the division could be sent into action only in large units and with Vlasov's consent. Its assignment to the front could lead only to its senseless annihilation. Bunyachenko refused to obey the command. He summoned the division's senior officers, and various plans were discussed. Among them was the possibility of seizing weapons, arming the second division, and marching to the Swiss frontier in order to contact the Western Powers. A staff battalion was set up, armed with automatic and antitank weapons, to defend staff headquarters.

Herre was considered a sincere friend, but helpless to do anything against an order from Himmler. The Russians did not know that Herre himself, who had done his utmost to make the division a reality, had in fact instigated the combat order. Without consulting Vlasov or Bunyachenko, he had kept pushing Köstring to use the troops, in the belief that if they proved themselves, the organization of additional divisions might be accelerated. Köstring had advised him to appeal directly to Himmler. Herre had explained to Himmler that what he wanted was a successful, limited operation which would not endanger the existence of the division—perhaps the elimination of a Soviet bridgehead. Himmler did state that the reliability of the Russians already had been proved by the successful action of the light-armored unit; but then he agreed. Thus it was Herre's well-meaning initiative that produced a chain of dramatic events.

179

Vlasov finally calmed his officers down and pointed out that a refusal might lead to reprisals against the Eastern workers. He succeeded in having the division's assignment switched from the Stettin to the Cottbus area. The division was also permitted to march as far as Nuremberg, since the rail line through Ulm was under steady bombardment. During the march, contacts with Eastern workers and war prisoners were inevitable; many of them joined up as volunteers, so that more than three thousand men swelled the division's ranks. They were given makeshift uniforms and organized in reserve units. (Ultimately, however, many of them had to be discharged in order to maintain discipline.) On March 19 the division was assembled in the entrainment area outside Nuremberg, and on March 26 its last units arrived at the Lieberose training area.

When Bunyachenko's German liaison officer, Major Helmut Schwenninger, established contact with the staff of Army Group Vistula, he learned that Himmler had resigned as its commander a few days earlier. His successor, Colonel General Gotthard Heinrici, knew nothing of Himmler's order and was against this kind of experiment. He did not believe that Russians would still fight at this time and in this situation and was uninformed regarding the political aspects of the Russian liberation movement. Heinrici's chief concern was the impending Soviet attack, which might begin any day. He would agree to deployment of the Russian division only if Himmler explicitly assumed responsibility for this action. Schwenninger traveled to Berlin, but could only get to see Berger, who had been briefed on the situation and referred him to the commander of the Ninth Army, General Busse.

Busse proposed as the only possibility the liquidation of a Soviet bridgehead south of Frankfurt-an-der-Oder, which a cadet officer regiment had vainly attempted to take. The terrain could be targeted and shelled from the high bank opposite, so that strong artillery support was required for a successful operation. Bunyachenko suspected that the division was intentionally being given an impossible mission. His main preoccupation was the strength of the enemy units, and he kept asking when the Soviet attack could be expected. He was obsessed by a nightmarish fear that the division might perish needlessly. Vlasov planned to join the division shortly before it moved south and complete the march with it.

On March 25, in Karlsbad, Vlasov met with Zherebkov, who reported to him on his attempts to make contact with the Western Powers. After his return from Paris, Zherebkov had placed himself at Vlasov's and KONR's disposal and had been appointed director of the "Section for Relations with Government Agencies," which was part of Malyshkin's Administrative Department. This linguistically talented man turned diplomat also served as KONR's representative in dealing with the Russian Section of the German Foreign Office and in attempts to establish relations with the Western Powers in order to clarify as much as possible the inevitable postwar questions. His efforts till then had been unsuccessful, as also had been those he had made in December 1944 through the Swedish military attaché in Berlin, Colonel von Danenfeld, to Gustav Nobel, and through Ambassador Marzahn to the Russian-born wife of the American ambassador in Madrid, Norman Armour. The purpose of these contacts was to explain the Russian liberation movement to the Western Allies and prevent its members from being handed over to the USSR. With the same idea in mind, Zherebkov also wrote to the president of the International Red Cross, Dr. Burckhardt,[9] through the Foreign Office, requesting the latter to secure him a Swiss visa so that he could negotiate in person.

He also wished to establish direct contact with the diplomatic representatives of the Western Allies in Bern. When he received no answer, Zherebkov went to see the Swiss chargé d'affaires in Berlin, who told him to forget about a visa, since granting visas to anti-Communist Russians might have unpleasant consequences for future Swiss relations with the Soviet Union. It was for the same reason that Grand Duke Vladimir

---

[9] The text of this letter, dated February 26, 1945, is in the author's archives.

had also been refused a visa. However, the chargé did advise him to attempt a crossing of the Swiss frontier, and he provided Zherebkov with a letter of recommendation indicating that a visa had been requested, but that no action had as yet been taken on it. After receiving the necessary authorization from Vlasov, Zherebkov returned to Berlin. Before his departure, Kroeger informed him that the RSHA, too, no longer had objections to contacts with the West.

KONR's last meeting took place on March 28. Over it lay the shadow of the imminent German collapse. The decision was made to assemble all elements of the ROA in the Innsbruck area, make contact with the Cossack Corps, and, depending on the course of events, either surrender to the Western Allies or join the fight in Yugoslavia.

The next day, Vlasov traveled with Kroeger to Berlin in order to secure the quick withdrawal of the first division from the Oder front. Only a small KONR force under the command of Colonel Kromiadi and the newly appointed intelligence chief, Lieutenant Colonel Nikolai Tenzorov, still remained in Berlin. They were busy evacuating Russian families to Württemberg. On March 31, Vlasov received a Cossack Corps delegation headed by Kononov and Colonel Kulakov, who were authorized to transmit to KONR and the German government a declaration by the delegate assembly of the Cossack units.[1] At this congress, held on March 29 in Verovititsa, Lieutenant General von Pannwitz had become the first non-Cossack in history to be elected a field ataman of Cossack armed forces; Colonel Kononov had been chosen as chief of staff.

It was unanimously voted to place the Cossack formations under Vlasov as commander in chief of the KONR armed forces and to suspend the Cossack administration headed by General Krasnov, which refused to accept Vlasov's authority. This decision, however, had practical meaning only for Pann-

---

[1] The text of this declaration was published on April 24, 1945, in *Kazachii Vestnik* ("Cossack Bulletin").

witz's Cossack Corps. In an obvious thrust at Rosenberg's plans, it was emphasized that the Cossacks were a part of the Russian people. The pro-Vlasov resolution was in no way directed at Pannwitz, whom the Cossacks idolized. (Himmler did not approve the transfer of command until April 28.)

Vlasov agreed that Kononov should assume command of all Cossack units when the Germans surrendered and, with Guderian's approving countersignature, promoted him to major general. Before his trip to the Oder front, Vlasov succeeded in securing from Kaltenbrunner the release of the NTS leaders. Only the argument that these convinced anti-Communists could not be allowed to fall into Soviet hands changed Kaltenbrunner's attitude.[2] Had they not been freed, Vlasov would have been prepared to implement Tenzorov's plan to rescue them, by force if necessary, before the Soviets appeared. An armed body of Russians escorted the NTS leadership to Karlsbad on April 4. Despite Kaltenbrunner's decision, justifiable fears existed that the Gestapo might be planning a kidnapping in the style of the Zykov affair.

On April 8, Vlasov traveled with Kroeger and Kononov to the Oder front, where he had a long conversation with Colonel General Heinrici. When Heinrici asked him why he still wanted to fight, Vlasov explained that Himmler had insisted on this combat operation as a condition for creating more units. In any case, he had been deceived in the most scandalous fashion by the German leaders.[3]

Vlasov subsequently discussed the combat plan with General Busse. The terrain was most unfavorable for an attack, especially since floods had reduced the potential attack area in that sector to a one-hundred-yard stretch. The mission called for strong artillery fire to knock out the Soviet positions on the eastern shore. But artillery batteries were no more available than dive bombers. Vlasov considered the operation futile under these

[2] Buchardt, letter to author.
[3] Gotthard Heinrici, interview.

circumstances and wanted to order a return march south. Kroeger, who feared Himmler's reaction, had to summon every ounce of his persuasive powers to wrest agreement from Vlasov for the mission.[4] Even though finally consenting, however, Vlasov insisted on leaving the division before it went into action. In this way he expressed his protest and also became inaccessible in case of a conflict with the German commander because of the attack's failure and the division's pulling out of the front lines.

After conferring at length with Bunyachenko, Vlasov summoned the regimental commanders and told them the operation was required whether it succeeded or not, whether it was futile or not. Refusal might threaten ROA's expansion. What he discussed with Bunyachenko is not known, but he probably ordered him to withdraw from the front once the attack failed, and march south. Bunyachenko could then fend off further German orders by asserting that the division could not enter combat without Vlasov's instructions, as stipulated in the agreement.[5]

On April 11, Vlasov traveled to Berlin with Berger, who had delivered Himmler's written guarantee to Heinrici. He was back in Karlsbad on the 12th, and he married Adeleide Bielenberg the following day. He had visited her again between Christmas and the New Year, bitter and disillusioned. "How gladly," he had said, "would I live a quiet life here as a peasant. My cares oppress me." Yet, he was not completely without hope. He believed he would be able to continue the struggle "on the side of an ally whose policy would be more intelligent than that of the Germans."[6] Shortly thereafter he had asked Frau Bielenberg to marry him. Kroeger, who had at first opposed the marriage on political grounds, then obtained approval from

---

[4] Kroeger, letter to author.

[5] Helmut Schwenninger has expressed his conviction that Bunyachenko, in his subsequent actions, was in fact following Vlasov's orders (letter to author).

[6] Dellingshausen, interview.

Berger. And so, in the very face of approaching catastrophe, the union quietly took place.[7]

Vlasov met with the freed NTS leaders on the 14th. It was decided to arrange for the capture of some NTS members on the advancing western front in order to make contact with the Allies. On the 16th, Vlasov left for Prague. Those accompanying him included Fröhlich, who was to establish communications with the Czech resistance. Among other possibilities discussed was that of defending, together with non-Communist Czechs, the so-called Bohemian basin against the Soviets until the Americans occupied Bohemia. This plan assumed that a conflict would soon arise between the Western Allies and the Soviet Union. Russian émigrés helped Fröhlich meet the Czech general Klečanda, who had fought under Kolchak during the Russian Civil War. He declared that the Czechs would welcome the Russians joyously because President Beneš would be returning with them. Their eyes would be opened later, but nothing could be done now. He himself could not abandon his post because he commanded the underground army of Prague and its environs.

Klečanda was quite pessimistic about Vlasov's prospects. He had been in Rome when the Germans occupied Czechoslovakia and had implored the Western Allies to rescue twenty thousand Czech officers whom they would need later, but they had not been interested. They would not help Vlasov either. Just as they had not believed in war with Hitler then, so now they would not believe in a conflict with the Soviets.[8]

On the 17th, Vlasov received Kromiadi and Tenzorov in Prague's Hotel Acron. They had arrived with the rear-guard group after managing to evacuate the endangered Russian families from Berlin. Zherebkov had joined them, bringing with him a written communication from Dr. Burckhardt. This stated that hopes were slight for preventing the handing over of liberation

[7] A. Bielenberg, interview.
[8] Fröhlich, letter to author.

movement members to Stalin, since the movement had arisen with the help of the Third Reich. Still, the negotiating position would be better if Vlasov appealed to Himmler to stop the killing of concentration camp inmates as the Third Reich crumbled. Zherebkov had assured the Red Cross representative that Vlasov would do everything in his power to fulfill this request. Vlasov asked Kroeger, who was with him, to make representations of this kind to Himmler.

Zherebkov talked in Vienna with Professors Eibl and Raschhofer, who had suggested that on April 25, Vlasov broadcast an appeal from Prague to the nations gathered in San Francisco for the founding of the United Nations. Soviet propaganda had apparently succeeded in keeping not only the public, but even the Allied leaders, ignorant of the aims and significance of the liberation movement. Vlasov should therefore describe the political program of KONR and explain the reasons for collaboration with the Germans. He was to protest the Soviet Union's acceptance into the UN and the continued existence of the Stalin regime.

Zherebkov asked Minister of State Frank for approval of this step; but the latter did not wish to decide by himself on so important a political action. Nor could he be moved when Zherebkov pointed out that Hitler was cut off in Berlin and unreachable. Frank did, however, give Zherebkov a document declaring him to be on an important state mission, so as to facilitate his journey to the Swiss border. He also presented him with a new car as a gift for Vlasov.[9]

Meanwhile, Vlasov had traveled to staff headquarters, located south of Landsberg, because the second division, the staff and personnel of the officers school, and the replacement brigade had all been mobilized by the OKH and dispatched toward Linz, where they were to join Army Group Rendulic. Vlasov had no objection to their heading in this direction, since he had meanwhile learned that the first division was also marching south.

[9] Zherebkov, interview and unpub. rept.

In the interim, the first division's attack against the Soviet bridgehead had begun as scheduled at 5 a.m. on April 14. As Vlasov had anticipated, the battalions were stopped by the enormous wire barriers which had previously brought the Germans to a standstill. For four hours the ROA units tried to surmount this obstacle, despite flanking fire from the opposite bank. Finally Bunyachenko, realizing the mission could not be accomplished, asked Busse for permission to break off the attack. Permission, however, was refused. The positions had to be held, since the division was there to take over this front sector from the Germans.

Bunyachenko's old distrust was once again aroused—the Germans wanted to bleed the division to death. Zhukov's great offensive might begin at any hour and would bring destruction. The order to take over a section of the front was a violation of KONR's agreement with the Germans. Bunyachenko therefore defied Busse's instructions and ordered a withdrawal from the division's initial position. That night, Busse demanded that Bunyachenko report to him and explain himself. Bunyachenko invented an excuse for refusing and informed Busse the next day that the Ninth Army order conflicted with Vlasov's instructions and that in the future he would only obey Vlasov, his superior, whom he was going to contact immediately. He pressed Schwenninger to obtain Busse's permission for a march south. Then he summoned his senior officers to a conference at which the decision was made to march south and, if necessary, to commandeer food supplies. Schwenninger finally did win consent from the Ninth Army staff for a withdrawal toward Cottbus. A Russian attack was expected at any hour, and the staff was genuinely happy to get rid of the troublesome division. When Schwenninger returned with the order, he explained dryly to Bunyachenko that the army undoubtedly understood that the division was already on the move.[1]

[1] There are two reliable sources on the first division's march south: Schwenninger's diary and an unpublished report written in 1946 by the commander of the division's Second Regiment, Colonel V.

★

In leading the division south, Bunyachenko displayed great courage, cunning, and tactical skill. It would be no fault of his own but rather the political shortsightedness of the Allies that would, in the end, defeat him. The division, fully combat-ready, covered over sixty miles in the first two days. It eventually took up quarters in the Klettwitz area, in the territory of Army Group Schörner. At this point, Bunyachenko received a communication from the staff of the German 275th Infantry Division informing him that the 600th Infantry Division (Russian) was now under its command and was to take up positions behind the German unit. Bunyachenko lost his self-control and shouted at Schwenninger that he would never obey this order, that it was sheer effrontery to put him under the control of a division. Schwenninger drove to the 275th's headquarters, where he learned that Field Marshal Ferdinand Schörner had personally issued the order and only he could change it.

Schwenninger succeeded in getting to talk to Schörner at division headquarters. He had heard much about the crudity, tactlessness, and fanatical loyalty to the Führer of this youngest of German field marshals. Schörner's sole interest was in the size and arms of the division and whether or not it would fight. When Schwenninger tried to explain the political problems involved, he would not let him finish. "Well, then, I don't want the Russians," he snapped. "How would it be if I had Bunyachenko shot for not obeying my orders?" But then he abruptly broke off the discussion. He had to go to the Führer's headquarters and couldn't waste any more time on the Russians. When he returned, he would teach them how commands should be obeyed. He rescinded the order placing them under the 275th Infantry Division.[2]

Artyemyev. They agree on all essential points. Other pertinent information was obtained in an interview with F. Schörner and from a letter to the author by Kroeger.

[2] Schörner states (interview and letter to author) that the OKW ordered the division into combat. He did not know it was under Vlasov's

The division was already on the march toward Peitz when Schwenninger returned. Bunyachenko listened to his report and then declared that he did not fear execution—Stalin, too, wanted to have him shot. He asked Schwenninger to drive to the Fifth Corps, to which the division was now supposed to be attached, and inform them that he took orders only from Vlasov and would continue marching south. When Schwenninger reached Fifth Corps headquarters, however, more serious problems preoccupied them: The Soviet offensive had started at dawn on April 16. Schwenninger immediately received permission for the march to continue into the Hoyerswerda area, which the division reached on the 17th.

Here, Bunyachenko received his first direct personal command from Schörner: to take the division into combat in the Kosel area. Bunyachenko, instead, led his men toward the area west of Kamenz. Then a new order arrived: "Division to move into Radeberg area near Dresden for entrainment to Operation Czech Lands." This time Bunyachenko obeyed, since he wanted to go in this direction anyway. The division reached the area around Radeberg on the 19th. But Bunyachenko refused entrainment with the excuse that fighting was in progress near Bautzen and the division could be wiped out. Shortly before this, Sakharov's regiment had joined up with the division. How Sakharov had managed to break away from the front has remained a mystery. Volunteers he had recruited en route had swelled the regiment to more than three thousand men, so that the division as a whole was now about twenty thousand strong.

Under normal conditions, Schörner undoubtedly would not have hesitated to turn his guns on the insubordinate division. But in the present situation he wanted to avoid conflict. Since he saw no way of bringing Bunyachenko to reason, he sent an officer to General Aschenbrenner requesting that he exert pressure on the division commander through Vlasov. Vlasov, how-

---

command. In the confusion of those days he did not have time to deal with political problems.

ever, had transferred KONR headquarters to Füssen on April 20. Aschenbrenner sent a plane to drop a message to Bunyachenko, imploring him to obey the combat order; but Bunyachenko ignored this appeal as well. Aschenbrenner went to Füssen and arrived there in time to accompany Vlasov, Trukhin, Malyshkin, Zhilenkov, Boyarsky, and Kroeger on a visit to Strikfeldt, who had found lodging on a nearby farm. Now, with the catastrophe inevitable, Vlasov wished to consult his friend once more.

Malyshkin and Boyarsky met with Cossack Corps officers and the Yugoslav leader Mihailovich to decide on the best way out. Aschenbrenner and Strikfeldt believed that no solution was possible without the sanction of the Western Allies, and recommended immediate negotiations for surrender on a single condition—assurances that no one would be handed over to the Soviets. It was at last decided to assemble all the units in the Innsbruck area in order to march them, if need be, through the Brenner Pass to join with the Cossack Corps. At the same time, truce emissaries were to be dispatched to the Americans and the English. Aschenbrenner had Professor Theodor Oberländer, who spoke English, brought from Prague to act as such an emissary; he proposed, in addition, that Strikfeldt and a Russian officer seek to contact some influential American. Strikfeldt knew the risks involved in such an attempt, but was ready to perform this last service for his friend. Vlasov appointed Malyshkin head of the delegation. Kroeger made out an official authorization to protect them from the Nazi "Werewolves" and other fanatics.[3]

The next day, Vlasov, Kroeger, and Buchardt drove to Innsbruck to prepare for the moving of KONR headquarters. There they chanced to meet SS General Wolf, who was on a visit to his family. Through him an attempt was planned to establish contact with Field Marshal Sir Harold Alexander, commander in chief of the Allied forces. For this purpose, Kroeger's representative, SS Major von Sivers, and a Russian officer, Captain Baron Lüdinghausen-Wolf, were sent several days later to Bozen

[3] Strik-Strikfeldt, interview.

with a memorandum signed by Vlasov. Sivers had fought in the Baltic states as a volunteer in Baltic forces under Alexander's command in 1921. The two men were unable to see Alexander, however, and talked instead with Colonel Lehmann, a Canadian intelligence officer on his staff. Sivers and Lüdinghausen were subsequently interned.[4]

Wolf agreed to let the ROA troops march through the Brenner Pass to the South Tyrol. This kept open the possibility of being able to operate jointly with the Cossack Corps, which was fighting its way toward the Austrian border.[5] Vlasov was in Füssen again on April 24. Trukhin dictated the last order to ROA units, ordaining the move to the Innsbruck area.

Malyshkin selected several officers, among them Colonel Kromiadi and General Zakutny, as truce emissaries. Their mission was to establish contact with the Western Allies and inform them that, by Vlasov's order, General Malyshkin was ready to negotiate the surrender of the ROA, though only with the commander in chief.

That evening, Strikfeldt came to Füssen once again, to bid Vlasov a last farewell. He found him apathetic and without hope; Vlasov no longer believed in the Americans, or, for that matter, in any other possibility of salvation. He thanked Strikfeldt for everything he had done and said he would go his own way to the end. "If you survive," he concluded, "let the truth be known about what I wanted to do." These were Vlasov's last words to Strikfeldt, and this was the last time they saw each other.[6]

Meanwhile, Major Neuner, Schörner's liaison officer, had appeared at the headquarters of the first division on April 22 to negotiate with Bunyachenko. Neuner brought an order for the unit to take over a rear position in the Haida area. Schörner wished to brief Bunyachenko himself and requested the latter

---

[4] Erich von Sivers, letter to author.
[5] Buchardt, op. cit., p. 341.
[6] Strik-Strikfeldt, interview.

to visit him at 5 p.m.; he considered their previous misunderstandings over and done with. Bunyachenko agreed to the visit.

At 5 p.m., however, the commander of the first division's reconnaissance detachment, Major Kostyenko, appeared at Schörner's headquarters and explained that General Bunyachenko, to his deep regret, could not come himself because he had been hurt in an auto accident. Schwenninger, who was present, saw that Schörner was having a hard time controlling himself. After Kostyenko left, he exploded: "What crap! If I had just one air squadron, I'd bang them around until they knuckled under."

In the meantime, Soviet tanks had appeared less than eight miles from the division's encampment. Late that evening, Bunyachenko informed the field marshal that because of the situation at the front he would wait till 2 a.m. for the order to continue south. Although no order arrived, Bunyachenko gave his combat-ready men the signal to move out. Now, with the front rapidly approaching, he had to get across the Elbe, come what may. If Schörner intended to stop the division, he would do so there.

A bridge near Bad Schandau was chosen for the crossing. However, it was occupied by a German engineering detachment, which refused to let the advance party cross because the bridge was mined and there were no orders to let the division through. Bunyachenko himself drove up to talk to the detachment's commander, but the latter, citing his orders, politely refused to budge. Thereupon, Bunyachenko had thirty ambulances roll forward and requested that the wounded be let through. This was permitted, and a narrow strip of the bridge was cleared of mines. But as the last of these vehicles drove onto the bridge, Bunyachenko had the tanks and cavalry battalion follow. The Germans, seeing themselves outwitted, contacted the Army Group by phone while the tanks were moving into position to protect the division as it crossed. Bunyachenko stood on the west bank as the columns filed by. Meanwhile, Lieutenant Colonel Nikolayev was managing, though with considerable effort, to stall a colonel of the Army Group who was insisting on the immediate recrossing of that part of the division already on the west bank. Bunyachenko simply refused to talk to the colonel. The columns kept crossing till well into the night— the maneuver had succeeded.

Once across, the division enjoyed a good strategic position. The Elbe provided cover from the north and east, and the division controlled the bridge. During the night, however, a battered SS armored division moved into the surrounding villages, and the next day more SS units appeared in the neighborhood. It was rumored that these units had come to disarm the division. Bunyachenko ordered the march resumed toward the area of the Schneeberg.

Shortly thereafter, Schörner informed the division by radio that he would visit the unit the following day, April 27. It was not the field marshal, however, but his chief of staff, Lieutenant General Oldwig von Natzmer, who appeared. Bunyachenko, his head and arm bandaged, had an honor guard and a military band waiting to welcome him.

Natzmer demanded that the division go into combat in the Brno area and made it unmistakably plain that another refusal would have grave consequences. Since the division was immobilized by a lack of gasoline and rations, Bunyachenko agreed; but he still refused to allow his men to be entrained, and Natzmer yielded on this point. It was arranged that the division should, instead, immediately march south behind the front.

The situation was indeed serious. Attempts to communicate with Vlasov had failed, and the division's fate was now at stake. Bunyachenko, feeling that he no longer had the right to make a decision by himself, summoned his regimental commanders. He described the situation to them and declared that under these circumstances he was prepared to break his word if it would save the division, but that he did not feel justified in making this decision alone.

With the exception of Lieutenant Colonel Arkhipov, the

officers all agreed that an operation at the front would lead to the senseless annihilation of the division. Nothing remained, therefore, but to attempt a quick march south, by force if necessary, in order to reach the Americans. The division began its march that day. The strictest orders were issued against looting, theft, and hostile acts toward the German population. Keyed to the highest pitch physically and psychologically, the division covered some seventy-five miles in two days, taking only a single, five-hour break.

One question disturbed the soldiers: Where was Vlasov? To raise their morale, they were told during the march that Vlasov had arrived. A cheer swept the ranks, and their spirits rose. The Czech border was passed without incident. On the evening of April 28, the division pitched camp south of the town of Lobositz. That same evening a radio message arrived unexpectedly from Schörner: He would personally visit the division the next day. When he appeared, he acted as if nothing had happened.

Bunyachenko was obviously enjoying the situation. The arrogant field marshal had been forced to come to him, thereby confessing his impotence. The Russian commander expressed his pleasure at the visit, especially since, shortly before, a different treatment had been planned for him. When Schörner irritatedly asked what he meant, Bunyachenko replied: "But the Herr Field Marshal wanted to have me executed!" Schörner harshly asked the Germans present who had passed on this information. When Schwenninger stepped forward, he merely snarled, "That was very clever," and again turned to Bunyachenko: Naturally, that was nonsense, a misunderstanding, or he wouldn't be there. Then he asked whether or not the division was ready to fight. "Certainly," replied Bunyachenko—leaving open the question of where and under what conditions. Nonetheless, this answer satisfied Schörner; he seemed happy to be able to end the conversation and remarked that this, after all, was what counted. He agreed to let Bunyachenko choose his own route of march toward Brno.

VI

MARCHING TOWARD DOOM

On the same day, Bunyachenko had a long talk with two delegates of the Czech partisans. The population had shown unusual interest in the division since it crossed the border. Its conflicts with the Germans were not unknown, and there was hope that the Russian soldiers would help the insurgents. Events at the front encouraged the Czechs to open resistance, but it was badly organized. Furthermore, there were both nationalist and Communist partisan groups, with the latter being better organized, though numerically small. The Czech partisans informed Bunyachenko that an uprising was due to occur in Prague within the next few days and asked him for support, since their own forces were inadequate. They expected the Americans to occupy Prague. If a national Czech government held Prague when they arrived, argued the Czech negotiators, the Americans would not allow it to be ousted. The Czechs expressed their willingness to grant asylum to the division in a democratic Czechoslovakia.

Bunyachenko was well aware of the mood prevailing among his men and knew that an order to help the Czechs would be received enthusiastically. The psychological strains of the past few years, the humiliations and breaches of faith by the Germans, the almost hopeless situation of the Russians for which the Germans were to blame—all had taken a toll. But Bunyachenko still refused to commit himself. He was waiting for Vlasov, with whom he had finally succeeded in establishing contact. He continued marching southward, taking up quarters in the vicinity of Beroun, some twenty miles southwest of Prague.

Meanwhile, Vlasov was visiting the units of the second division, which—together with the officers school and the replacement regiment—was moving toward Linz. He met with Zherebkov in Fernpass on April 27 and gave him complete authority for the conduct of negotiations in Switzerland. Vlasov, however, could no longer bring himself to hope for any success.

Zherebkov begged Vlasov to fly to Spain before the collapse; but he would not abandon his men. He then received a Cossack delegation from North Italy headed by Colonel Bocharov, whom he had appointed liaison officer to Krasnov. Bocharov transmitted the request of Ataman Naumenko that KONR assume authority over the North Italy Cossacks, a majority of whom, it seemed, disapproved of Krasnov's attitude. But, as with everything else, it was too late. The course of events had rendered all such concerns irrelevant. Vlasov gave orders to assemble KONR forces in the Innsbruck area, and then went to spend two days with his wife in lodgings she had found at Reit im Winkl, near Reichenhall. For her sake he pretended to be optimistic, but she could sense the hopelessness in him.[1] On April 30, Vlasov met again in Bad Reichenhall with Kroeger, who had consulted with Köstring on Schörner's complaints to the latter. The decision was made to negotiate directly with Schörner.

[1] Bielenberg, interview.

Quite unawares, Vlasov and Kroeger traveled through a partisan-occupied area to Schörner's headquarters in Königgrätz. On May 1 they spoke there with his chief of staff, Natzmer, from whom they learned that Schörner had already ordered the first division disarmed the next day. That would mean, almost certainly, a battle. Colonel General Hermann Hoth, the commander of the "Ore Range" Combat Group, had been assigned to carry out the order.[2] Hoth, who knew nothing of Vlasov's presence at Schörner's headquarters, had meanwhile asked Kleist, the security officer of the Dabendorf Propaganda Section, to talk to Bunyachenko and, if possible, prevent a clash.

Kleist was quite willing and, after an excited phone conversation between Hoth and Schörner in which Kleist participated toward the end, Schörner finally agreed to postpone action for several hours—although he still considered negotiations pointless; the Russians had always been traitors, and he was now determined to mop them up.[3] Toward evening, Schörner told Kroeger he was going to act and saw no reason to negotiate with Vlasov. Not until Kroeger had explained the political aspects of the ROA and urgently advised him against using force was he willing to talk to the Russian general.

At their meeting, Vlasov guaranteed the loyalty of the division as long as it was not attacked. He again pointed out the possibilities the Germans had failed to exploit and indicated that he hoped to continue his struggle with the aid of the Western Allies. The impulsive Schörner was swayed by these arguments. He was impressed that this man in this kind of situation still had plans and aims, whereas the Germans could no longer have any. He grasped the political significance of the Russian liberation movement and agreed not only to withdraw the attack order, but also to release the division from his command.[4]

[2] O. von Natzmer, letter to author.
[3] Kleist, letter to author.
[4] Schörner, interview.

Immediately afterwards, Vlasov and Kroeger drove through the night to Kozojedy, where the first division's headquarters had been moved. At dawn the next day, Kleist also appeared in Kozojedy, waving a white flag. He was unaware of the cancellation of the order to attack, and was very surprised to meet Vlasov and his group. He reported on his conversation with Hoth, whereupon Vlasov and Kroeger drove with him to "Ore Range" headquarters in Kriegern to explain the situation there, too. But Hoth had already been informed, and so they returned to Kozojedy.

Meanwhile, with the division to back them, the Russians felt themselves to be masters of the situation. They disarmed smaller German units and sent them home. There had also been some shooting, for the Russians were discharging long-accumulated rancor. Kroeger himself almost fell victim to this hostile mood: A hand grenade was thrown at night into what was believed to be his room, but he happened to have changed rooms. To the Russians, who were unaware of his real attitude, Kroeger represented the hated Nazi regime and shared responsibility for the obstructionism of the German leadership. The following morning, Kroeger traveled to Prague to learn from Frank how matters stood. The uprising there a few day later took him by surprise, and he never saw Vlasov again.[5]

That same morning, Vlasov and Bunyachenko received a delegation of Czech officers, who informed them that the uprising was set to begin on May 5. They pressed for support; the Czech people would never forget their help at such an hour. Vlasov, however, would make no promises. Afterwards he and Bunyachenko had a heated exchange, the latter insisting that they intervene in Prague—it would be the only, and perhaps the last, chance to save the division; the Americans could not be trusted. Vlasov did not share this view. He did not believe that the Czechs, especially if the Americans occupied Prague, could act without the latter's approval. The Americans would

[5] Kroeger, letter to author.

have the last word in any case, and that was why it was more sensible to establish contact immediately with them. Still, when Nikolayev and other senior officers of the division spoke out in favor of fighting, he reluctantly gave Bunyachenko a free hand. In this desperate situation he did not want to stop him from taking advantage of any opportunity that arose.

The next morning, May 4, a plane carrying Lieutenant Buschmann and General Shapovalov landed near Kozojedy. Trukhin had sent Shapovalov, who was to have headed an originally projected third division, to receive instructions. Vlasov advised him that a transfer of the ROA to the Innsbruck area had become meaningless and that all units should therefore be assembled in Bohemia. In a talk with Buschmann that night, Vlasov expressed a feeling of depression over the imminent operation in Prague, seeing nothing good coming from it. Besides, he did not want to fight the German army. If any slight hope still existed, it lay in resort to the Western Allies. He told of the efforts to contact these powers to determine whether they would be willing to accept the ROA's surrender without turning its troops over to the Soviets. "But," he concluded, "I will have to surrender in any case, put myself at their mercy even if they offer no guarantee. Perhaps the rank and file can be saved if they hand me over. I don't know. I can't do anything but wait, and that is the worst thing for a man." Buschmann was shaken to see Vlasov so despairing.

The following morning he told Vlasov that Maltsev and the other officers felt he should seek safety. A plane was ready to take off for Spain. But Vlasov remained adamant. "A leader who abandons his people at the critical moment is useless later on as well," he said. "I had every chance for victory. The Germans, or—if you please—fate, decided against it. Now I must follow my course to the end." [6] Shortly thereafter, Buschmann and Shapovalov flew back to Trukhin.

At dawn that same morning, Bunyachenko had ordered the

[6] Buschmann, interview.

march on Prague, after coming to an agreement with the insurgent representatives. A little later, Nikolayev asked Major Schwenninger for his weapon. He voiced his regret—the measure was not directed against him, but was meant, rather, to insure his safety. He begged Schwenninger to understand the reason for Bunyachenko's decision. It was the one chance remaining to salvage something.[7] On the evening of May 6, marching from the west and southwest, the division reached the outskirts of Prague and prepared for battle. On the way it had been enthusiastically greeted by the population and showered with flowers and gifts.

In some sections of the city the uprising had already started on the evening of May 4, triggered by news that planes carrying badly needed arms had left from Bari in Italy. When the planes failed to arrive—Churchill had canceled the take-offs at Stalin's behest—the fighting was temporarily halted; the superiority of the Germans was too great.

As the uprising began, the insurgents opened negotiations with the Narodny Rada ("National Council"), the provisional parliament of the Czech government-in-exile in London. Professor Albert Prazak was president of the Rada, and his deputy, and representative of the Rada's minority Communist faction, was Josef Smrkovsky. The government-in-exile had appointed Captain Nechansky its top military leader and had him dropped by parachute into Czechoslovakia.

The Rada had to decide whether to ignore the action of the insurgents or to take over leadership of the struggle. It opted for the second alternative. After hard negotiations—the military distrusted the Rada because some of its members were Communists—it was recognized as the political leadership. In turn, the Rada accepted General Kutlvasr as military head of the revolt, although Captain Nechansky had nominally equal authority.

The intervention of the Russian division was a decisive factor

[7] Schwenninger, letter to author.

in the revolt's success. By the afternoon of May 7, after bitter fighting, most of the city was in the hands of the insurgents. At his command post in the suburb of Jinonice, Bunyachenko worked closely with the rebel staff. Although Vlasov took no part in directing the fighting, he was kept informed of developments.

On learning that the Rada had assumed political authority, Bunyachenko assigned Vlasov's adjutant, Captain Antonov, to establish liaison with it. On the morning of May 7, Antonov accidentally met Smrkovsky in the lobby of the Rada building. Smrkovsky told him that the Rada rejected the help of traitors and mercenaries of the Germans and wanted nothing to do with them. Soviet forces under Marshal Konev would soon reach the city and replace the insurgents. When the dismayed Antonov pointed out that the rebels themselves had asked Vlasov for assistance, Smrkovsky replied: "But not the Rada. It alone has political authority. You yourself confirm that you are fighting Communism. Many members of the Rada are Communists. Therefore, you are our enemies."

As they stood arguing, Dr. Otokar Machotka, a member of the Rada, came up to inform them that the issue had been resolved: The Rada, overruling the Communists, had voted to accept the help of Vlasov's forces. However, Communist pressure had sufficed to make it refuse to sign a formal agreement.

This was a harsh blow for Bunyachenko. He demanded a written apology as well as an agreement. The Rada refused on the grounds that it had not made any insulting statements. When Bunyachenko learned that the Americans had stopped their advance on Prague near Pilsen, he ordered his men to cease fighting, and that night the division began marching back to its starting positions.[8] News of Germany's capitulation reached

---

[8] On the Prague Uprising: Antonov, interview; Artyemyev, op. cit., p. 16; *Prazke Povstani*, 1945, O. Machotka, ed., published in Czech by the Czechoslovak National Council, Washington, D.C., 1965; Prince Frantisek Schwarzenberg, letter to author; O. Machotka, letter to author. After the Communists seized power in Czechoslovakia, Captain

them on May 8. The following day the division again reached the Beroun area, but continued its march south. Now Bunyachenko also understood that the Americans were their one last hope.[9]

During the march, part of the division passed through the city of Przibram, some thirty-five miles southwest of Prague. While in search of gasoline, Captain Buderatsky of the division's Third Regiment entered the yard of a prison on the city's outskirts. Suddenly, from a barred window there came a cry for help: It was Romashkin, Trukhin's adjutant. Buderatsky went off and returned with reinforcements, and his threat to use force freed not only Romashkin but also a number of other adjutants and chauffeurs.[1] From them, Bunyachenko learned the fate of their generals.

Trukhin had made contact with the Americans on May 5 and received an ultimatum to surrender within thirty-six hours with the entire second division. When Shapovalov brought him Vlasov's order to march into Czechoslovakia, he sent Boyarsky to Kozojedy to induce Vlasov to lead the first division to the Americans as well. When Boyarsky did not return, Trukhin drove off himself, accompanied by Shapovalov. They were stopped in Przibram by Czech partisans, and, accustomed to a friendly reception from the Czechs, they unsuspectingly entered a building. But inside they ran into a Red Army captain and were overpowered. They learned that Boyarsky had been hanged. Shortly afterwards, Shapovalov was shot and Trukhin handed over to

---

Nechansky was sentenced to death, General Kutlvasr to twenty years at hard labor. Smrkovsky, who could hardly be accused of collaboration with Vlasov's troops, was sentenced to eight years at hard labor.

[9] Details on the last days before Vlasov's capture are reported by: Tenzorov and Antonov, interviews; Ressler, letter to author; Artyemyev, op. cit.; V. Pozdnyakov: "Posledniye dni" ("Last Days") in Golos Naroda, 1951, No. 25 ff.; Y. Fominych: Kak Byl Po-iman Vlasov ("How Vlasov Was Captured"), Izvestia, October 7, 1962. Thorwald's description of Vlasov's capture (op. cit., p. 544) is inaccurate.

[1] Buderatsky wrote an account of this incident in Golos Naroda, 1949, No. 33.

the Red Army. When Trukhin, too, did not return, his deputy, Meandrov, sent off General Blagoveshchensky. But Fate overtook him in Przibram as it had the others; the Czechs delivered him to the Soviets.

While the first division moved south in forced marches, Vlasov drove ahead to Pilsen. He was accompanied by General Kononov, who had at last found Vlasov after following many false leads. Kononov had intended to advise him to link up with the Cossack Corps, which was then fighting its way back to Austria from Yugoslavia. However, all plans had now become meaningless, since Germany's capitulation had come faster than expected. Now all Kononov wanted was to join his Cossacks once more, to be with them in the last hours. He took leave of Vlasov just in front of the American lines. They embraced, and Vlasov asked him, also, to let the truth be known if he survived.[2]

Vlasov reached the first American outpost in the late evening. A major escorted the column to Pilsen. There Vlasov was received by a colonel who, having not the slightest inkling that a Russian liberation army existed, at first mistook him for a Soviet general. After the misunderstanding had been cleared up, a meeting with the commanding general was arranged for the next day. When Vlasov entered the house in which his companions had been lodged—the villa of a former Nazi Party official—he found them dressed in civilian clothes. Tenzorov explained that nothing would be accomplished if they were turned over to the Soviets. He did not trust the Americans. The German border was nearby, they were not being guarded, there were civilian clothes for all of them in the villa, and he had laid out a suit for Vlasov. But Vlasov once again refused: He would stay until the fate of the army had been decided. He would not restrain anyone in this situation, everyone was free to go. . . . Antonov began to prepare a bed for the general. The others silently took off their civilian clothes.

[2] Kononov, letter to author.

At ten o'clock the next morning, Vlasov was received by an American general who told him he could offer no guarantees against his being delivered to the Soviets, that was a matter beyond his control. He could only recommend unconditional surrender; in that case he would do his best to have the division declared American prisoners. Vlasov thereupon returned to his quarters. Toward 2 p.m. an American officer appeared and informed Vlasov that his division had arrived outside Schlüsselburg, and that the general left it to Vlasov to decide whether he wished to drive there. But he was free to go anywhere he liked and would receive gasoline if he needed it. It was tacit sanction for Vlasov's flight. To be sure, this reflected merely one officer's personal attitude, but this gesture was the first sign of human sympathy Vlasov had received here. He passed back the message that he was joining his division.

As Vlasov got into his car, a passerby recognized him. To the Czechs, he was still the hero who had liberated Prague. A rapidly growing crowd surrounded the car. Loud cheers went up, fists were raised in the Communist salute, a woman threw flowers into the car. Vlasov, fully aware of the tragicomic overtones of this ovation, stared impassively at the crowd. At first, the Americans looked on in bewilderment and incomprehension, but then they pushed the crowd back and hurried to get the column started on its way.

They arrived in Schlüsselburg in the late evening. The Americans went into a castlelike building on the outskirts of town while the column waited on the side of the road with headlights out. Through the warm evening air could be heard the shrill screams of girls having a good time with soldiers—and in the distance, Russian songs. Now and then people passing on the road approached the cars, but turned away when they saw the silent figures in them. They waited four hours in this fashion. No one spoke. It was a breathing space before the last, hardest stage of their journey. No one could know whether he would survive. Finally, near midnight, they were informed that they could spend the night in the castle. There the commandant of the city, Captain Donahue, received them.

While their sleeping quarters were being prepared, they waited in Donahue's office. The American commandant asked Vlasov why he had fought against his country. Vlasov, sunk in total apathy, indicated to the interpreter that he considered a reply pointless. The American leaned forward, his expression calm and sympathetic, without arrogance. He said his question implied no criticism. He had understood Vlasov to be an enemy of Stalin, and he was interested in his reasons. Vlasov realized that the captain's interest was sincere, and he began to speak, at first slowly and dispassionately, but then with growing intensity. For one last time, he spoke of all the prospects, hopes, and disappointments of his countrymen. He summed up everything for which countless Russians had fought and suffered. It was no longer really to the American that he was addressing himself—this was rather a confession, a review of his life, a last protest against the destiny that had brought him to a wretched end. The American listened intently, and something like admiration seemed to be moving him. He rose and shook Vlasov's hand: "Thank you, General. I will do what I can for you."

The next day, May 11, Vlasov learned that the division had assembled four miles north of Schlüsselburg and laid down its arms on American orders. Discipline was excellent; the men considered themselves interned by the Americans. Donahue informed Vlasov, however, that the area would be turned over to the Soviets on the evening of the following day, and that he still lacked permission for Vlasov and his men to enter the American occupation zone before then. He offered to permit Vlasov to travel with a transport of liberated British POW's into the British zone, where he could get in touch with senior British officials. But Vlasov declined this offer and drove over to the division's camp—prompted particularly by the increasingly critical situation in the castle, where Czech partisans and Soviet officers were constantly entering and leaving. At the camp he learned about the fate of Trukhin and the other generals. He and Bunyachenko agreed that, should the Americans refuse to grant the division passage, the men should try to make their way into the American zone in small groups.

He returned to the castle in the afternoon. Captain Donahue told him that army headquarters had inquired as to whether Vlasov was in Schlüsselburg. "Are you here?" he asked. Vlasov understood that this courageous officer still wanted to make flight possible for him. But again he refused. "I am here," he said, and shook hands with him. Toward evening, Vlasov had to negotiate with General Reimann and Captain von Pastor, representing the German Twenty-ninth Corps, which was bivouacked alongside the division. Donahue had ordered both units supplied with rations in common and called for a report of their strength. The discussion was fruitless, since neither the Germans nor Vlasov saw any value in submitting such a joint report.[3]

Toward 7 p.m. of the same day, some of Bunyachenko's reconnaissance patrols reported the approach of Soviet tanks. Division headquarters was immediately moved from the village of Khvozhdian to the nearby woods; Bunyachenko summoned the regimental commanders, but they could not find him. The 162nd Soviet Armored Brigade set up camp for the night less than two miles from the American lines. Contact could not be established with Vlasov, so Bunyachenko drove up to the American antitank barriers and demanded to be taken immediately to see the American commander. After a long exchange he was told a meeting could not be held until the next morning at ten o'clock. Then the decision would also be made as to whether the division could pass through. In any case, Bunyachenko had to win time. There was the danger that the Soviets would advance at dawn to the American lines and overwhelm the division.

[3] Herbert von Pastor, letters to author. Pastor's war diary, in which Donahue is mentioned, has been preserved.

Chance came to his aid. Lieutenant Colonel Vyacheslav Artyemyev, commander of the Second Regiment, while searching for division headquarters, unexpectedly came face to face with Soviet officers. So as not to be taken prisoner, he quick-wittedly pretended to be a truce emissary and was immediately conducted to the commander of the Soviet armored brigade, Colonel Mishchenko. Mishchenko's manner was cordial though patronizing. He guaranteed life and liberty to all who voluntarily surrendered, and urged a quick decision. He obviously knew nothing of either the division's being disarmed or the American refusal to protect it.

Artyemyev asserted that he had to discuss everything thoroughly with Bunyachenko and was promptly released. Bunyachenko sent Artyemyev back to Mishchenko with the task of winning, at all costs, a delay until 11 a.m. of the next day. Artyemyev was to insist on a written guarantee, to make the request more plausible, and to fix 11 a.m. as the hour for the change-over to the Soviet side.

Artyemyev arrived in Khvozhdian again at 1 a.m. and was served supper. Afterward Mishchenko scribbled the guarantee on a scrap of paper and agreed to the proposed time, with the proviso that the division was to bring all its weapons. After the official business had been concluded, Mishchenko began daydreaming aloud about the marvelous life in the Soviet Union, where everything had now changed. Finally, quite drunk, he proposed to Artyemyev not to wait for Bunyachenko's decision but to bring his regiment over immediately. If he did so, this would be very much in his favor and he might be able to return to the Red Army with his old rank. Mishchenko finally let Artyemyev leave at dawn. Time had been won: The Soviets would do nothing until 11 a.m.

During the night, Vlasov had drawn up a memorandum in which he stated that the leaders of the ROA were ready to appear before an international court, but that it would be a monumental injustice to turn them over to the Soviets and thereby to certain death. It was not a question of volunteers who had served the Germans, but of a political organization, of a broad opposition movement which, in any event, should not be dealt with under military law.

Donahue immediately transmitted the text by radio. Soon afterwards, however, he had to inform Vlasov that the supreme commander had refused to give the division permission to pass through and enter American custody. His own advice was that they slip into the American zone in small groups. Vlasov himself was to be taken to the Army High Command for talks at 2 p.m.

At 10 a.m., Bunyachenko was admitted into the castle, where Vlasov briefed him on the American decision. There was no way out—only dissolution remained. Bunyachenko returned to the division to give the last order. With the command "Break ranks!", a completely intact and disciplined combat unit disintegrated in minutes.

Thrown back upon themselves, the men were bewildered. Should they head south? But then what? Officers and men removed the insignia from their uniforms, tried to find civilian clothing, burned papers. Shots echoed through the woods— some preferred suicide to fear and uncertainty. Although bitter feelings were expressed, there was no word of reproach for the officers, who were not to blame for this collapse.

That night the great hunt began. Special Red Army commandos searched for them, and the Czechs who just a few days earlier had feted them as liberators beat them to death or turned them over to the Soviets. About ten thousand men were executed or fell into Soviet hands. Some succeeded in saving themselves temporarily by reaching the American zone, but more than half of these soldiers were later forcibly repatriated to the USSR.

About two o'clock that afternoon a column of eight automobiles set out from the castle, escorted by an American armored scout car at its head and another bringing up the rear. In the first automobile sat Bunyachenko and Nikolayev, who had managed to get through to the castle with several other division officers; in the last were Vlasov, Antonov, Vlasov's driver, and First Lieutenant Viktor Ressler, an interpreter. Vlasov had left Tenzorov and several others behind in the castle, under Donahue's protection, to render whatever assistance they could to men of the now-dissolved division. Donahue had said good-bye to Vlasov with an expression of regret that the general had not taken his advice while there was still time.

Not far from the castle, Vlasov's column was stopped by a car carrying Major Yakushev, the commander of the motorized rifle battalion of the 162nd Armored Brigade, and an ROA captain named Kuchinsky. To save his own skin, Kuchinsky had called Yakushev's attention to the departure of the column. Yakushev demanded that Bunyachenko follow him. Nothing would happen to him, he was the liberator of Prague. Bunyachenko categorically refused; he was a prisoner of the Americans and on the way to American Army Headquarters.

At a sign from Kuchinsky, Yakushev then turned to Vlasov's car and tore open the door. Vlasov got out and, accompanied by Ressler, headed toward the American officer at the head of the column. Resistance was senseless, since all the Russian officers had been forced to surrender their weapons. Ressler begged the American officer to intervene: Vlasov was his prisoner and on the way to Army Headquarters. The American did not understand Ressler's poor English—or else did not want to understand. Silent and immobile, he simply watched the scene.

When Yakushev saw that the American would not act, he turned his submachine gun on Vlasov. Vlasov calmly opened his coat and said: "Shoot!" At this moment a young nurse threw herself in front of him. "No!" she screamed. "Don't shoot!" Vlasov carefully pushed her aside. But Yakushev said angrily: "Comrade Stalin will judge you, not I!"

Meanwhile, Ressler noticed that several cars had turned

around and were driving back to Schlüsselburg, while others had been abandoned. In the hope that Captain Donahue would be informed, he tried by every means to gain time. Once again he pleaded with the Americans to intervene; but they did not move, as though what was happening was none of their business. Vlasov stood alone, beside Yakushev. As if under a compulsion, Ressler walked over to him, and together they got into Yakushev's car. They overtook the nurse, who was running sobbing along the side of the road, and drove past the castle, in which nothing was stirring, and through villages in which Soviet and American soldiers were happily fraternizing.

Ressler was an ethnic German from the Soviet Union who had gone to Germany before the war and worked there as a cab driver. A simple man, he now displayed extraordinary qualities. For giving way to his feelings of sympathy and decency, he would pay a heavy price—ten years in prison. He was not sent back to Germany until 1955.

As they entered corps headquarters, a victory celebration with American officers was just coming to an end. Bottles, champagne glasses, and left-over food still covered the long tables. Several high-ranking Soviet officers, obviously still in the best of moods, rose as Vlasov entered. "Are you Vlasov?" a colonel asked. Vlasov nodded. The officer immediately demanded that Vlasov sign a surrender document. Vlasov explained that the army no longer existed; it had been disarmed and dissolved. The Soviet officers continued to insist that he sign, and Vlasov yielded. It no longer seemed very important to him.

Antonov had driven back to the castle and reported Vlasov's capture. Donahue left immediately, but it was too late—he found only the escort vehicles. That night he personally drove the Russians still remaining in the castle over thirty-five miles into the American zone, provided them with food, and left them. Among this group were Tenzorov, Antonov, and Vlasov's driver; the interperter Rostovtseva and her husband; Major

Savelyev; and the medic Donarov and his wife. Bunyachenko and Nikolayev were later captured by the Soviets, but just how is still unknown. They were not handed over.[4]

Shortly before Vlasov fell into Soviet hands, Strikfeldt and Malyshkin had spoken to the commander of the U.S. Seventh Army, General Alexander Patch. Malyshkin explained to him the motives of those who had supported the liberation movement. He requested protection not for himself, but for opponents of the Soviet system who were asking for political asylum. He appealed to the American people, who had always cherished the idea of freedom.

Patch seemed moved; but only Washington could make this decision. Nonetheless, he was ready to assume responsibility for the Russian units under the same conditions that applied to the Germans. Malyshkin and Strikfeldt were to inform Vlasov. Day after day, however, one pretext after another was invoked to postpone their release. And on the day the Germans surrendered, they were told they were no longer truce emissaries but prisoners of war.[5]

Professor Oberländer had better luck; he had himself taken by the Americans to the estate of Prince Leopold of Bavaria, and by April 23 was negotiating with the commander of the U.S. Second Armored Corps, General Kennedy. Kennedy said he was prepared to take over Maltsev's group and would not hand them over to the Soviets. He would do so on his own responsibility and would not report it to his superiors. However, he required that General Aschenbrenner appear in person.

---

[4] All the descriptions of Vlasov's capture agree in their essentials: Ressler, letter to author; Tenzorov and Antonov, interviews. The account by Lieutenant General Y. Fominych (op. cit.) confirms the major details provided by Vlasov's officers, but the description of Vlasov hiding in a rug at the back of the car behind two women, and then seeking to escape, is Fominych's own invention. Fominych's report makes it clear that the Americans had not planned to turn Vlasov over to the Soviets in this way.

[5] Strik-Strikfeldt, interview.

Oberländer returned with Aschenbrenner on the 24th; both talked on the 25th with Kennedy, who repeated his promise. On April 27 the ROA air force unit marched in closed ranks, bearing white flags, to Münsingen, where they laid down their arms.[6]

General Kennedy's promise was not kept. Most of the officers and men, including Maltsev, were later forcibly repatriated to the USSR. The KONR headquarters staff, led by Zhilenkov, withdrew from Innsbruck to Zillertal and was interned there by the Americans. The remaining units of ROA—the second division, the replacement brigade, the officers school, and the General Staff—also marched into American-occupied territory. Meandrov had given the order to move on May 8, after failing to establish contact with Vlasov.

Zveryev, the commander of the second division, had ordered his men to proceed but had himself remained overnight in his quarters—his wife had taken poison and lay dying. The division headquarters was attacked during the night by the Soviets and captured after a brief fire-fight, with only one officer escaping. The rest of the division, with the exception of some camp followers, succeeded in crossing the American lines. They gave up their weapons near Krummau.

The replacement brigade, commanded by Lieutenant Colonel Sadovnikov, reached the Friedberg area. There the American commandant, ignoring his orders, provided small groups of Russians with transit passes to Munich. Eight hundred enlisted men and fifteen officers managed to escape in this way.

All the remaining ROA forces eventually assembled in the Landau area. There Meandrov asked Herre—who could not bring himself to abandon the Russians to their fate—to request Köstring to intercede with the Americans. Herre obtained civilian clothing and, after a slow journey of eleven days, got through to Köstring, who was waiting to be taken prisoner by the Americans at his home near Marquartstein.

[6] Oberländer, interview and his war diary.

Köstring, however, did not believe the Russians would benefit
in the slightest from his intervention. A few days later his pessimism was borne out when he was assigned to the POW
camp of the U.S. 101st Airborne Division. His interrogation was
perfunctory. His experiences and his knowledge of the problems
in the Russian territories were obviously of no interest to his
American interrogators, who merely wanted to know what
means of compulsion the Germans had used to make the Russians fight. It seemed pointless to Köstring to explain the deeper
aspects of these problems. He did, nonetheless, state that the
German leadership by its greed and stupidity had squandered
a great resource in the struggle against Bolshevism. Now the
Americans were about to dissipate this resource a second time,
because they were disappointing those who had hoped for their
help and understanding after they had been deserted by the
Germans. Perhaps the Americans would soon have cause to
regret this. "Perhaps," his interrogator answered. It was no more
than a polite rejoinder.[7]

The various truce emissaries experienced similar failures.
Zherebkov was stopped at the Swiss frontier after Bern had
been called for instructions, and when he tried to cross the
border illegally, was arrested and brought back. Dr. Poremsky
and Colonel Milishkevich, who had attempted to establish
contact with the English military authorities in Hamburg, were
also arrested, as were Bykodorov and Captain Lapin. Milishkevich and Lapin were turned over to the Soviets shortly thereafter. Colonel von Renteln, whom General von Pannwitz had
sent to British Field Marshal Alexander, never reached him
and was also given over to the Soviets.[8] He died in prison.

While the ROA units were surrendering to the Americans, the

---

[7] Köstring, unpub. rept.; V. Pozdnyakov: *"Posledniye Dni,"* in *Golos
Naroda*, 1951, No. 25 ff.
[8] First Lieutenant Gerhard Petri, officer on Pannwitz's staff, letter to
author; Field Marshal Alexander, letter to author. Alexander states that
none of the truce emissaries reached him.

Cossack Corps was fighting its way over the Austrian border. In contrast to the disorder of the fleeing Germans, order and discipline prevailed in its ranks. Its first contact with Allied forces came on May 9, with the British Eleventh Armored Division, in the Lavamünd area.

Pannwitz drove ahead to meet the British. It was inconceivable to him that the Cossack Corps, which had never fought the Western Allies, should be delivered to the Soviets. On May 10, the corps's First Division marched up, and Pannwitz watched their arrival in the company of several British officers.

The Cossacks presented a fantastic spectacle in the midst of the surrounding chaos. The bugle corps, on white horses, ranged themselves in regulation fashion behind their commander. Then they followed him, squadron by squadron at parade gallop, as the British watched in utter astonishment.

The conduct of the British was at first impeccable. The corps was left free to move about in the area around Klagenfurt, and there was no talk of repatriation. On May 27, however, the commander of the First Division, Colonel Wagner, was ordered to relocate his men in a camp near Weitensfeld, and a British officer gave him to understand that this was a prelude to repatriation. Wagner thereupon set everybody free to do what he thought right. He and several other German officers succeeded in crossing the Alps to Germany. Colonel Sukalo assumed command of the division, with the understanding that each man could act as he saw fit. Yet, at roll call the next morning, almost the whole division assembled. Sukalo also stayed, and led the men into the camp.

On their way there, some of the men were rescued by a British major who asked each soldier where he had been born and if he was an old émigré. Those who said yes were released. The rest were handed over to the Soviets a few days later. Pannwitz himself refused to seek safety, although he was not being guarded. He explained: "I have shared many happy days with my Cossacks, and I will also remain with them in this time of misfortune." [9] Shortly afterward he was arrested and passed on to the Soviets in Judenburg. The other German officers of the corps, on the pretext of a transfer to Germany, were assembled near Neumarkt and also turned over, under heavy guard, to the Soviets in Judenburg.

At about the same time that Pannwitz's Cossack Corps was crossing the Austrian frontier, Domanov's group was also reaching Austria from North Italy, after an exhausting march. The group—numbering some 35,000 people, including women and children—pitched camp in the broad valley near Lienz. These people, too, were allowed at first to move about freely. They trusted in the pledge given by a British officer, Major Davis, that none of them would be repatriated to the Soviets.

On May 28 the group's officers were ordered to attend a meeting with Field Marshal Alexander; they were to return in a few hours. Several skeptics were ridiculed by the old émigrés: An officer of the Crown does not break his word, that is unthinkable. So it was that a little later, 2,200 officers—Domanov himself among them—climbed aboard the waiting trucks. Only the seventy-six-year-old General P. N. Krasnov seems to have had a premonition of the imminent catastrophe. As they were saying good-bye, he asked his wife: "Smile once more, I have always loved your smiles so much."

On the road the column was surrounded by tanks and turned over to the Soviets. No more than a few managed to save themselves.

The following day, Major Davis informed those who remained that their officers had been arrested and would not return. Now each soldier could express his opinion freely; each had the right to repatriation. At first, the people were stunned. Then they sent delegates to Davis to ask that the officers be freed. They would only follow their officers, and none wanted to return voluntarily to the Soviet Union.

[9] Petri, letter to author.

Davis set May 31 as the date for the transport of the Cossacks to the point of transfer. The operation was postponed to the following day, however, at the request of the Catholic priests of Lienz, since the 31st was Corpus Christi Day. Then black flags and banners were raised with the inscription: "Better dead than return to the Soviet Union." When Davis appeared at the camp, the people told him: "We will not go voluntarily." Davis explained that he was a soldier with an order to carry out.

The Cossacks went on a hunger strike. In their barracks, which had been made into a church, uninterrupted prayer services were held. Messages were written to the Pope, Churchill, the International Red Cross—all of which ended in the wastebaskets at British headquarters.

During the night of May 31 a deathly silence prevailed in the camp. Now and then a figure vanished into the darkness. A group numbering hundreds, perhaps even a few thousand, might have managed to escape; but an assemblage of thirty-five thousand people—among them many women and children—was in no position to flee over the snow-covered mountains.

On the day of the forced repatriation, religious services were celebrated at dawn in the square in front of the barracks. Major Davis appeared at 8 a.m., bringing with him a column of trucks. Soon afterwards, armored scout cars and soldiers of the Eighth Scottish Artillery Battalion drove up. The Cossacks were instructed through loudspeakers to get into the trucks. Resistance was senseless—yet nobody moved. The crowd began to chant the liturgy for the dead, their own dirge. The priests raised the cross, and the younger men formed a chain around the old people, women, and children.

The British advanced, struck out with clubs and rubber truncheons, pulled some people out of the crowd, and threw them into the trucks. Children were torn out of the arms of women, even the women and priests were mercilessly beaten. The horrified crowd retreated. In the press of their withdrawal a platform built for the priests collapsed, and many people were buried beneath it. Finally, the wire fence enclosing the camp gave way, and the crowd ran in wild panic toward the bridge across the Drava River and the woods and mountains beyond it.

But the armored scout cars arrived first and blocked the road. Nonetheless, many crossed the bridge. Women with their children fell into the Drava and drowned; some Cossacks shot their families and themselves. British commandos hunted the refugees in the woods, and shots filled the forest. The unfortunates remaining in camp were forced into the trucks. Many collapsed into unconsciousness because they had gone without food for days. Finally, at about 3 p.m., loudspeakers announced that the operation was being cut short for the day: "The soldiers are tired."

There were 134 dead. A small cemetery was established on the bank of the Drava, which is still tended today by some Cossacks who managed to remain in Lienz. The next day, repatriation continued until the operation was ended. Thirty-seven generals, most of them old émigrés who had never been Soviet citizens, 2,200 officers, and about 30,000 Cossacks were handed over to the Soviets.

General Shkuro tore a British decoration from his chest and threw it down in front of a British officer. He asked for a gun, so he would not fall alive into the hands of the Soviets. Colonel Kulakov, a legendary figure of the Civil War, both of whose lower legs were amputated, was surprised by the Soviets in a sanatorium in the East Tyrol. He and a handful of Cossacks defended themselves to the last bullet, and all of them perished. A few days later, Pannwitz and the Cossack generals were flown from Baden, near Vienna, to Moscow. Field Marshal Schörner was on the same flight. In contrast to the Cossack generals, he was well treated.[1]

---

[1] Schörner, interview. Reports on the forced repatriation of the Cossacks come from: Ivan Gordyenko, interview; N. N. Krasnov: "Nezobyvayemoye 1945–1956," *Russian Life*, San Francisco, 1967 (Krasnov,

★

On January 17, 1947, *Pravda* published a bulletin from the War Collegium of the Supreme Court of the USSR:

> Ataman P. N. Krasnov, lieutenant general of the White Army, A. G. Shkuro, major general of the White Army, Sultan Kelech Girei, major general of the White Army, S. N. Krasnov, and Major General Domanov, as well as Helmut von Pannwitz, general of the German Army and SS member, have been found guilty of "fighting the USSR, engaging in active espionage, and committing terrorist acts, with the help of groups they formed, on behalf of the German Intelligence Service." The sentence—death by hanging —has been carried out.

a nephew of General P. Krasnov, was, as a Swiss citizen, released from captivity in 1956); M. Rotov: "How the Cossacks' Surrender to the English Was Carried Out" (Russian) in *Donskoi Atamanskyi Vestnik*, 1954, No. 22; S. Ungermann, unpub. rept., IfZ; Colonel C. Wagner, unpub. rept., IfZ; Kern, op. cit.; N. Petrovsky: *Unvergessener Verrat, Schutzverband der Kosaken*, Munich, 1965; V. Naumenko: *Velikoye Predatyelstvo*, New York, All-Slavic Publishing House, 1962; B. Kuznetsov: *V Ugodu Stalinu*, Verlag Voyenny Vestnik, New York, 1958, part II, with sources on forced repatriation; Masyanov: *Gibel Uralskovo Kazachevo Voiska*, Slavonic Bazaar, Bridgeport, Conn. The All-Slavic Publishing House has an extensive Archive on the Tragedy of Forced Repatriation.

EPILOGUE

Shortly after the Cossacks had been repatriated, the British turned the 162nd Turkic Division over to the Soviets in an assembly camp near Tarent. There, too, many suicides and desperate attempts at flight occurred. The Russian Corps and the Second Ukrainian Division of General Shandruk were luckier; they were not forcibly returned as units because both consisted primarily of old Russian émigrés.

Under the Yalta Agreement of February 11, 1945, the United States and Britain committed themselves (later France also became a party to the agreement through a special treaty) to repatriation, by force if necessary, of those persons who had been citizens of the Soviet Union on September 1, 1939, and at the same time either had been captured in German uniform, were members of the Red Army on June 22, 1941, or had collaborated voluntarily with the enemy.

However, in practice, a great many persons who did not fulfill these conditions were affected. Many Cossacks, women, children, and old people, as well as émigrés who had never been Soviet citizens, were indiscriminately turned over. The initial repatriations may perhaps be explained by the intoxication of victory and by bitterness against Germany and those who had allegedly helped the Nazis. But this argument is inapplicable to subsequent forced transfers, which extended into 1947. These represented a clear breach of international law and the Geneva Convention on prisoners of war.

Only a few voices were raised in protest. In *Le Monde* of June 12, 1947, the jurist Galinyak pointed out that the concept of "forced repatriation" does not exist in international law, only voluntary repatriation. In Britain, just the day before, the Conservative MP Harold Nicolson had directed a question in the House of Commons to the foreign secreary, Ernest Bevin, as to whether he knew that forced repatriation to any country was contrary to English tradition. Bevin replied: "It is also contrary to our views. On the other hand, I cannot permit these people to benefit from that. . . . I am prepared to grant the right of asylum, but I cannot endure people who will exploit this right in order to ride on our backs for a long time to come." Nicolson then asked whether the government could not give assurances that at least those people who faced certain death as a consequence of repatriation would not be forcibly handed over. Bevin: "I don't believe we will do so [give such assurances]. There have been cases where people committed suicide because they preferred death to being taken back to their country, but my duty is clear in light of the Yalta Agreements."[1]

The U.S. government was aware of the illegality of the forced repatriations. This is confirmed by a State Department note submitted to the Soviet Embassy in Washington on February 1, 1945, in which explicit reference is made to the Geneva Convention to explain why Russian prisoners in Ger-

[1] Quoted by Kuznetsov, op. cit.

man uniform should not be repatriated against their will.[2] The attitude of the U.S. government was also unequivocal with respect to the demands of the North Koreans and Chinese Communists that all their nationals captured in the Korean War be returned to them: It refused to hand over those who did not wish to return. Secretary of State Dean Acheson declared to the United Nations on October 24, 1952: "So far as I know, there is not one member of the UN, outside the states of the Communist bloc, that has ever asserted forced repatriation of prisoners of war to be legally admissible and necessary under international law."

What the U.S. government regarded as self-evident in 1952 had not been at all self-evident to it in 1945. The forced repatriations from 1945 to 1947 were clearly the consequence of an arbitrary interpretation of the Yalta Agreement by the U.S. High Command and the chief of staff, General Eisenhower. On August 25, 1945, the Seventh Army commander, General Patch, asked Supreme Headquarters whether he should order the repatriation of Soviet troops who did not wish to be returned. Supreme Headquarters in turn queried Washington. The Joint Chiefs of Staff took four months to compose its answer, which read: "All Soviet citizens who were in the territory of the Soviet Union on September 1, 1939, must be repatriated, without regard to their personal wishes and, if need be, by force." This order went far beyond even the terms of the Yalta Agreement. And it was not the U.S. military authorities alone that carried out such a policy, but the United Nations Relief and Rehabilitation Administration as well, as the top-secret Order No. 199 proves.[3]

---

[2] The text of this note has not appeared in the Yalta documents published so far, nor has there been any reference to it to the effect: Note not published. The text was presented for the first time in German by Julius Epstein, in the New York German-language newspaper *Staatszeitung und Herold*, December 4, 1955. It was made available to Epstein by Secretary of State John Foster Dulles.

[3] Cf. Epstein, op. cit.

The American historian George Fischer has called the forced repatriations "an indelible stain on the honor of the West." Yet, to this day, there has been no identification of those actually responsible or any public acknowledgment of the breach of law. The efforts of a journalist, Julius Epstein, led the U.S. Senate to adopt an amendment to the McCarran-Walter Act in 1956, under which forty thousand Eastern refugees who had come to the United States with forged documents in order to escape forced repatriation, were no longer deportable. The amendment was signed into law by President Eisenhower on September 11, 1957. But tens of thousands of Russians who might have saved themselves fell into Soviet hands because they believed in the humaneness and political understanding of the Western Powers.

Meandrov, at the end the senior-ranking officer of the ROA, appealed to his subordinates not to flee because he had faith in the liberal principles of the Western Allies and the moral unimpeachability of his own position:

. . . I am repeatedly asked why I have not fled, although I have had the chance to do so. I will answer this question:

Even before the war ended, our units went over to the American side. They believed the democratic nations would grant us political refuge. It can be held against me that more than eight months have already passed without our fate being decided. Even worse, there have been instances of forcible repatriation. That is true, but there has been no general, final decision. We must wait for this, since I am convinced we will achieve more through calm, restraint, and discipline than through attempts at flight and an illegal existence in freedom.

We are not traitors, not criminals, but members of a political movement aiming at a better future for our people. This movement grew with an elemental force. Tens of thousands, hundreds of thousands of people without any leadership, moved only by the consciousness of the falsehood of their lives, rose up in struggle against a power they considered

unjust and not stemming from the people. We are not criminals, because there are hundreds of thousands of people who
share our views, because we did not seek our own advantage
but the welfare of our people and country. Only those flee
detention who fear justice. Should we flee under these circumstances and hide like criminals? No!

Imagine what would happen if we were all to flee. Sooner
or later, most of us would be caught and people would consider all Russians criminals. And even if only those fled who
occupy positions of authority in our movement, the others
would say: "They have abandoned us to our fate." We cannot continue the struggle, but we are obliged to leave it with
honor. Our departure must reflect the honorableness and sincerity of our ideals.

It is hard to sit behind barbed wire. We all hover between
life and death, and sometimes it seems as if we will break under the strain. But one can overcome these psychological weaknesses, one can be ready to die, if that must be. But it is imperative to die with dignity and in the sure belief that our
truth must conquer in the end, that our Russian people will
yet be free. . . .[4]

As late as November 1945, Meandrov was still hopeful, still
believed the decision would be positive.[5] But he began to fear
the worst in January 1946, when news leaked out from Dachau
that three hundred persons there had been slated for repatriation.
Of this number, forty committed suicide and a hundred either
deliberately injured themselves or were beaten viciously by the
Americans.[6] It was at this time that Meandrov wrote his "Notes
of a Man Afflicted to the Point of Death":

. . . We are accused of treason. We are called German

[4] Text in: *Posev*, No. 46, November 15, 1959.
[5] Meandrov's letter to Colonel Aldan, November 25, 1945, MiD, p. 41.
[6] Kuznetsov provides thorough documentation on the forced repatriation
in Dachau, op. cit., pp. 30 ff.

mercenaries. This is a superficial view, because there was no place to arm ourselves except in the camp of the enemy. But no one who knows the true spirit of Bolshevism can honestly maintain this accusation. . . .

But should this legalistic, superficial attitude prevail, we are lost. Our ideas, however, will not be destroyed. They belong to the people. They mirror the centuries-old advance of the Russian people to social justice and freedom. The day will come in which those who regard us as traitors and criminals will have to give us worthier names. It is sad to think that we ourselves may not live to see this day. . . .

Many will prefer death to forced repatriation. How unjust that will be! For it is not just we who refuse to return to the Soviet Union; there are tens of thousands of "traitors to the people." Nothing like this has ever happened before in the history of any nation. Aren't the reasons for this mass defection clear to the world? Or does the world not want to understand? Where is the principle of freedom of political conviction?

Streams of blood will flow with the approval and support of the democracies. The Soviet Union will try to keep it a secret, but the blood will seep through and besmirch the democratic slogans of the freedom-loving nations. But we will know how to die with dignity.

Meandrov and other Russian officers sent letters to the governments of the Western Allies, to the Pope, to the International Red Cross. They received not a single answer.

In August 1945, in Kempten, a group of Russians was seized in church during religious services and transported. Some were injured, and the church was destroyed.[7] On February 23, 1946, two thousand Russians were loaded onto trucks for repatriation in the Natternberg camp near Plattling. Many of the Russians, refusing to accept their fate passively, cut their wrists or stabbed or hanged themselves.

[7] Kuznetsov, op. cit., pp. 6 ff.

At first, the wounded were taken to a military hospital to be treated, but there were too many. The living, the wounded, the dying, and dead were all dragged onto the trucks. The vehicles drove to the railroad station, straight to the platforms where freight cars with bars were waiting in long rows. In a short time the two thousand Russian officers and men were rolling toward the Soviet Union.[8]

But the Russians were not repatriated from Germany alone. They were turned over as well from Italy, France, Denmark, Norway, even Sweden and the United States.[9] The total number will never be known. At the end of the war, according to an OKW estimate received by the Allies, there were close to 700,000 volunteers serving with the German armed forces: 600,000 with the army, 50,000–60,000 with the air force, and 15,000 with the navy.[1] (Actually, however, the number was larger, since many units had not reported their Hiwis.) In addition, there were tens of thousands of refugees—men, women, and children—who had joined in the German retreat to the west because they feared Stalin's regime. Also to be taken into account are the POW's, as well as the Eastern workers conscripted for service in Germany.

Overall, perhaps six to seven million were repatriated. There are no statistics to show how many went voluntarily and how many would have remained in the West if they had been given the choice. A few thousand escaped repatriation because Western officers defied their orders and covered up for them.

The last to be handed over were the generals: In April 1946, Meandrov, Sevastyanov, and Assberg; in May, Maltsev; in June, Malyshkin and Zhilenkov. Each of them tried to kill himself, but the wounds in each case were not fatal. They were all nursed back to health, and then repatriated. On August 2, 1946, the

[8] Kuznetsov, op. cit., p. 57 ff.

[9] Sources of information on the forced repatriation in Denmark include N. Rebikov: "Tagebücher eines Offiziers des Ostbataillons 28, 1942–1945," unpub. ms.; *Borba*, "Forced Repatriation from Denmark" (Russian), Nos. 1–2, 1950. On forced repatriation in Sweden: ". . . überfiel uns das Grauen," in *Baltische Briefe*, April, 1964.

[1] OKW/WFSt/Org. Dep't. No. 2085/45, May 20, 1945; cf. Dallin, op. cit., p. 674.

Soviet government paper *Izvestia* carried the following item, under the heading "Announcement of the Military Collegium of the Supreme Court of the USSR":

> The Military Collegium of the Supreme Court of the USSR reviewed the indictments against
> Vlasov, A. A.—Malyshkin, V. F.—Zhilenkov, G. N.
> —Trukhin, F. I.—Zakutny, V. I.—Bunyachenko,
> S. K.—Zveryev, G. A.—Korbukov, V. D.—and Shatov,
> N. S.[2]
> for treason as well as active espionage and terrorist activity against the Soviet Union in the service of the German Intelligence Service, crimes which are described under Art. 58–11 of the Penal Code of the RSFSR. In accordance with Point 1 of the decree of the Presidium of the Supreme Soviet of the USSR of April 19, 1943, the Military Collegium of the Supreme Court of the USSR condemned the accused to be hanged. The sentence was carried out.

Thus Vlasov died. For understandable reasons he and his closest associates were not subjected to a show trial. It would have inevitably evoked the memory of millions in the Russian territories occupied by the Wehrmacht initially greeting the invaders with joy. This fact and the remarkable extent of "collaboration" with the Germans were no inventions of Goebbels's propaganda. Although the implications were never grasped or exploited, it cannot be erased from history—neither that of Germany, of Soviet Russia, nor of the victorious Western Powers of the Second World War.

The fact that Vlasov, his Russian colleagues, and the members of the Russian volunteer units cooperated with representatives and agencies of the Third Reich and, given the circumstances, were compelled to do so, does not justify equating them with collaborators like Quisling, who were National Socialists

[2] Korbukov and Shatov were officers on Trukhin's staff.

and wanted to impose National Socialism on their peoples. In German captivity, Vlasov and his associates succeeded in drafting a political program which deliberately rejected the Nazi ideology and aimed at a genuine democratization of Russia. They were able to do so because they moved in a protected sphere beyond the direct reach of the Nazi Party—the same sphere in which active resistance against Hitler and his policies began to take form. This meeting on a common ground of Russian and German opponents of dictatorship and despotism was not surprising, under the circumstances. For it was occasioned, at least in part, by the fact that the Red Army and the Wehrmacht were compelled to go through similar—though outwardly different— experiences with their respective political leaderships. Organizations whose task it is to ensure the security of their nations react alike when they are thrown into a state of uncertainty. This was true for the Red Army, which had not yet recovered from the Tukhachevsky Affair, and it was true for the Wehrmacht, which had been more deeply shaken by the ousters of Generals Blomberg and Fritsch in 1938 than appearances indicated at the time.

Possibly, also, the memory of a historical parallel may have played a role. In 1917 the imperial German government had permitted the Russian revolutionary Lenin to travel back to Russia in order to stir up trouble in the Tsarist empire. The plan had exceeded all expectations: The Tsar had been overthrown, and a separate peace concluded. The subsequent, unintended developments—the collapse and end of the German monarchy, the Kaiser's flight—evoked the prospect of parallel events that, in the different context of the Second World War, were altogether to be desired.

The situation at the beginning of the Soviet-German War was even more favorable in comparison with that in the First World War. An enormous part of Soviet territory, with a population of tens of millions, was beyond Stalin's reach. The readiness of this population to create a new, free social order, within the framework of a national Russian state, was genuine and spontaneous.

It required no revolutionary leader to effect this repudiation of the existing regime—just a representative leadership able to act, and a corresponding organization.

Vlasov wished to assume this task; his German friends and associates wanted to help. He formulated his goal and intentions clearly. He did not strive for power for the sake of power. He wanted to lead Russia back to a normal state which had been denied her despite all the promises of the October Revolution. Vlasov always emphasized that afterwards others, more qualified, would govern, and looked upon himself merely as someone preparing the way.

His fate, it must be pointed out, in the final analysis was inevitable, stemming as it did from the nature of National Socialism, which Vlasov and his Russian colleagues failed to understand. They and Vlasov's German friends erred in expecting that Hitler's *Ost* policy could be influenced or radically changed by military realities or rational considerations.

And so Vlasov did not make history, and history did not make of him what he might have become. However, this man's tragedy lies perhaps most truly in the slow, agonizing process of attrition to which he was subjected. For many reasons he felt helpless before its onslaught, as it wore away his ideals, his hopes, his moral force and legitimacy.

The man whom the Soviets captured on May 12, 1945, was no more than a shadow; he had lost the will to live, the ability to act. But his brief life was bound up with one of those rare moments in which history seems to pause—a moment that can, if it is understood and seized, lead to the beginning of a new impulse, a new rhythm.

The Stalin era now belongs to history. Today the Russian people would no longer greet an attacker as a liberator. The younger generation in Russia condemns Stalin and his despotic methods just as German youth condemns Hitler and his crimes. Vlasov, the Russian liberation movement, and the Russian liberation army were an outgrowth of the Stalin regime. They are part of the "unmastered past" which still haunts the Soviet Union.

Chronological Table

September 1, 1900	Vlasov's birthday
March 1919	Joins the Red Army
November 1938	Assigned to Chinese mission—until November 1939
June 4, 1940	Major general
January 24, 1942	Lieutenant general
March 6, 1942	Deputy commander of northwest front
July 12, 1942	Captured after battle of Volkhov
January 12, 1943	Rosenberg approves Smolensk Proclamation
February 25, 1943	Vlasov begins first tour of occupied areas
March 1, 1943	Dabendorf Propaganda Department begins operations
April 19, 1943	Vlasov sets out on second tour of occupied areas
May 25, 1943	Mauerwald conference
June 8, 1943	Hitler forbids all activity by Vlasov and the liberation movement
July 24, 1943	Malyshkin addresses Russian émigré colony in Paris
September 19, 1943	Hitler orders transfer of all volunteer units to western front
September 16, 1944	Vlasov meets Himmler
November 14, 1944	Prague Proclamation
January 17, 1945	Financial agreement between German Reich and KONR
January 28, 1945	Authority over ROA transferred to KONR with Vlasov as commander in chief
February 6, 1945	KONR shifts to Karlsbad
February 16, 1945	Vlasov given command of first division
March 28, 1945	KONR holds last meeting

March 28, 1945	Cossack congress in Verovivitsa
April 14, 1945	First division goes into action on Oder front
May 6, 1945	First division supports Czech uprising in Prague against Germans
May 12, 1945	Vlasov captured by Soviets; dissolution of first division
June 1, 1945	Forced repatriation of Cossacks in Lienz
August 2, 1946	Vlasov and colleagues executed
January 17, 1947	Cossack generals executed in Kiev

Abbreviations

IfZ	Institute for Contemporary History, Munich
KONR	Komitet Osvobozhdyeniya Narodov Rossii (Committee for the Liberation of the Peoples of Russia)
MiD	Materialy i Dokumenty ODNR v Gody Vtoroi Mirovoi Voiny (Materials and documents of the ODNR in the Second World War, All-Slavic Publishing House, New York, 1966)
NKVD	Soviet Secret Police
NTS	Natsionalnyi Trudovoi Soyuz (Organization of Russian Solidarists)
OKH	High Command of the Army
OKW	High Command of the Armed Forces
OD	Ordnungsdienst (armed Russian militia in occupied areas)
RSHA	Reichssicherheitshauptamt (Reich Security Main Office)
ODNR	Osvoboditelnoye Dvizheniye Narodov Rossii (Liberation Movement of the Peoples of Russia)
ROA	Russkaya Osvoboditelnaya Armiya (Russian Liberation Army)
ROD	Russkoye Osvoboditelnoye Dvizheniye (Russian Liberation Movement)
SD	Security Service of the SS

Index

A Note About the Author

Sven Steenberg's experience as a German army interpreter on the eastern front in World War II brought him into contact with many individuals associated with the Russian liberation movement. Subsequently, he interviewed and corresponded with Germans and Russians who worked with General Vlasov in 1942–5. Born in 1905 in Riga, Latvia, where he studied law, Mr. Steenberg has been a businessman in Germany since the end of the war. He now lives in Stuttgart, where he also lectures and writes film scripts.

A Note on the Type

The text of this book is set in Electra, a typeface designed by W. A. Dwiggins for the Mergenthaler Linotype Company and first made available in 1935. Electra cannot be classified as either "modern" or "old style." It is not based on any historical model, and hence does not echo any particular period or style of type design. It avoids the extreme contrast between "thick" and "thin" elements that marks most modern faces, and is without eccentricities which catch the eye and interfere with reading. In general, Electra is a simple, readable typeface which attempts to give a feeling of fluidity, power, and speed.

Composed, printed, and bound by
The Colonial Press Inc., Clinton, Massachusetts.

Typography and binding design by
Richard-Gabriel Rummonds.